The Age of the Parthians

This Volume is dedicated to the memory of

A. Shapur Shahbazi

(1942-2006)

The Age of the Parthians

Volume II

Edited By

Vesta Sarkhosh Curtis

and

Sarah Stewart

I.B.TAURIS
LONDON · NEW YORK · OXFORD · NEW DELHI · SYDNEY

in association with The London Middle East Institute at SOAS
and
The British Museum

I.B. TAURIS
Bloomsbury Publishing Plc
50 Bedford Square, London, WC1B 3DP, UK
1385 Broadway, New York, NY 10018, USA
29 Earlsfort Terrace, Dublin 2, Ireland

BLOOMSBURY, I.B. TAURIS and the I.B. Tauris logo
are trademarks of Bloomsbury Publishing Plc

First published in Great Britain 2007
Paperback edition published 2021

Copyright © London Middle East Institute, 2007

Vesta Sarkhosh Curtis and Sarah Stewart have asserted their right under the Copyright,
Designs and Patents Act, 1988, to be identified as Editors of this work.

The publication of this book was generously supported
by the Soudavar Memorial Foundation.

For legal purposes the Acknowledgements on p. ix constitute
an extension of this copyright page.

All rights reserved. No part of this publication may be reproduced or
transmitted in any form or by any means, electronic or mechanical,
including photocopying, recording, or any information storage or retrieval
system, without prior permission in writing from the publishers.

Bloomsbury Publishing Plc does not have any control over, or responsibility for,
any third-party websites referred to or in this book. All internet addresses given
in this book were correct at the time of going to press. The author and publisher
regret any inconvenience caused if addresses have changed or sites have
ceased to exist, but can accept no responsibility for any such changes.

A catalogue record for this book is available from the British Library.

A catalog record for this book is available from the Library of Congress.

ISBN: HB: 978-1-8451-1406-0
PB: 978-1-3501-9777-0
ePDF: 978-0-8577-1018-5
eBook: 978-0-8577-3308-5

Series: The Idea of Iran

Typeset by P. Fozooni

To find out more about our authors and books visit
www.bloomsbury.com and sign up for our newsletters.

Contents

List of Figures	vi
Acknowledgements	ix
Map of the Parthian Empire	x
Introduction	1
1 - The Iranian Revival in the Parthian Period	7
2 - Gondophares and the Indo-Parthians	26
3 - Fars under Seleucid and Parthian Rule	37
4 - Friend *and* Foe: the Orient in Rome	50
5 - Parthia in China: a Re-examination of the Historical Records	87
6 - The *Videvdad*: its Ritual-Mythical Significance	105
List of Abbreviations	142
Bibliography	143

List of Figures

Gold coin of Andragoras	7
Silver coin of Arsaces I	8
Silver coin of satrap Tissaphernes	8
Silver coin of satrap Autophradates	8
Silver coin of satrap Tarkamuwa (Datames)	9
Silver coins of Mithradates I (Mihrdad)	9
Silver coin of Mithradates I (Mihrdad)	10
Silver coin of Kamnaskires I of Elymais	10
Silver coin of Artabanus (Ardavan) I	11
Silver coins of Mithradates (Mihrdad) II	12
Silver coin of Phraates (Farhad) IV	13
Silver coin of Artabanus (Ardavan) IV	14
Sasanian rock-relief of Ardashir I at Naqsh-i Rustam, Iran	14
Silver coin of Ardashir I	15
Silver coin of Artabanus (Ardavan) II	17
Silver coin of "unknown King", perhaps Darius of Media Atropatene	17
Gold coins of Kanishka I	17
Silver coin of Bagadates of Persis (Pars)	18
Sliver coin of Kamnaskires and Anzaze of Elymais	19
Bronze coins of Elymais, southwestern Iran	20
Silver coins of Persis (Pars)	22
Coloured lithograph of King Otto of Greece	52
Statue of Augustus, from the imperial villa of Livia at Prima Porta.	55
Statue of Augustus. Detail of the Roman and the Parthian.	55
Bronze statue of a Parthian prince from Shami	56

Fragment of a monumental relief. A Parthian fights against Romans (not extant). From Rome, *c.* CE 60 — 57

Ivory frieze. Captive Parthians in front of Trajan(?) and Roman soldiers. From Ephesus — 58

Relief of local stone. A Parthian proffers gold bars. From Coblenz, *c.* CE 170 — 59

Two bars of gold of Valentian I. From Czófalva, Romania. — 59

Glass gem. Two kneeling Parthians present Roman standards to Victory — 61

Marble table-leg. Oriental servant with wine ladle. From Pompeii, *Casa del Camillo (VII.12.22-27, room "e"), c.* CE 50-70 — 62

Stone figure. Parthian servant with jug and wine ladle. From Palmyra — 62

Statue made of "marmor Phrygium". Ganymede in the clutches of Zeus' eagle. From the villa in Sperlonga — 64

Reconstruction of the grotto at the villa in Sperlonga, showing the statue of Ganymede — 64

Rome, Ara Pacis Augustae. Relief to the right of the main entrance. Aeneas, behind him Iulus/Ascanius — 65

Rome, plan of the Forum Augustum — 66

Marble relief. Aeneas carrying his father Anchises and holding the hand of his son Iulus/Ascanius. In the background Aphrodite — 67

Grand Camée de France made of sardonyx. In the centre Tiberius and Livia seated, above them Iulus/Ascanius in Oriental dress carrying Divus Augustus — 69

Statue made of "marmor Phrygium". Kneeling Oriental. From Rome — 71

Reconstruction of a victory monument (now lost). Originally in Rome and Athens. Three kneeling Orientals made of "marmor Phrygium" carrying a bronze tripod — 71

Reconstruction of the Delphian tripod. Dedicated at the sanctuary of Apollo at Delphi — 72

Torso made of "marmor Phrygium". Standing Oriental ("telamon") originally shown in the gesture of support. From Rome, Basilica Aemilia — 73

Reconstruction of the support gesture of the standing Oriental from the Basilica Aemilia — 73

Marble relief. Two Oriental "telamons" support the inscription of a Roman magistrate. From Nuceria Alfertana — 74

Wall painting. Attis holding a sickle in his right hand 77

Wall painting. Mithras subdues the bull 77

Acknowledgements

The editors would like to thank a number of people whose assistance in the planning and production of this volume has been invaluable. In particular, Mrs. Fatema Soudavar Farmanfarmaian, Narguess Farzad, Elizabeth Pendleton, Elizabeth Errington and Louise Hosking. We are also grateful to Mr Mohammad-Reza Kargar, the Director of the National Museum of Iran, Tehran, for allowing us to use the photograph of the Shami bronze statue.

We would also like to thank Dr Parvis Fozooni for his expert handling of the text and for typesetting and formatting the book. Without his generous support, these volumes would not materialise.

We are grateful to Iradj Bagherzade, Alex Wright, Nicola Denny and Elizabeth Munns for their help in producing the publication.

Finally, we are indebted to the Soudavar Memorial for their sponsorship of the lecture series.

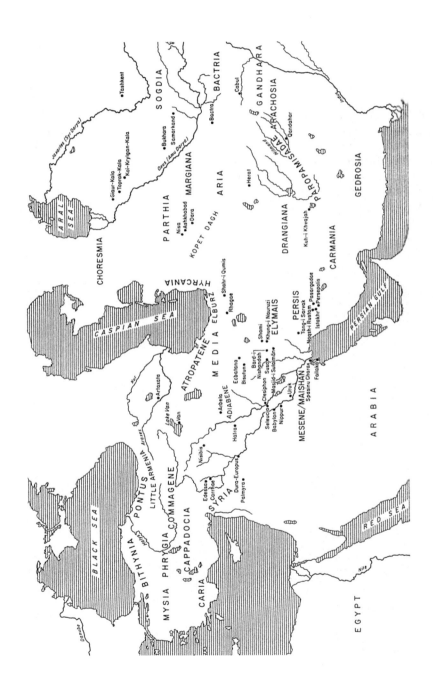

Map of the Parthian Empire. From J. Wiesehöfer, Ancient Persia, London, 1996: 116.

Introduction

Vesta Sarkhosh Curtis (The British Museum)
and
Sarah Stewart (The London Middle East Institute at SOAS)

The Parthian era is worthy of considerable attention, partly because of the survival of many artistic expressions and styles.

This evaluation by E.J. Keall of Parthian artistic expressions and styles and the impact these had on the Islamic art of later centuries was an innovative approach in 1977. More than forty years before, Michael Rostovtzeff[1] had also drawn attention to the importance of Parthian art as an art style in its own right, but such views have largely been ignored by the majority of scholars in the field.

By far the most prevalent attitude to the post-Hellenistic era, including the Parthian period, is encapsulated in a passage about the architecture of the site of Khurha in western Iran written by Ernst Herzfeld in 1941:[2]

> When the Iranians attempted to accept everything Greek, as they do with everything European, they did not grasp the significance and proportion, but were entirely satisfied with semblance. The depth of things remained hidden to them. The result is a hybrid art, if art it can be called, which is neither Greek nor Iranian; it is of no inner or aesthetic value, and is worthy of study only for historical or psychological interest... It is amazing to see how quickly, in not more than two or three generations, a handicraft of unlimited power can be completely lost, and with the mere technical skill the artistic judgement also.

Such a negative view of Parthian artistic representation is the result of a number of factors. First, the Parthian era and its art have mainly been the preserve of classicists who naturally analysed and evaluated Parthian material culture from the viewpoint of classical archaeology and Hellenistic and Roman art. Similarly, archaeologists working in the Near East were not interested in the Parthian period and largely ignored Parthian levels on sites where they did exist preferring to reach more ancient structures below.[3] In Mesopotamia for example, Assyrian and Babylonian levels were the main goal of archaeologists;

in Iran, Achaemenid, Median, Elamite and earlier prehistoric levels attracted far more attention than Parthian levels. Second, the fact that the Parthian period provides historical and cultural continuity with both the pre-Hellenistic Near East and Achaemenid art has been evaluated in a mainly negative way. Although Keall saw the importance of a period where "Greek traditions were being replaced by new ideas deriving from both Mesopotamia and Iran",[4] others claimed that the Parthians "as individuals ...seem to have had little cultural impact, appearing now and again in documents as governors, royal representatives and the like, but hardly energetic patrons" and that "Parthian art was not truly Parthian at all, even from the viewpoint of patronage", or again "the Parthians imposed no common language or art, and let diverse traditions flourish..."[5]

It is no exaggeration to say that Parthian art is more often than not regarded as derivative, with no original contribution of its own. It is also true to say that the long lasting lack of scholarly interest in the Parthian period has been exacerbated by the paucity of archaeological evidence for this period of Iranian history. Thus we know little about the local regional arts that might have followed an artistic style that developed under the Arsacid kings or the patronage that they may have attracted. In this vacuum, assumptions have been made largely based on the extent of known patronage of Greek art and according to western ideals of artistic expression. Although there is little doubt about the impact of Greek art on the art of the ancient Near East, particularly among the ruling classes, it is uncertain to what degree this Hellenisation had influenced the everyday life of the ordinary people of Iran and Mesopotamia

Neglect of the Parthian period is not confined to western scholars. In fact, the Sasanians themselves have contributed to our distorted view of 400 years of Parthian history and tradition. Neither the *khwaday namag* nor Firdowsi's later *Shah-nama* have much to say about the Parthians. Officially, only 27 distiches are given to the petty rulers, the "Ashkanian" (Arsacids), "the shortest account of any phase of Iranian history".[6] In fact the entire heroic part of the *Shah-nama, The Book of Kings*, dates to the Parthian period. It begins with the rule of King Manuchihr, finishes with the tragic death of Rustam and his family, and features many heroes and noble families, who are associated with the Parthian aristocracy.

The rich minstrel tradition of the Parthian period, through which the stories and legends later embodied in the *khwaday namag* were disseminated, has also been neglected by scholars.[7] The reason for this neglect is possibly because the legends and stories of the time were in oral transmission and so it is not easy to source the origins of works that did not appear in written form until much later. The Parthian *gošan*s were highly trained musicians and poets who transmitted traditional material as well as extemporising and composing new works. However, it seems that most of their work was memorised and, by the time it found its way into later literature, had been subject to an unknown number of redactions. The epic romance, *Vis u Ramin,* is perhaps the best known example of a text that has its origins in the Parthian period but which draws on ancient

INTRODUCTION

3

oral traditions for much of its imagery and storyline. This love story, which is centred first in Media, western Iran, and then at Merv, now in Turkmenistan, was finally put into modern Persian rhyme by Asad-Gurgani in the middle of the eleventh century, reflecting the traditions of the Parthian period with its feudalistic set-up.

It is hoped that the present book will draw attention to the importance of this particular period of Iranian history which deserves as much recognition as both the earlier Achaemenid period as well as the following Sasanian period.

The following chapters are based on a collection of six papers delivered at a symposium held at the School of Oriental and African Studies between March and May 2005, and generously sponsored by the Soudavar Memorial Foundation. They can broadly be divided into two categories. Vesta Sarkhosh Curtis, David Bivar and Josef Wiesehöfer discuss aspects of the Parthian period drawing on new evidence gained from the fields of art and numismatics, archaeology and historical documents. The remaining three authors, Rolf Michael Schneider, Wang Tao and Oktor Skjærvø use their material to describe the power of representation. Skjærvø discusses the different approaches adopted by scholars to the dating of the *Avesta* and the impact these views have had on our understanding of this religious corpus. Schneider and Wang Tao explore the political propaganda employed by Imperial Rome and China, respectively, towards Parthian Iran.

Vesta Sarkhosh Curtis discusses the significance of Parthian material culture by examining Arsacid Parthian coins and the information that this important primary source reveals about the history and iconography of the period. The influence of Hellenistic art and culture, particularly in the early Parthian period, cannot be denied and is exemplified by the fact that the Parthian kings adopted the Greek language for their official inscriptions, but the impact remained on the surface. At the same time, there is an interesting revival of pre-Hellenistic and characteristically Iranian features in the official court art of the Parthians, as illustrated in their coinage. From the very beginning a similarity exists between the iconography of the Parthian silver drachms and the satrapal coins of the fifth and fourth centuries BCE. Particularly interesting is the official costume of the Parthian kings, as seen on their coins, which at the end of the second century BCE is no longer a Greek outfit, but consists of the v-necked jacket, which was worn with trousers. Artabanus (Ardavan) I and Mithradates (Mirhdad) II wear as their official costume this nomadic trouser-suit, which was associated with Iranian-speaking peoples in the pre-Hellenistic period.

By reinstating ancient traditions, the Parthians developed a material culture which was imitated by those in close political and geographical contact with them. Their costume of tunics and trousers and their tri-partite hairstyle became so popular in the ancient Near East that it was adopted outside the political boundaries of the Parthian empire, for example at Palmyra and Roman Dura-Europos. At Hatra in northern Mesopotamia, the Parthian *eyvan* was adopted for the architecture of the sanctuary of Shamash, the sun god, and the worshipping statues of royals and non-royals are clad in elaborate Parthian costumes.

Reliefs and sculpture from Elymais also show strong Parthian influence, combined with local traditions, and the local kings of Persis (Pars), who ruled in the Achaemenid homeland first under the Seleucids and then under the Parthians, brought together Achaemenid and Parthian motifs on their coinage. These were then passed on to the Sasanians at the beginning of the third century. Curtis concludes by suggesting that it was the degree of "autonomy and self-expression" granted by the "King of Kings" to the local rulers that made an Iranian revival in the Parthian period possible.

David Bivar begins by exploring the origins of the eastern Indo-Parthian kingdom at the heart of which was Sistan: "...to this day archaeologically one of the least known...and also one of the most desolate regions of ancient civilisation". He traces the lineage of the House of Suren, the Parthian dynasty that ruled over Sistan, and who struck silver drachms in the Parthian fashion, with the portrait of the king wearing a bejewelled headdress on the obverse and an enthroned ruler on the reverse. It was the head of the Suren family who first placed the royal tiara on the head of the founder of the Arsacid dynasty sometime in the third century BCE thereby founding a tradition that was continued by his descendants. It was also Suren who defeated the army of the Roman general, Crassus, at Carrhae in 54 BCE. It is Bivar's hypothesis that the legendary family of Garshasp, Nariman, Sam, Zal and Rustam, who feature prominently in the Iranian epic of the *Shah-nama*, have a historical origin and that Rustam of the Persian epic may be identified with the Suren of Carrhae.

Josef Wiesehöfer looks at Persis (Parsa/Fars) under Seleucid and Parthian rule, the most poorly documented period of a region that had been the heartland of Achaemenid Persia. The main issue raised in this article is that of dating the *fratarakā*, the local rulers of Persis, who struck coins showing their portrait on the obverse and either a king in a worshipping or enthronement scene on the reverse. Names of these local kings and the title *fratarakā*, meaning governor, also appear on the reverse. Traditionally, the *fratarakā* coinage was dated to around 300–280 BCE, but Wiesehöfer argues that the Seleucids had not lost Persis during this time. Instead he follows Michael Alram's dating of the *fratarakā* coins to the beginning of Parthian rule in southwestern Iran and Mesopotamia in the second century BCE.

Rolf Michael Schneider addresses the power of image looking specifically at how and why the Romans transformed images of the Orientals, including the Parthians, and "how these images functioned within, and contributed to, the culture of imperial Rome". It was after the defeat of Crassus at Carrhae and the loss of the army that "the ideology of revenge on the Parthians" was developed. When Augustus retrieved the lost Roman standards and a large number of captive Romans, this diplomatic achievement was publicised as a victory which gave him the legitimacy he needed in order to rule. "Portrayals throughout the Roman empire propagated the Parthian settlement as the ultimate triumph of the Roman West over the East, and as one of the greatest achievements of

INTRODUCTION

5

Augustan foreign policy". Schneider finds in the rhetoric of orientalism that marked Roman supremacy over the east a strong resonance with the way in which the "Orient" is depicted in our visual and written media today: "in today's media the Orient(al) is mostly present as an exotic Other, a stranger and foe, whereas the image of the Orient(al) as friend is almost missing."

Oktor Skjærvø's article draws attention to the way in which western scholarship has represented the ancient world. In his discussion of an ancient Zoroastrian text, the *Videvdad* or "Law against the demons" Skjærvø refers to the nineteenth and twentieth century perceptions of the prophet Zarathushtra as a law-giver and exalted teacher who rejected "what was perceived as the primitive and mindless ritualism of the *Videvdad*". Attitudes towards this text included the fact that it was judged according to the norms of western literary merit and was also considered to be a "late text" and, therefore, not a reliable source for what had been construed as Zoroastrian "orthodoxy". Skjærvø discusses the age and transmission of the *Videvdad* in light of the fact that it was in oral transmission for centuries before being committed to writing probably during the late Sasanian period. The text is structured according to the Zoroastrian cosmological world view of the "three times": the perfect creation of the world, the chaos caused by the Evil Spirit and the final Renovation. It is also a ritual of purification and "a treasure trove of archaic lore" that includes remnants of Indo-European poetic heritage.

Wang Tao returns to the theme of representation in his re-examination of historical records for evidence of Parthia in China. Although there are numerous accounts of the Parthians written in traditional Chinese records, few archaeological remains have been cited in previous studies of the cultural exchanges between China and the Parthians. Wang Tao re-visits these records in order to find out why this is the case, and also to examine their significance in the cultural history of ancient Iran. He finds that, contrary to the western perception of historical records as a chronological narrative, the Chinese compiled their records in order to aid the administration in such matters as tax and military services. While they might record the strange behaviour of alien peoples, such as the Parthians, there was no requirement to produce their information chronologically so that material from different periods was often interwoven. Nevertheless, this material is: "...particularly important when we want to understand the complex geographic-political history of the Western Regions and the Parthian empire".

The collection of articles presented here will show the reader that many aspects of the "Persian renaissance" attributed to the Sasanians originated in the Parthian period. The popularity of themes of Parthian origin in the post-Parthian period explains the continuation of these familiar motif in Islamic art and architecture. We hope that this book will shed light on what has become known as the Dark Age in Iranian history and give the Parthians something of the recognition they deserve.

Notes:

1. M. Rostovtzeff 1935: 157-304.
2. Herzfeld 1941: 286-287.
3. Exceptions to this rule were the expeditions to Ashur and Babylon under Walter Andrae and Robert Koldewey at the beginning of the twentieth century.
4. Keall 1974: 124.
5. Colledge 1977: 143.
6. Shahbazi 1991: 116.
7. The exception here is Mary Boyce 1957: 10 ff.

1

The Iranian Revival in the Parthian Period

Vesta Sarkhosh Curtis (The British Museum)

After the conquest of the Achaemenid empire by Alexander of Macedon in 330 BCE and during the subsequent rule of the Seleucid dynasty over the former Persian empire, the two former Achaemenid satrapies of Hyrcania (modern Gurgan) and Parthava (Khurasan) were amalgamated into the province of Parthia.[1] According to Justin (12.4.12), the Seleucid ruler Antiochus I (281-261 BCE) appointed a Persian named Andragoras as satrap of the province of Parthia. Andragoras' name appears on coins and is also attested in a Greek inscription.[2]

Towards the end of the reign of Antiochus II (261-246 BCE) Andragoras rebelled against his Seleucid overlord and minted gold and silver coins. A gold stater bearing the inscription ΑΝΔΡΑΓΟΡΟΥ shows on the obverse a bearded figure wearing a diadem looking to the right (Fig. 1). The reverse depicts a chariot drawn by four galloping horned horses. Nike/Victory drives the chariot and an armoured figure, wearing a cuirass, stands behind her. Andragoras' name appears below the chariot. Silver tetradrachms show on the obverse a goddess wearing a stepped mural crown looking right. The reverse has a standing Athena with helmet, long *chiton* and mantle holding an owl in her outstretched right hand, the left hand resting on her shield. Here, the name appears vertically on the right, behind the goddess.[3]

Fig. 1. Gold coin of Andragoras. The British Museum.

Meanwhile, a man called Arsaces, of Scythian or Bactrian[4] origin, was elected leader of the Parni tribes in 247 BCE. This date marks the beginning of the Arsacid era. The Parni or Aparni were part of the confederacy of the Dahae and lived along the river Ochus southeast of the Caspian Sea. Less than ten years after the rebellion of Andragoras against the Seleucids, in 238 BCE, Arsaces and his brother Tiridates invaded the satrapy of Parthia, killed Andragoras and established control over this province.[5]

The language of Parthia at this time was Parthian, which linguistically is related to Median and belongs to the family of West Iranian languages.[6] The

Parni newcomers abandoned their own language in favour of Parthian.[7] The Parni, whose speech was described by Justin as "midway between Scythian and Median, and contained features of both", now became known as the Arsacids or Parthians.[8]

Their kings all took the throne name Arsaces, following the founder of the dynasty. This has made it difficult to identify many Arsacid Parthian kings on coins and cuneiform inscriptions. Strabo (XV.i.36) writes:

> ...such is also the custom among the Parthians; for all are called Arsaces, although personally one king is called Orodes, another Phraates, and another something else.

The earliest coins are those of Arsaces I (*c*. 238-211 BCE) and Arsaces II (*c*. 211-191 BCE) which were perhaps minted at Mithradatkirt or Nisa, now in the Republic of Turkmenistan. They show the head of the ruler on the obverse and a seated archer on the reverse, both turned to the right in the Seleucid fashion. Soon, however, the direction of the king's head is changed to the left (Fig. 2).[9]

The soft cap with the top bent over to one side, worn by the ruler, seems to have derived from the tall, pointed Scythian hat, which appears on late sixth-century and fifth-century Achaemenid reliefs (e.g Bisitun and Persepolis).[10]

Fig. 2. Silver coin of Arsaces I. The British Museum.

The coin legends are in Greek, giving the throne name "Arsaces", and sometimes the additional title autocrat.[11]

Fig. 3. Silver coin of satrap Tissaphernes. The British Museum.

Fig. 4. Silver coin of satrap Autophradates. The British Museum.

Both the obverse and reverse type of these early coins are remarkably similar to the pre-Hellenistic coins of the Persian satraps. The combination of a soft hat with earflap and neckguard and diadem can be seen on coins of the satraps Tissaphernes, *c*. 420-395 BCE (Fig. 3), Spithridates, *c*. 440-330 BCE,[12] and Autophradates, *c*. 380-320 BCE (Fig. 4).

This type of headdress is not unlike the soft hats worn by Delegation I, the Medes, and other Iranian peoples on the reliefs of the Apadana at Persepolis.[13] Perhaps Arsaces adopted this type of hat after his conquest of Parthia.[14] The seated figure on the reverse resembles the archer shown on coins of Tarkamuwa, formerly known as Datames, of the fourth century BCE (Fig. 5).

This could indicate that the coins of the western satraps of the Achaemenid empire must have been known to the early Arsacids once they took over power in Parthia.

The geographical expansion of Parthia and the political consolidation of the early Parthian kingdom is associated with Mithradates (Mihrdad) I (*c.* 171-138 BCE). Silver drachms of this ruler show him first with a soft hat (Fig. 6),

Fig. 5. Silver coin of satrap Tarkamuwa (Datames). The British Museum.

similar to coins of Arsaces I and II, but soon a new type of portrait appears on his coins. Mithradates abandons the floppy hat and instead appears with only a diadem (Fig. 7). He adopts the image of a Hellenistic ruler,[15] but appears bearded in the Iranian/Near Eastern tradition. A fragment of a male head from the excavations at New Nisa may represent Mithradates.[16] Both here and on his coins he looks remarkably similar to the bearded Andragoras (cf. Fig. 1), the satrap of Parthia, who was deposed by Arsaces I. The long beard was not uncommon amongst the Seleucids and Demetrius II is shown as a bearded ruler on tetradrachms from Antioch.[17]

The progression of titles employed on the coins of Mithradates is also

Figs. 6-7. Silver coins of Mithradates I (Mihrdad). The British Museum.

interesting. First we read the plain "of Arsaces", then "of King Arsaces", and finally "of the Great King Arsaces" (Figs. 6-8). We also find on these coins the extended title "whose father is a god" (ΘΕΟΠΑΤΟΡΟΣ), an epithet which is repeated again under Phraates (Farhad), Mithradates' son, and Artabanus (Ardavan), Mithradates' brother. This particular epithet was not usual amongst

Fig. 8. Silver coin of Mithradates I (Mihrdad). The British Museum.

the Seleucid kings,[18] but coins of the Greco-Bactrian ruler Antimachus I (*c.* 180-170 BCE) have as part of the legend the title ΒΑΣΙΛΕΩΣ ΘΕΟΥ "of divine king".[19]

In June 149/8 BCE, the western part of Iran, that is Media, was still under the control of the Seleucids. This is indicated by a dated Greek inscription from Bisitun, which mentions a certain Kleomenes as "Viceroy of the Upper Satrapies".[20] But soon afterwards, in 148 or 147 BCE, Mithradates took Ecbatana (modern Hamadan) and the region came under the control of the Arsacid Parthians.

Southwestern Iran was still under Seleucid rule around 150 BC, but internal struggles between Demetrius I (162-150 BCE) and Alexander Balas (150-145 BCE), who claimed to be a son of Antiochus Epiphanes, ended in the death of Demetrius and a short rule of Alexander Balas.[21] In 147 BCE Kamnaskires, a local ruler of Elymais, seized Susa from the Seleucids and issued coins there. Kamnaskires appears on his tetradrachms like a Seleucid king, beardless and wearing a diadem (Fig. 9). On the reverse of his tetradrachms he calls himself

Fig. 9. Silver coin of Kamnaskires I of Elymais. The British Museum.

"Great King Kamnaskires, the Saviour" (ΒΑΣΙΛΕΩΣ ΜΕΓΑΛΟΥ ΚΑΜΝΙΣΚΙΡΟΥ [ΣΩ]ΤΗΡΟΣ).[22]

Meanwhile, Mithradates was also able to capitalise on the internal struggles of the Seleucids and in 141 BCE invaded Babylonia and occupied Seleucia-on-the-Tigris. An attempt in 140-139 BCE by the Seleucid ruler Demetrius II to recover lost territories proved a failure. He was taken prisoner by the Parthian army and sent to Mithradates, who by this time had returned to Hyrcania in northeastern Iran. The capture of Demetrius ended resistance in Babylonia and Mithradates was able to extend Parthian control over Iran, including Characene on the Persian Gulf, Susa and Elymais.[23] The Arsacids were now in control of both Iran and Mesopotamia.

Tetradrachms of Mithradates I struck at Seleucia-on-the-Tigris (Fig. 8), a Hellenistic city founded by Seleucus I (312-281 BCE), use the epithet "philhellene" (ΦΙΛΕΛΛΗΝΟΣ). It seems likely that Mithradates needed the support of the Greek population in that particular part of his empire and therefore adopted this epithet once he conquered Seleucia.[24] The title philhellene continued on coin legends until the reign of Artabanus II at the beginning of the first century CE.[25]

During this time, Hyspaosines (Spaosines), the son of Sagdodonacus, was the governor of Antiochea-on-the-Tigris, a city founded by Alexander of Macedon on the Persian Gulf.[26] Hyspaosines whose name, like that of his father, is of Iranian/Bactrian origin, broke away from his Seleucid overlords between 141 and 139 BCE, when Demetrius was defeated by the Parthians.[27]

At the end of his reign, Mithradates encountered trouble from nomads in the northeastern parts of his empire. Movement of nomads, including the Yuezhi confederation, had pushed the Saka, who were of Iranian origin, into Parthian territory.[28] Phraates (Farhad) II (*c.* 138-127 BCE) was now faced with both unrest along the eastern borders as well as an attack by the Seleucids under Antiochus VII Sidetes (139/8-129 BCE) in the west. Phraates put an end to the initial Seleucid victory in the western part of his empire by killing Antiochus in battle, but once again nomad trouble erupted in the east where Phraates was

Fig. 10. Silver coin of Artabanus (Ardavan) I. The British Museum.

killed in 128 BCE. Artabanus I (*c.* 127-124 BCE), a brother of Mithradates, succeeded his nephew Phraates on the throne, but was also killed on the eastern front while fighting the Tocharis (Fig. 10).

Figs. 11-12. Silver coins of Mithradates (Mihrdad) II. The British Museum.

When Mithradates (Mihrdad) II (Figs. 11-12) came to the throne in 122/1 BCE, Hyspaosines of Characene had rebelled against Himerus, the Parthian governor of Seleucia-on-the-Tigris. Cuneiform tablets from Warka[29] of 127/6 BCE mention Hyspaosines as ruler of Babylonia. His silver tetradrachms from Charax of the Seleucid era 184, that is 129/8 BCE, as well as undated tetradrachms from Seleucia-on-the-Tigris,[30] also mention him by name. He appears like a Seleucid ruler, unbearded and wearing a diadem. The reverse depicts a nude Herakles seated on a rock, which has been linked with a similar iconography on Greco-Bactrian coins.[31] This does not take account of Seleucid coins, such as those of Antiochus I (281-261 BCE) and Antiochus II (261-246 BCE),[32] where Herakles is also sitting on a rock.

This short-lived autonomy was brought to an end by Mithradates II the Great, who overstruck bronze coins of Hyspaosines.[33] Characene, once again, became part of the Parthian empire until its collapse in the early third century CE.[34] Mithradates also conquered parts of northern Mesopotamia, including the Hellenistic city of Dura Europos around 113 BCE.[35] The Parthian empire now stretched from the river Euphrates to eastern Iran. It was also during this period that the quarrel over Armenia began. This dispute was to last for many centuries and became the most important source of contention between Rome and Parthia and was to continue under the dynasty of the Sasanians.

By the end of the second century BCE the seat of power lay firmly in the western part of the empire and Ctesiphon became the capital. Mithradates, the "Great King", is also depicted on a badly eroded relief at Bisitun.[36] Here he receives homage from a row of standing figures, which, according to the accompanying Greek inscription, includes the satrap of satraps, Gotarzes (Godarz). According to cuneiform tablets from Warka, Gotarzes succeeded Mithradates II to the throne in 91 BCE. He struck tetradrachms and remained in power in Babylonia. Another Parthian ruler, Sinatruces I, controlled the eastern part of the empire. Coins bearing the title ΘΕΟΠΑΤΟΡΟΣ ("whose father is a god"), which probably refers to Mithradates II, were originally attributed to Gotarzes but recently have been dated to the reign of Sinatruces.[37]

In the middle of the first century BCE, Roman forces received a heavy blow from the Parthian army of King Orodes II. Under the command of Surena, the Parthians defeated and humiliated the Romans at Carrhae, modern Harran in southeastern Turkey, in 53 BCE and Crassus, the Roman consul and general, was killed. The Roman standards were lost to the Parthians and were not returned to Rome until 20 BCE. This military humiliation was then turned into a political victory by the Roman emperor Augustus, when after lengthy negotiations, the Parthians agreed to return the standards (see below, Schneider: figs. 5-6). Augustus successfully portrayed them as barbarians and a defeated enemy.[38]

An invasion of Parthia via Armenia took place under Mark Antony, who advanced through northwestern Iran and came face to face with the Parthian army of Phraates (Farhad) IV (c. 38-2 BCE) (Fig. 13). But Antony was forced to withdraw with his army when they suffered heavy losses during the unsuccessful siege of Praata/Praaspa, perhaps at Takht-i Solaiman near modern Takab or Maragheh in northwestern Iran.[39]

Fig. 13. Silver coin of Phraates (Farhad) IV. The British Museum.

Roman-Parthian relations were often tense as both powers laid claim to and fought over Armenia. This continued during the reign of Artabanus (Ardavan) II (10-38 CE). In 115 CE the emperor Trajan invaded Armenia and turned it into a Roman province. He then advanced towards northern Mesopotamia, conquered Dura Europos on the river Euphrates, and then took the capital Ctesiphon. Trajan was presented with the title "Parthicus" by the Roman Senate, but after an unsuccessful siege of the city of Hatra in 117 CE, he was forced to retreat.[40]

More confrontation between Parthia and Rome took place in the second half of the second century, when in 161 CE Marcus Aurelius destroyed and burnt Seleucia-on-the-Tigris and Ctesiphon. This took place during the reign of the Parthian king Vologases (Valgash) IV (147-191 CE). Dura Europos was by now firmly part of the Roman empire on their eastern frontier. In 197 CE northern Mesopotamia was invaded by Septimius Severus and after capturing Seleucia and Babylon, he received the title "Parthicus Maximus" from the Roman Senate. Once again a siege of Hatra in northern Mesopotamia proved unsuccessful. The Roman forces withdrew and peace was made by the Romans under the emperor Caracalla in 211 CE.[41]

By now Parthian central authority was no longer in the hands of one ruler. Vologases VI (208-228 CE) struck coins at Seleucia-on-the-Tigris and controlled Mesopotamia even after the defeat of his brother Artabanus (Ardavan) IV (Fig. 14) by Ardashir, a local king from Pars/Fars, in southern Iran.[42]

Fig. 14. Silver coin of Artabanus (Ardavan) IV. The British Museum.

Ardavan controlled Media and also Susa and his name appears on a stele from Susa of 215 CE. The relief shows the king seated on a throne supported by winged mythical beasts. The "King of Kings" is offering a ring of power to Khwasak, the satrap of Susa.[43] In 224 Ardavan was finally defeated by Ardashir, the son of Papak, a local king in Pars. The historic battle of Hormizdgan appears on the early Sasanian jousting relief of Firuzabad, south of Shiraz. Here, the saddle bag of the toppled Parthian king bears the same royal crest that also appears on the tiara of the dead opponent lying under the horse of Ardashir on his Naqsh-i Rustam relief (Fig. 15).[44]

Fig. 15. Sasanian rock-relief of Ardashir I at Naqsh-i Rustam, Iran.

Evidence for an Iranian revival in the Parthian period is found on coins of this dynasty, as already mentioned above. Under Mithradates II, the ancient

Near Eastern title "King of Kings" or "Great King of Kings" reappears on both drachms and tetradrachms.[45] Cuneiform tablets from Warka in southern Mesopotamia of *c*. 94 BCE also mention these royal titles,[46] which were not used by the Seleucids,[47] but became popular also to the east of the Parthian empire. The title "King of Kings" was also common amongst Kushan kings of the first and second centuries CE, who ruled over Bactria.[48]

The costume of the Parthian kings is further evidence of an Iranian revival in this period.[49] Coins show how the trouser-suit became the most popular outfit of the Parthians and was worn by the king himself. While the archer on the reverse of coins appears in tunic and trousers from the very beginning, the ruler on the obverse of the earliest coins wears a Hellenistic over-garment fastened at one shoulder. This can be seen on coins of Arsaces I, Arsaces II and Mithradates I. From the time of Artabanus I (*c*. 127-124/3 BCE) this type of dress is replaced by a v-necked jacket, which must have been part of the Parthian trouser-suit (Fig. 10). As such, it is shown on the reverse of Parthian coins and is particularly clear on tetradrachms of the second and first centuries BCE and first century CE (Figs. 13 and 17).[50] Mithradates II introduced a new royal headgear, the tiara or *kolah*, which was bejewelled around the edge and in the centre (Fig. 12). This type of hat, which remained popular until the end of the Parthian period, was sometimes decorated with astral designs and pearls and even rows of stags.[51] The tiara was presented by the Parthian King of Kings as one of the royal insignia to local kings.[52] When Ardashir I of the Sasanian dynasty rose to power as the new King of Kings, he struck gold dinars, silver drachms and billon tetradrachms on which he appeared with the Parthian tiara (Fig. 16).[53]

Fig. 16. Silver coin of Ardashir I. The British Museum.

A mixture of Iranian and Hellenistic traditions is noticeable in the art of Commagene in the first century BCE. The Commagenian rulers had Iranian and Greek names (Mithradates I Kallinikos and his son Antiochus I Theos) and worshipped gods with Zoroastrian / Iranian connections but with mixed Greek and Iranian names. Antiochus I (69–31? BCE) refers in an inscription from the Nimrud Dagh Hierothesion[54] to gods worshipped by him:

> I have set up these divine images of Zeus-Ormasdes and of Apollo-Mithra-Helios-Hermes and of Artagnes-Herakles-Ares...

The Commagenian rulers claimed descent from the Persian kings Darius and Xerxes, while also being related to the Seleucids on the maternal side.[55] An inscription from Arsameia-on-the-Nymphaios mentions the "Persian costume" and that Antiochus I gave orders to the priests to wear this on his and his father's birthday.[56] A combination of a long-sleeved long overcoat and baggy trousers appears on the Mithra-Apollo relief from Arsameia-on-the-Nymphaios,[57] as well as the ancestral relief at Nimrud Dagh.[58] It is interesting that the ancestral relief of Darius from Nimrud Dagh shows the Persian king wearing a tall hat, which is decorated with stars and a row of eagles.[59]

The costume of the kings of Commagene was a variation on the Iranian trouser-suit. Here, a long-sleeved and belted tunic is pulled up in the centre by straps suspended from a looped belt and is worn over tight trousers. In addition, the king wears an elaborately decorated cuirass or over-shirt, a shoulder cloak and a tall hat with the top ending in five pointed rays and a diadem tied around the tiara. Lion heads decorate the looped belt, while walking lions appear on his tiara. The earflap is tucked in at the top.[60] The royal headgear, which has been interpreted as sun rays, a symbol of Apollo-Mithra-Helios, could easily be a variation of the crenellated crown. A type of vegetation decorates the crown. Apollo-Mithra-Helios and Herakles-Artagnes-Verethragna were frequently shown clasping the hand of the king.[61] At Nimrud Dagh Apollo-Mithra also wears the Commagenian trouser-suit, but his head is covered with a "Phrygian" cap which has long earflaps and neck guard. Sun rays decorate his headgear and nimbus.[62]

During the reign of Artabanus (Ardavan) II (10-38 CE), who was from Media Atropatene (Azarbaijan) in northwestern Iran and an Arsacid through his mother, the process of Iranisation continued. Artabanus dropped the title philhellene from the reverse legends of his tetradrachms.[63] The king on the reverse is shown seated on a throne, as well as riding a horse (Fig. 17). Here he receives a symbol of kingship from a deity, who is iconographically similar to Tyche the goddess of Fortune, or Nike the goddess of Victory.[64] Some tetradrachms of this ruler show him in frontal pose, similar to silver drachms of an earlier Parthian king of the early first century BCE (Figs. 17 and 18).[65]

The large bronze statue from Shami, found in the Bakhtiari region of Iran and now in the National Museum of Iran, shows a larger than life-size male figure facing the spectator (see below, Schneider: fig. 4).[66] He wears the Parthian trouser-suit consisting of a long-sleeved short jacket and leggings. His crossed-over top with its v-shaped opening and wide lapels, a belt made of plaques, a dagger worn on each side and the suspenders of his wide leggings are all clearly seen on Parthian coins of the middle of the first century BCE. These details are especially clear on tetradrachms of Phraates (Farhad) IV (Fig. 13). A similar outfit is also worn by a small statuette from Susa and a figure on a limestone stela from Parthian Ashur in northern Mesopotamia.[67]

Terracotta figurines from Parthian sites in Mesopotamia, such as Ashur, Babylon, Warka, Nippur and Seleucia, of the first to second centuries CE often

Fig. 17. Silver coin of Artabanus (Ardavan) II. The British Museum.

Fig. 18. Silver coin of "unknown King", perhaps Darius of Media Atropatene. The British Museum.

wear Parthian costume. The hair of these figures is sometimes arranged in the Parthian tripartite fashion.[68]

There are many examples of reliefs, statues and wall paintings showing figures in frontal pose and wearing the Parthian costume during the first to early third centuries CE. To the east of the Parthian empire, the art of the Kushan kings of Bactria depicts worshipping figures wearing trouser-suits.[69] The Kushan kings themselves appear in such outfits both on their coins (Figs. 19 - 20) as well as their sculptures.

To the west, at Palmyra, Dura Europos and Hatra we find many elaborate examples of male figures wearing Parthian tunics, jackets and trousers.[70] The wealthy merchants of Palmyra, ancient Tadmor, in the Syrian desert were keen to show themselves and some of their gods in the fashion of the time (see below, Schneider: fig. 12). They followed the Parthian style of frontality and both gods and mortals, who appear on architectural and funerary reliefs, wear the Parthian trouser-suit.[71]

Fig. 19-20. Gold coins of Kanishka I. The British Museum.

At Dura Europos, which was part of the Parthian empire from c. 113 BCE until 165 CE, the influence of Parthian art continues during the Roman occupation of the city. Examples of Parthian frontality and the Parthian costume are found in various religious and private buildings at Dura. The most famous of these are the Jewish Synagogue and its magnificent wall paintings, the Mithraeum, the temple of the Palmyrene Gods, as well as graffiti in private houses of the early third century CE.[72]

At Hatra the local rulers are shown wearing lavish trouser-suits, where the tunic and trousers have geometric and floral designs.[73] The decoration may have been embroidered, woven, or created by sew-on-plaques and pearls.[74]

A popular item of clothing in the second and early third centuries was the long-sleeved coat, worn over a round-necked and knee-length tunic. It appears on reliefs from Bard-i Nishandeh and Tang-i Sarvak in southwestern Iran and at Hatra a wavy pattern on the lapels indicates fur. To the east, Kushan sculpture often shows worshipping figures in such overcoats. Statues and coins of the Kushan king Kanishka I (127-150 CE), for example, show him wearing a long-sleeved coat over long trousers. On the reverse of coins of Kanishka deities described in the legends as Orlagno (Iranian Verethragna) and Pharro (Iranian *khvarrah/farr*) are dressed in the same way as the ruler on the obverse (Figs. 19-20).

The long-sleeved coat appears on the very first Parthian coins of the late third century BCE, where it is part of the outfit of the archer on the reverse of coins of Arsaces I and II (Fig. 2). The way the over-garment is slung over the shoulders reminds us of coins of early local kings of Persis/Pars (Fig. 21), the *frataraka* of the post Achaemenid period,[75] as well as early fourth century BCE satrapal coins from Tarsus in the Achaemenid empire. Tarkamuwa is shown as a seated archer wearing a long-sleeved coat over his shoulders (Fig. 5).

This type of coat, the *kandys*, is widely represented in the art of the Achaemenid period. On the Apadana reliefs at Persepolis it is worn by Delegation I (the Medes) and is presented as tribute to the king by other Iranian delegations. It is also shown on the Pazyrik carpet, Greco-Persian seals, on

Fig. 21. Silver coin of Bagadates of Persis (Pars). The British Museum.

reliefs and wall paintings from Daskyleion and Karabarun in the western satrapies, as well as on statuettes and gold plaques from the Oxus Treasure.[76]

More evidence of Parthian-style art is also known from southwestern Iran, including the region of the Bakhtiari mountains. Here, the local rulers of Elymais minted coins during the Hellenistic period, when they were probably still under the yoke of the Seleucids. Antiochus III was murdered while raiding the temple of Bel in 187 BCE.[77] In 164 BCE Antiochus IV repeated the plundering on the temple of a goddess called Artemis/Aphrodite/Nanaia.[78]

Under Mithradates I Parthian supremacy was established over Elymais soon after 140 BCE, but there were attempts by some Elymaian local rulers to break away from their Parthian overlords.[79] Towards the end of the reign of Mithradates II, Kamnaskires II/III struck coins showing him with his queen Anzaze. The name of the Elymaian king and his consort appear in the Greek legend on the reverse of their tetradrachms (Fig. 22).

An anchor-like symbol, one of the dynastic insignia of the Seleucids, appears on the obverse behind the heads of the royal couple. This symbol seems to disappear temporarily from Elymaian coins with the growing

Fig. 22. Silver coin of Kamnaskires and Anzaze of Elymais. The British Museum.

influence of the Arsacids in this area around the middle of the first century BCE. It soon reappears on coins of the Elymaian kings in the first and second centuries CE with an added moon crescent with and without a star.[80] From the middle of the first century CE Parthian coins were no longer struck at Susa. The local kings of Elymais issued their own coins and enjoyed a certain degree of independence under the supremacy of their Parthian overlords.[81]

Elymaian coins show strong local iconographic features, such as the over-emphasised and outward curling moustache and geometrically shaped beard, as well as the *kolah* or tiara rounded at the top, paralleled on both architectural and rock-reliefs from this region. At the same time, Parthian influence shows itself in the way the diadem is worn around the tripartite bushy hairstyle (Figs. 23-25).

The diadem remains a popular symbol of kingship throughout the rule of these local kings. On second to early third century CE coins the portrait on the obverse is frontal and the Elymaian ruler is shown with his tripartite hairstyle, long moustache and full beard. Other coins of this period depict him with a kolah or tiara decorated with rows of pearls.[82]

The costume of the Elymaian kings consisted of the Parthian trouser-suit, as seen on reliefs and statues from the Bakhtiari region of southwestern Iran. Many rock reliefs were commissioned by the local rulers. They also built two sanctuaries at Masjid-i Sulaiman and Bard-i Nishandeh.[83] Here dedicatory statues and reliefs were discovered in and around temples. They show male figures with beard and moustache in frontal pose wearing elaborately decorated tunics and trousers, similar to those on Elymaian coins.

An item of clothing which seems typically Elymaian, as it is also shown on coins of the Elymaian kings, consists of a twisted sash that hangs over the left shoulder.[84] This is best seen on an architectural relief from Bard-i Nishandeh showing a sacrificial scene and rock reliefs from Tang-i Sarvak and Tang-i Butan (Shimbar), where male figures, perhaps priests, are shown in worshipping pose.[85] Here, the iconography and style of sculpture ties in well with late Parthian material of the second and early third centuries CE from Parthian Mesopotamia and further west at Palmyra.

Figs. 23-25. Bronze coins of Elymais, southwestern Iran. The British Museum.

The rock reliefs of Tang-i Sarvak, Hung-i Azhdar, Hung-i Kamalvand, Shimbar and Bid Zard show combat scenes, investiture scenes, religious scenes and banquet scenes.[86] Amongst a number of important and newly discovered Elymaian rock reliefs are those of Shaivand and Shirinow Movri in Iran, as well as two reliefs of frontally facing figures wearing a diadem from Algi.[87] The similarity of the diademed heads to second-century Elymaian sculpture from Shimbar, Shirinow Mowri, Bard-i But and other sites has rightly prompted Ja'far Mehrkiyan to suggest a second-century CE date.[88]

This semi-independence applied to a number of kingdoms within the Parthian empire, where the local kings enjoyed a certain degree of autonomy. This is usually seen as a sign of the political weakness of the Parthian overlords and the consequent growing independence of the local kings, but perhaps one should move away from such modern interpretations and see the existence of various local kingdoms within the political framework of the Parthian empire.

From the reign of Mithradates I onwards, when the Parthians controlled Mesopotamia and Iran, local kingdoms were granted a certain amount of

The Iranian Revival in the Parthian Period

freedom, as long as they recognised the Parthian sovereign as their overlord. The semi-independence of local kingdoms should not be interpreted as a sign of weakness of Parthian central government. The political framework of the Parthians allowed local kings a degree of independence within their region, as long as they accepted Parthian central authority.

It is also within this political framework that we should understand the position of the local kings as subordinates of the Parthian King of Kings. We should be cautious of interpreting the flourishing of local art as an indication of a decrease in central power. This has been suggested in the case of the late Parthian site of Qaleh Yazdgird in western Iran.[89]

The wealth of material from this site in the form of plaster sculpture, elaborate figural and floral decorations painted in polychrome colours and engaged column capitals with female figures, similar to those found to the east at Marv and to the west at Seleucia and Warka in southern Mesopotamia, may simply indicate the growing economy as a result of the flourishing east-west trade, rather than a decline in central power.

While the art of Elymais undoubtedly shows local features, the influence of Parthian art on the iconographic details of the hairstyle, regalia and costume cannot be denied. Elymais, as well as Persis, was able to continue with its own local traditions, while at the same time absorbing iconographic and stylistic features of Parthian art, which were then passed on to the Sasanian period that followed. Local kings also adapted certain features of the pre-Hellenistic tradition from the Arsacid Parthians. The Parthians' apparent awareness of this tradition is best seen in the revival of iconographic features known from the Achaemenid period, e.g. the trouser-suit and slung-over coat on early coins, and the revival of the royal title "King of Kings".

The Parthian-period coinage of Persis is of great interest in any discussion of an Iranian revival in post-Hellenistic Iran. Here, the second and third series of drachms of the local kings are of particular relevance, as they show clear parallels with Parthian coins from *c.* 140 BCE to the beginning of the third century CE. The obverse of the drachms from Persis depicts the local kings in similar fashion to the Parthian "King of Kings". The ruler is bearded looking to the left, either wearing an elaborate tiara and diadem, or a diadem only (Figs. 26-28). His costume consists of a jacket, where often the v-necked opening is visible.

The most obvious difference to Parthian coins is the iconography on the reverse. On later coins of Persis we have either a bearded figure holding a *barsom* bundle (the sacred twigs) and standing in front of a fire altar, or astral signs − sun and moon crescent − as symbols of divinities (Figs. 26-28). In addition, the coin legends are in Middle Persian. The legends on Parthian coins are in Greek, but Parthian letters and words appear from the late first century BCE / first century CE onwards.[90]

The portraits of the rulers of Persis show Parthian influence, while the scene with the worshipping figure and fire altar remind us of Achaemenid tomb reliefs and Persian seals of the fifth century BCE. On Parthian bronze coins altars are occasionally shown in the early first century during the reign of Phraataces.[91] They also appear on bronze coins of Artabanus II.[92] Bronze coins of Vologases III depict a male figure standing at an altar, which is sometimes shown by itself.[93] The astral signs are known from Parthian coins of the first century BCE, where they either appear on the obverse of silver drachms next to the king's head, or they are shown on their own on the reverse of bronze coins.[94]

Figs. 26-28. Silver coins of Persis. The British Museum.

The iconography of the coins of Persis brings together Parthian and local motifs. This has long been seen as a sign of a revival of Persian iconography, which is then passed on to the Sasanians. The contribution of the Parthians to this process is often ignored. Perhaps such a revival would not have been possible under a different dynasty than the Arsacid Parthians, as they allowed their sub-kings a certain degree of autonomy and self-expression. The local kings created on their coins and reliefs an iconography which was a mixture of Iranian, Hellenistic and local traditions.

Notes:

1. Bivar, 1983: 24.
2. Robert 1960: 85-91. Ghirshman 1974:7 sees the name Andragoras as a Greek translation of the Old Persian Narisanka and Avestan "nairya-sanha-" (one of the messengers of Ahura Mazda). Cf also name of the Sasanian King Narseh. See Frye 1987:26.
3. Hill 1922: pl. XXVIII, 1-3.
4. For Scythian or Bactrian origin and discussion of various classical sources, see Drijvers 1998: 285; also also Shahbazi 1987: 525.
5. Bivar 1983: 28-9.
6. Schmitt 1998: 164.
7. The language of the Parni/Aparni was probably related to Khwaresmian, Sogdian and Saha. This assumption is based on surviving loan words in the Parthian language, see Schmitt 1998: 164-5.
8. Bivar 1983: 27.
9. Abgarians and Sellwood 1971: 115-16, pl. 20; Sellwood 1980, types 1-3, 4.
10. Curtis and Tallis 2005: figs. 2, 39-40.
11. Abgarians and Sellwood 1971: 111-12; Sellwood 1980, types 1-6.
12. See Curtis and Tallis 2005: 204, nos. 341-434.
13. Walser 1966: pl. 31.
14. Curtis, forthcoming.
15. The diadem already existed in Achaemenid iconography and before that appears in Assyrian art, but the Arsacid Parthian rulers imitated Hellenistic rulers, and in particular the Seleucids, when they tied a diadem around the head as symbol of kingship.
16. Invernizzi 2001: pls. I-IV.
17. Messina 2003: p. 23.
18. Mørkholm 1991: 31.
19. Bopearachchi 1991: 183, 187.
20. Bivar 1983: 33.
21. See Bivar 1983: 33-34.
22. See detailed discussion by Assar 2006a: 27-91.
23. Bivar 1983: 34-5.
24. Sellwood 1980: 29, 35, type 10.i-iv.
25. Curtis 2000: 24.
26. For Sagdodonacus and his son Spaosines, see "Arsacids and Sasanians" in Shayegan, forthcoming. Schmitt 1990: 246-247 sees the earliest evidence of the Iranian name Hyspasines in Bactrian. He equates it with Vispa-čanah, meaning finding pleasure in all ("an allem Gefallen habend"), related to the Old Persian name Aspačanah (finding pleasure in horses, "an Rossen Gefallen habend"). I am grateful to Professor Rahim Shayegan for drawing my attention to the above references. Aspačanah (Greek Aspathines) is named as the bow-bearer of Darius in his Naqsh-i Rustam inscription (DNd); see Kent 1953: 140; Hinz 1973: 162.
27. Hansmanm 1992: 363.
28. Bivar 1983: 36.
29. Schuol 1998: 407.
30. See Assar 2006b: 105-108, figs. 10-11.
31. Schuol 1998: 410.
32. Houghton and Lorber 2002: 208: pl.17, no. 313.

24 THE AGE OF THE PARTHIANS

33. See Sellwood 1980: type 23-4.
34. Bivar 1983: 40; Sellwood 1983: 310-11.
35. Curtis 2000: 25.
36. Curtis 2000: 25, fig. 7.
37. For a detailed discussion of coins of Mithradates II, Gotarzes, Sinatruces and the so-called Parthian dark age, see Sellwood 1983: 284-286, Assar 2005: 51-55.
38. See in this volume, Bivar: 27-28 and Schneider: 54.
39. See Bivar 1983: 63-4.
40. See Bivar 1983: 89, 90-1.
41. Bivar 1983: 94.
42. Bivar 1983: 94.
43. Curtis 2004: 349.
44. For the jousting relief, see Ghirshman 1962: 125-130, figs. 163-166.
45. Curtis 2000: 25.
46. Van der Spek 1998: 214-24.
47. Coins of Alexander of Macedon and the Seleucids bear the title "of the king" (ΒΑΣΙΛΕΩΣ), see Price 1991: 32-33.
48. See for example, Rosenfield 1967: pls. 1-2.
49. For a detailed analysis of the Parthian costume, see Curtis 1988.
50. See also Sellwood 1980: types 39.1, 46-8, 50-7, 60-5, 68-70, 72-9, 84.
51. Sellwood 1980: type 34.
52. Curtis 1998: 65.
53. It is usually assumed that Ardashir adopted the tiara of Mithradates II as a symbol of legitimacy, but it should be remembered that the kings of Persis/ Parsa in the second and early third century CE wore the tall hat on their coins. See above: Fig. 28.
54. Boyce and Grenet 1991: 323.
55. Doerner and Goell 1963:70-71.
56. Doerner and Goell 1963: 47.
57. Doerner and Goell 1963: 201, fig. 28, pl. 52B.
58. Humann Puchstein 1890: pls. XXXVI,1 and XXXV, 3.
59. Ghirshman 1962: fig. 78.
60. Doerner and Goell 1963: pl.50.
61. See Ghirshman 1962: figs. 79 -80. This gesture is generally described as *dexiosis*, but may have been the Zoroastrian *hamazor*, see Errington and Curtis, in press.
62. I am grateful to Dr Elizabeth Pendleton for drawing my attention to these details.
63. Sellwood 1980: types 62-3.
64. Sellwood 1980: type 63.
65. Sellwood 1980: type 35; 1983: 286, known as "the unknown ruler" or "Darius of Media Atropatene".
66. Curtis 2000: 26, fig.8; 2004: 347-348.
67. Curtis 2000: 27, pls.3-4.
68. Curtis 2000: 29, pls.6-7.
69. Rosenfiled 1967: pls. II-XII, 1-2.
70. Curtis 2000: colour plates III-IV.
71. Curtis 2000: 33, fig.9.
72. Curtis 2000: 32.
73. Safar and Mustafa 1974; Curtis 2000: pls. 9 and III.
74. Curtis 1998: 65.

THE IRANIAN REVIVAL IN THE PARTHIAN PERIOD

75. For a second century BCE date of these coins, see Wiesehöfer in this volume: 42. The date of these coins is far from certain and remains disputed. See also Curtis forthcoming.
76. Curtis 1998: 66.
77. Houghton and Lorber I, 2002: 354.
78. See Hill 1922: clxxxiii with references to classical sources such as Polybius, Josephus, Appian and the Old Testament (2nd Maccabeans).
79. Sellwood 1983: 307.
80. Hill 1922: pl. xxxviii – xlii; Sellwood 1983:308.
81. Augé et al. 1979: 426; Curtis 2000: 31.
82. Hill 1922: pl.XL, nos. 8-19, 20-24; Alram 1987: 121-122.
83. See Ghirshman 1976; Curtis 1994: pls. I-IV.
84. Hill 1922: pl. xxxviii, nos. 1-3, 7-8; Curtis 2000: 31.
85. Vanden Berghe and Schippmann 1985: pls. 2 (Hung-i Azhdar) 13, 22; Curtis 2000: pl. 10.
86. Vanden Berghe and Schippmann 1985.
87. Mehrkiyan 1381/2003: 82-4, figs. 1-3.
88. Mehrkiyan 1381/2003: 85.
89. Keall 1975: 627-32; also Curtis 2000: 28.
90. Sellwood 1980: type 71.1.
91. Hill 1922: pl. XXIII, 15.
92. Hill 1922: pl. XXV, 10; Sellwood 1980: type 63.22.
93. Sellwood 1980: types 78.13; 78.15.
94. Hill 1922: pls XIII, 13-15; XV15-17.

2

Gondophares and the Indo-Parthians

A.D.H. Bivar (Professorial Research Associate, Department of Art and Archaeology, SOAS)

When the Greek philosopher and miracle-worker Apollonius of Tyana crossed the River Indus on his journey to visit the Brahmans in India, he was impressed by the smooth contacts between his caravan leader and the officer of the kingdom they were about to enter.[1] Apollonius had travelled in a caravan under the protection of the Parthian king Vardanes, who ruled from 39 to 47 CE. He had visited the king in Babylon in 42 CE. His caravan leader presented the king's letter of introduction, presumably in Parthian, to the Indian official, who understood it, and received it respectfully, though as the biographer Philostratus reports, he was not himself a subject of Vardanes. There was, indeed, a separate Parthian kingdom beyond the Indus, independent of the Arsacid kingdom, but in friendly alliance with it. Thus Apollonius travelled to Taxila and beyond with official hospitality. His description of the Indo-Parthian capital is convincing in the main, though he does not name the celebrated ruler Gondophares reigning at that time, unless his arrival was in fact after the latter's demise. He mentions as king a certain Phraotes, previously not known to the historic record, but who could be identified with a name lately read as Phraates on a poorly preserved coin.[2] That a citizen of the Roman east could travel so far was entirely possible at that time, for we shall see that Apollonius was not the only such visitor.

Sceptical scholars, it is true, have been reluctant to accept the story of Apollonius as fact, as it has some doubtful associations.[3] In later decades, pagan apologists had been inclined to inflate the legend of Apollonius as a counter to the propaganda of Christian evangelists. It is true, also, that his *Life* was compiled many years after his time from a variety of pamphlets and memoirs. Still, one should not be too hasty in dismissing his story as fantasy. For example, we are told that on arrival in India, Apollonius was invited by his hosts to join in a dragon-hunt. Yet this episode is not as fantastic as it seems. The Greek word which gives rise to our term "dragon" is described in earlier sources as a coiling serpent. Only at a far later date is the creature visualised with legs, wings, and breathing fire, an image probably inspired by Chinese observations of dinosaur skeletons in the Gobi. The δράκων reported by

GONDOPHARES AND THE INDO-PARTHIANS

Philostratus was no doubt a king cobra, itself a formidable antagonist for a hunter unprovided with a shotgun, and no doubt even more plentiful in the first century CE than it is today. A hunt for such quarry was quite credible, and a dangerous adventure.

To explore the origins of the eastern Parthian kingdom we must look back to the rise of the Arsacids. In about 238 BCE, Arsaces and his six companions rose against Andragoras, the maverick Seleucid satrap of Hyrcania and Parthia. This Andragoras was a veteran officer of the Seleucid king Antiochus II,[4] left isolated by the king's death in Asia Minor in 247 BCE, when the Seleucid succession lay open, and Antioch and perhaps far to the eastward was taken by Ptolemy III. The satrap had no alternative but to declare independence, and reigned long enough to issue an interesting series of coins. The suggestion of Ghirshman seems plausible,[5] that Andragoras, a dedicated Seleucid officer who had served under two kings, was an Iranian, and that the Greek name appearing on his coins was actually a calque on an original name Narseh. This is supported by the fact he is shown bearded on his coins, a representation unfashionable for Hellenistic governors. Whatever his ancestry, however, Andragoras was defeated and killed by the Parthians. They never recognised his interregnum, and started their new era to replace the venerable era of the Seleucids from 247/246 BCE, the date of Antiochus II's death.

From subsequent developments we can infer that one of the six chiefs who helped the first Arsaces to power, the head of the Suren family, placed the royal tiara on the head of Arsaces after his victory, a function which became hereditary in his lineage. He may also have held a critical military command. We can further take the number of conspirators as significant. Including Arsaces, they numbered seven, a number identical with that of the conspirators who long before had helped the Achaemenid king Darius (522 – 486 BCE) to power in Iran. My own explanation would be – though I do not expect all colleagues to agree with me – that this number in a conspiratorial cell reflects the ideology and organisation of Mithraism, inherited from the administration of the Median Empire, and still deeply rooted in the ideology of Zoroastrian dynasties in Iran.

In 129 BCE a crisis arose in the affairs of the Arsacid kingdom. The ruler of the time, Phraates II, was engaged in war against the Seleucid Antiochus VII Sidetes, who had moved from Babylonia with a powerful army to regain Media for his kingdom.[6] At the same time, Phraates was threatened by the arrival on his eastern border of the large horde of the Sacae, displaced from what is today Kazakhstan by the formidable Yuehzhi or Tocharian confederacy, in turn expelled from China's Gansu Province after a crushing defeat by the Huns. By a clever manoeuvre, Phraates enlisted the nearest group of Sacae as mercenaries for his war against the Greeks, but before the contingents arrived, Antiochus was trapped and killed by the Parthian forces, and the war in the west was at an end. When the mercenaries arrived, they were too late to take part, and Phraates committed the fatal blunder of refusing these levies their pay. When he rejected their proposal either for compensation, or employment

28 THE AGE OF THE PARTHIANS

against another enemy, the mercenaries turned against him, and ranged across Iran ravaging the countryside. Phraates marched against them, bolstering his forces by the incorporation of Greek prisoners from the army of Antiochus, but these too had been cruelly treated, and at the height of the battle they deserted to the Sacae. The Parthians were routed, and Phraates himself was killed in the debacle.

With the Tocharians pressing on behind, the Sacae moved southwards into Drangiana, thenceforth to be known by their name as Sakastan, today Sistan. Next it was the Tocharians who collided with the Parthian eastern frontier, and in a battle to oppose them in 124/3 BCE the next Arsacid ruler, Artabanus II, was in turn killed, surprisingly as a result of a wound to the arm.[7] The next Parthian king Mithradates II, titled "The Great", was a powerful ruler. His personal campaigning seems to have been confined to the west, where he secured Babylonia, and overthrew the ruler of Characene, Hyspaosines, before pressing on to the Euphrates, where he defeated the late Seleucid ruler Antiochus X.

Events on the eastern border are not well attested, but fighting continued between the Iranians and the nomads – probably, at this stage, again the Tocharians. A clue may be derived from the *Shāh-nāma* stories of the battles between the Iranians and Afrasiāb in the time of Kay Ka'ūs. The Iranians, commanded by Ṭūs, Godarz and Fariburz, sustain a series of reverses, and are eventually besieged on the mountain of Hamāvān. In their extremity, they are eventually relieved by the invincible Rustam, already apparently installed in Sistan, and commanding the forces of the Parthian southeast border. The episode may reflect some bias from the Sistan epic, but it seems clear that in the aftermath of the nomad invasion, the stabilisation of the eastern frontier was entrusted to the family of the Suren, who were successful in restoring the situation, and repelling the invaders.

From the outcome it is evident that the Suren chiefs, whose names are not clearly transmitted, succeeded in expelling the Saca horde from Drangiana, and drove them eastwards into Arachosia and the Punjab. There the invaders established a powerful kingdom, known as Sakastan, and attested for us by inscriptions and a copious coinage. We can construct a list of the Saca kings: Vonones, Spalirises, Spalagadames, Azes I, Azilises, and Azes II.

Chronological pegs for this series are provided by two fixed dates. The date of the Vikrama Era, BCE 57, marks, as we shall see, the formal installation of the first Azes. The demise of Azes II appears to fall close to 9 CE, though this date[8] cannot be firmly substantiated. It is the event laconically reported in Prologue 42 of Trogus: *Interitus Sa(ca)raucarum*, "The destruction of the Sacaraucae".[9] We lack the full text to tell us by whom, and how, the Sacaraucae were destroyed, whether by the Kushans or by the Suren – that is to say by the Indo-Parthians – though their copious coinage disintegrates at around this moment.

So far as the lineage of the Suren is concerned, they next appear in the historic record in 54 BCE. The Roman triumvir, Crassus, was appointed

GONDOPHARES AND THE INDO-PARTHIANS

Governor of Syria, with a large force destined for an invasion of Parthia. The Parthian king, Orodes II, naturally called in his eastern supremo to support him in resisting the Roman attack. We know this spectacular figure only by his family name, in Greek Surenas, of whom Plutarch provides the following striking portrait:[10]

> Surenas was no ordinary person, but in fortune, family and honour, the first after the king; and in point of courage and capacity, as well as in size and beauty, superior to the Parthians of his time. If he went only upon an excursion into the country, he had a thousand camels to carry his baggage, and two hundred carriages for his concubines. He was attended by a thousand heavy-armed horse, and many more of his light-armed rode before him. Indeed, his vassals and slaves made up a body of cavalry little less than ten thousand. He had the hereditary privilege in his family to put the diadem upon the king's head when he was crowned. When Orodes was driven from the throne, he restored him; and it was he who conquered for him the great city of Seleucia, being the first to scale the wall, and beating off the enemy with his own hand. Though he was not then thirty years old, his discernment was strong, and his counsel esteemed the best.

It is notable how closely the Classical description coincides with the account of Rustam in the *Shāh-nāma*, where he is described as *pīltan* "elephant-bodied", *tājbakhsh* "bestower of the crown", *sipāh-sālār* "commander of the army", and *jahān-pahlavān* "champion of the world". His personal bodyguard consisted of a thousand cataphract cavalry with scale-armour and lances, like the horseman depicted on the coins of the contemporary Saca emperor Azes I (57 CE).[11] When they threw off the coverings of their armour and deployed for the charge, their helmets were seen glittering with "the steel of Margiana".[12] We may infer, if the helmets came from Margiana, that these horsemen also were Sacae recruited from the same area, no doubt enlisted as mercenaries to enhance the forces of this "Warden of the Marches".

Famously, the result of the battle was one of the most resounding defeats ever suffered by a Roman army, with proportionate enhancement of Parthian reputation and prestige. Although this Suren, having it seems by his eminence aroused the apprehensions of the Parthian king, was killed not long after the battle, there is no doubt that his successors continued to flourish in Drangiana, to maintain a formidable military force, and to press upon the borders of the Indo-Scythian kingdom in Arachosia and the Punjab.

We cannot determine the names of the Suren chieftains who preceded, or succeeded, the Suren of Carrhae. There are only some echoes of a lineage preserved in the Avesta, in the epic tradition, and in the local history, the *Tārīkh-i Sīstān*; but these, as we shall see, are difficult of interpretation. In the last source, the list of the dynasty appears as follows.[13] The original founder of Sīstān was one Garshāsp, whose son was Kurenk, who died young. He in turn was the father of Nariman, father of Sām, father of Dastān/Zāl, father of Rustam, father of Farāmurz. Earlier, in the Yashts (Yt. 9, 31; Yt. 13. 61) Sāma

30 THE AGE OF THE PARTHIANS

is an epithet or family name of Garshāsp, and Nairimana is another of his epithets. One may begin to suspect that separate epithets of several, or perhaps just one, historical character, have been developed into a series of distinct sagas. For the present, therefore, the earlier sequence of the Suren family remains obscure.

The next emergence of evidence relating to the Indo-Parthian rulers is in contrast admirably concrete.[14] The so-called Takht-i Bahi Kharoṣṭhī inscription, now in the Lahore Museum, is thought to have come from this site west of the Indus, and eight miles west of the city of Mardan. It is dated in the 26th year of the Maharaja Guduvhara, and in the 103rd year of an unstated era. It is evident that Guduvhara is a spelling of the royal name usually rendered in English as Gondophares. The probable explanation of the era date ascribes it to the so-called Vikrama Era of 57 BCE, still extant in India today. The conversion is then 103-57 = 46 CE. Since this was the 26th regnal year of Gondophares, his accession year would have been 20 CE. We shall see that these very precise dates fit well with independent evidence.

The inscription, recording a dedication by a local notable, mentions also a certain personage named *erjhuna Kapa* "the prince Kapa". It is possible to identify him with the Kushan chief known from his own coins as Kujula Kadphises. The Kushans seem to have travelled south from Bactria across the Hindu Kush mountains, and to have occupied the Jalalabad valley and the Peshawar area. There are even indications of coins issued for Kujula at Taxila, probably before the rise of Gondophares, though the attribution is far from certain.[15] The situation attested by the inscription is likely to be that after the expulsion of Kujula from Taxila, he remained in possession of the Indus west bank, acknowledging the suzerainty of Gondophares, whose influence was for a time dominant there.

Students of religious history will of course remember that Gondophares also appears in a New Testament context. One of the apostles, a certain Thomas, a skilled carpenter, fell into financial difficulties after the Crucifixion. Following the legal provisions of the time, he was sold into slavery to pay off his debt, and arrived in Taxila. There he became the slave of the emperor Gondophares, and was employed to superintend the construction of a splendid palace. After he had been working for some time, the work seemed to have advanced little, and it appeared he had been using his building funds to support the poor. When taken to task for this peculation, his defence was that he was building the king a palace in heaven, a defence confirmed when Gondophares dreamt of the palace in heaven on the very next night, and was mightily impressed by its magnificence. Accordingly he decided to remit the death sentence he had pronounced on Thomas. Still, the apostle does not seem to have retained his job as supervisor of buildings, and is next heard of in Madras, where he founded the Church of South India. In church iconography, there is a colourful representation of Gondophares in the stained glass of the cathedral at Troyes in central France.

GONDOPHARES AND THE INDO-PARTHIANS

As far as the chronology is concerned, we read in the Acts of Thomas that the apostle's journey began very shortly after the Crucifixion, currently dated in 30 CE. It is thus entirely feasible that on his arrival in Taxila, not more than one or two years later, he would have found Gondophares on the throne, associated as the Acts claim with his brother Gad, whose historicity is substantiated by the appearance of his name, seemingly as subordinate ruler, on several coin issues.[16]

Although the dates of Gondophares at Taxila are reliably fixed at 20 to 46+ CE, we have little precise information about the events of his reign. His coinage, the chief source of information, falls into three provinces, distinguished by their module and reverse types. To Sistan no doubt belong good silver drachms of typical Parthian format. They have on the obverse the royal portrait in jewelled tiara, and the crest adorned with figures of cervids. On the reverse are the name and titles of the Indo-Parthian king around the figure of the ruler, enthroned and crowned by a Victory. One special type has attracted attention recently for its possible link to the *Shāh-nāma* tradition. The unusual Greek inscription reads "Great King of Kings Hyndopheres, who is surnamed Sām". I must confess that this reading is my own, and is not yet widely accepted. It has, indeed, the advantage of making definite sense. The competing interpretation takes the debatable last character as an *eta*, and would convey, I suppose, the Middle Persian form *šāhī*, from Old Persian *Xšāyaθiya* , meaning "King". Yet after having designated the ruler by the exalted titles "Great King of Kings", the force of a "surname" again designating him "King" is hard to see. If my version is preferred, one sees a link with the ancestry of Rustam in the *Shāh-nāma*, since Rustam was son of Zāl or Dastān (both these names being found), who in turn was the son of Sām. The discovery that Indo-Parthian rulers had, beside their official names, also nicknames, is an interesting development. It may explain why names in the epic have not hitherto been equated with historical records. There is also, of course, the question of whether they could have been used to distinguish rulers with identical names. Some critics believe, for example, that there was more than one Gondophares (see n. 14). Beside the one whose dates are established, there could have been a later prince of this name, the two distinguished, perhaps, by different nicknames as well as by numismatic considerations. Though plausible, the identification of a second Gondophares is not everywhere accepted.

Besides the mint of Sistan, two or more minting provinces have been detected for the coinage of Gondophares I and his successors. That of Arachosia-Kandahar has been distinguished by its adhesion to the reverse type of a winged Victory, while that of the Punjab-Taxila employs reverses with anthropomorphic deities resembling Zeus or Athena. The key problem with the analysis of this coinage is of course to establish the correct sequence of the successive rulers. There seems so far no clue as to the predecessors of Gondophares I, but since Taxilan coins of Abdagases describe him as the nephew of Gondophares it appears that he should have been the immediate successor.

The sequence of rulers following Gondophares I, in each of the three main coinage areas, remains largely debatable. We have the names Abdagases I, Orthagnes, Hybouzanes (if correctly read), Pacores, Sanabares, Abdagases II, as we shall see Sanabares II, and Sarpedonos, but there are only tantalizing clues to their exact sequence and relationships. Abdagases (apparently the first of two namesakes) was a nephew of Gondaphares, so apparently a near successor. Orthagnes may have also been close in time, perhaps a rival, to Abdagases. Hybouzanes is reported as a son of Orthagnes: ΒΑΣΙΛΕΥΣ ΥΒΟΥΖΑΝΗΣ ΥΙΟΣ ΟΡΘΑΓΝΟΥ ΒΑΣΙΛΕΩΣ.[17] Abdagases II, as we shall see, is revealed as a son of Sanabares. So far as absolute datings are concerned, after the demise of Gondophares something after 46 CE, our only indication is provided by the fact that coins of Pacores are overstruck on issues of the Kushan Soter Megas, which may date from around 50-60 CE. It does seem evident that the Indo-Parthian princes retained their independence in Arachosia and Sistan even after the Punjab had fallen to the Kushans - and that in some style, as we shall see. While Macdowall's sequencing from the coin-weights may have fixed the succession of Gondophares I, Abdagases, Orthagnes and Pacores, and, as we saw, the probable Gondophares II, there are now the above minor and newly discovered rulers to be fitted in. The coinage is hard to analyse, as the specimens are scarce, poorly preserved, in scattered locations, and published in reproductions that are often poorly legible. The core of the Indo-Parthian kingdom in Sistan has been one of the world's most inaccessible and desolate regions, divided by the borders of Afghanistan and Iran, and practically closed to archaeological researchers. As we shall see, there are many possibilities for future discovery, but hardly, I imagine, in any of our lifetimes.

I return now to Abdagases, and another puzzle about his identity. In Book VI of the *Annals* of Tacitus[18] we read how, at the Parthian capital, the Arsacid Artabanus III had become unpopular owing to his unsuccessful wars, and cruelty to his opponents. A moving spirit in the campaign to remove him was one Abdagaeses, previously commander-in-chief under Artabanus, (Josephus XVIII, 333) with whose support Tiridates, an Arsacid hostage in Rome, was invited to replace him. Artabanus was driven into exile in Hyrcania, and this Abdagaeses led the movement to bring back, and crown, Tiridates. After the departure of Artabanus, Abdagaeses and his influential "house" (as Tacitus states VI, 43), were all-powerful at the Parthian court. The coronation was performed, according to the ancestral tradition, by the Suren. We are not told whether this Suren was in fact Abdagaeses himself, but even if it was not, it was evidently a close associate in the conspiracy, and the links of Abdagaeses with the house of Sistan are manifest. The functions of *sipāh-sālār* "commander-in-chief" and *tājbakhsh* "bestower of the crown" in the lineage of Rustam were of course traditional. However, this replacement did not succeed. The fickle Parthian nobility resented the aggrandisement of Abdagaeses, and the inexperience and effete lifestyle of the Romanized Tiridates. So Artabanus returned, expelling his rivals back to Roman territory. We are not told what became of Abdagaeses, but since those events took place in 36 CE, it is feasible that he could have returned to the Indo-Parthian kingdom. If he was indeed a prince of that line, he could have eventually succeeded Gondophares on the latter's demise some ten years later. We could interpret his role at Ctesiphon as that of the traditional Suren, commander-in-chief of the royal armies, and ceremonial crowner of the king at coronations.

This was the picture of the Indo-Parthians until two discoveries of recent years. It is, of course, axiomatic amongst numismatists that neither Parthian dynasty, issuers of silver currency in quantity, ever produced a coinage in gold. There are one or two doubtful exceptions, the genuineness of which remains debated, and it is conceivable that the Arsacids produced a very sparse inaugural gold coinage, with types similar to their usual silver, for ceremonial presentations. In 1996 there was reported, by Grenet and Bopearachchi, a remarkable gold coin, found, it appears, far away at Chilas on the Karakorum Highway.[19] The obverse shows a royal portrait facing left, wearing a rounded tiara, which we may, to differentiate from the modern usage of the term, call a "tea-cosy hat". Its surface would have been dotted with pearls, but owing to weak striking of the piece, this detail appears only at the side and back. The ties of the royal diadem extend at the back. In his right hand, close to the margin, the figure holds up an arrow, point upwards. The inscription above is in Parthian script: 'bdgšy MLKYN MLK' *Abdagaš Šāhān Šāh*, the spelling exemplifying the Parthian, rather than the Sasanian writing system.

The reverse type of the coin is rather basic. Within a plain dotted border, we see, in splendid isolation, the dynastic symbol of Gondophares and his dynasty. This *tamga*, as it is conveniently, but anachronistically, called, would originally have been a cattle brand like those of the Texan ranches. This would have marked the no doubt enormous herds of horses and cattle owned by aristocratic Iranian families; above all, those of the king. In this case, however, the form of the emblem appears rather distorted, apparently due to a break in the original die. However, the intention of the type is evident enough.

Only three years after the appearance of this slightly enigmatic coin, the same editors reported the appearance of yet a second, entirely distinct, gold coin in the name of Abdagases II.[20] This specimen, perfectly struck and preserved, displays on the obverse the figure of a mounted horseman spearing with a lance the fallen figure of a quadruped, which may be a wolf, or more probably a deer. He wears the rounded and jewelled tiara seen on the previous specimen, with diadem ties trailing behind. A miniature figure approaches from the front, the male Iranian version of the Classical Nike, extending a ring of sovereignty. Once again, the inscription is in elegant Parthian: 'bdgšy MLKYN MLK' BRY S'nbry MLK' *Abdagaš Šāhān Šāh puhr Sānabar Šāh* "Abdagases King of Kings, son of Sānabares, King". The reverse represents a human figure leading a bridled horse to the left; whether, as the editors suggest, for a sacrifice, or as a rendering of the deity Druvaspa as on coins of Kanishka, is uncertain. The inscription mentions "Abdagases, King of Kings, the Great" but the remainder, which might explain the image, is largely off the flan. To compare the headgear and splendid costume of such an Indo-Parthian prince we can look at the reproduction by E. Herzfeld of a mural painting discovered by him at the site of Kuh-i Khwaja across the Iranian frontier.[21]

This is again a spectacular and original coin, which together with his assumption of the elevated title King of Kings, suggests that this late Indo-Parthian achieved a quite unexpected level of affluence and prosperity. Despite the rather inconclusive discussion by the editors of this coin of the date of Abdagases II, one could, perhaps, taking him as contemporary with Soter Megas, place him around 70 CE. At this relatively late date the Indo-Parthians must have lost most of their possessions in the Punjab to the Kushans, but it appears that they retained undisturbed the regions of Kandahar and Sistan, and even enjoyed there considerable opulence.

The last echo of the kingdom of the Indo-Parthians is provided by a rather enigmatic coin-issue which for many years was known as the coin of "Ardamitra". The coin is of tetradrachm format, some 22mm in diameter, but apparently in bronze. There is a Parthian royal portrait on the obverse, and on the reverse a fire altar similar to those on the coins of the Sasanian Ardashir I. The inscriptions have baffled scholarship since the nineteenth century, its difficulties being aggravated by the fact that few specimens preserve more than a small part of the legend, and that it was hard to determine where the reading should commence. The problem was solved in 1994 by A.K. Nikitin of St. Petersburg,[22] who made a composite drawing from fourteen published specimens. The readings start at 10 and 11 o'clock and read, in translation "Farn-Sasan son of Ādur-Sasan / grandson of Tiridates, great-grandson of Sanabares King of Kings". This, perhaps the longest genealogy found on an ancient coin, establishes the ruler's claim to descent from a prominent king of the original Indo-Parthian dynasty. Despite the generally Sasanian appearance of the coin, there is no acknowledgement of Ardashir or his dynasty, and we must assume that Farn-Sasan resisted the Sasanian expansion, and was overwhelmed by it.

For the reasons already discussed, Sistan, the heartland of the Indo-Parthian kingdom, remains to this day archaeologically one of the least known, and also, plagued as it is by the drifting sands – the *rīg-e ravān* – and by the wind of 120 days, one of the world's most desolate regions of ancient civilization. Yet the appearance of the gold dinars of such a late, and relatively obscure ruler as Abdagases II reflects not only the independence, but also the enduring magnificence of this remote kingdom, the homeland of Rustam. The region, with its flourishing Parthian minstrel culture, obviously played a decisive role in the formation of the Persian epic. The lineage of its legendary chiefs, Garshāsp, Kurenk, Narimān, Sām, Dastān or Zāl, and Rustam, surely has a historical origin, but cannot for the moment be correlated with the names recorded in documents. The possible existence of nicknames, such as that I believe attested on the coin of Gondophares, adds a complicating factor. Such usages were convenient in popular poetry, often veiling politically dangerous allusions to actual personalities. If you could entertain my guess for an identification of Rustam, I would suspect he could have been a mythological treatment of the Suren of Carrhae, whose true personal name, let alone any nicknames, is unrecorded by western historians. Parthian ostraca have been found in the Syrian Jazira,[23] and perhaps one day that Suren's personal name will come to light. For the time being, as for so much else to do with the Indo-Parthians, we are reduced to conjecture. The main outlines of the picture are distinguishable. We can hope that the future will make more details clear.

Notes:

1. Philostratus: 2, 17.
2. Alram 1986: 268, n. 1215, with earlier references.
3. Bernard 1996: 505-519.
4. Robert 1960: 85-91. See also Curtis, V.S. in this volume: 7.
5. Ghirshman, 1974: 1-8, esp. 7-8.
6. Justin, Epitome: 42, 1-2.
7. Justin, Epitome: 42, 2: Artabanus Tochariis bello inlato in bracchio vulneratus statim decedit. See Curtis, V.S. in this volume: where this ruler is referred to as Artabanus I. This is due to different chronologies for the early Arsacid period.
8. Quoted by the medieval chronicler Roger of Wendover (d. 1237): Anno divinae incarnationis nono...Trogus Pompeius chronica sua terminavit. cf. Otto Seel (ed.) Pompei Trogi Fragmenta, Teubner, Leipzig 1956, p. viii, who, however, rejects the dating. This, whatever its source, remains plausible in the South Asian context.
9. Pompeius Trogus Fragmenta, Prologue 42: 180.
10. Plutarch, Crassus: 21, 6.
11. E.g. Whitehead 1914, I: pl. XI, 46. Numerous illustrations of the obverse type "King mounted with spear" in the classic article on this series, Jenkins 1955: 1-26, pl. I, 3; pl. II, 3, and pl. III, 7-8.
12. Plutarch, Crassus: 24, 1.
13. In the pedigree of Bakhtiyār the Commander, see Bahar: 8; the Tārikh-e Sistān: 6.
14. Konow 1929: 57 and 62.
15. Marshall 1951: 839-40. The coin was found with Indo-Parthian small silver coins of Sasan, Sapedanes and Satavastra.
16. cf. MacDowall 1965: 137-48, especially 139. However the name Gadana, which might be identified with Gad, appears in Kharosthī script on the reverse of coins there attributed to a second Gondophares, and placed after Pacores in the series, so probably dating around 60 CE. Alram 1986: 257, no. 1181 reports an issue of Pacores with apparently the name Gadana in Kharosthī on the reverse, so substantiating the placing of Gadana in a later generation than Gondophares I. Yet of course there could also have been an earlier Gad(ana).
17. Alram 1986: 255, no. 1176, with legend.
18. VI, 37, 3; VI,43, 2; 44, 6.
19. Grenet and Bopearachchi 1996: 219-231.
20. Grenet and Bopearachchi 1999: 73-82.
21. *Iran in the Ancient East* 1941: pl. CIV, in colour.
22. Nikitin 1994: 67-69.
23. Fuller and Bivar 1996:25-31.

3

Fars under Seleucid and Parthian Rule

Josef Wiesehöfer
(Christian-Albrechts University, Kiel)
For H.T. Wallinga

This article deals with the least documented period of ancient Fars, which is from Alexander the Great to the rise of the Sasanians. As we shall see this was the time when the former Achaemenid heartland had become a province under the Seleucids and then the Parthians. There was a short period of independence in between. The pre-Sasanian coins of Fars are our most important source of knowledge. Here, the names and titles of the sub-Seleucid dynasts and sub-Parthian kings of Persis are mentioned. Their respective reign and relationship with their Macedonian and Arsacid overlords should give us new insight into the history of southwestern Iran from the third century BCE to the third century CE.

In his small but, as usual, extremely important essay on "Alien Wisdom", the late Arnaldo Momigliano dealt with, *inter alia*, the Greek view of the Persians after Alexander:

> But if the Persians of old lingered on in the imagination of Hellenistic man, the contemporary Persians were almost forgotten.[1]

With this statement, Momigliano undoubtedly referred especially to Persis, the Persians' original province, the cradle of the Achaemenid "King of Kings". In fact, if one added up Greek and Latin literary and epigraphical testimonies referring to Fars and its history between 280 and 140 BCE - the Iranians themselves were relying on an oral tradition - there would be only twelve references, mostly comments made in passing or short impressions rather than coherent accounts. It is, therefore, not surprising that for a long time ancient historians have paid only little attention to this period of Iranian history. In addition, certain scholars of the past decades may have had a preference for Greco-Macedonian cultural achievements on Iranian soil. This does not seem tangible in Fars. In my *Habilitationsschrift*, I attempted to shed light on the "dark ages" of Fars and ever since have tried to make further progress.[2]

38   THE AGE OF THE PARTHIANS

However, before trying to judge anew the history of southwestern Iran in pre-Sasanian times, we have to go back to the time of Alexander's arrival in Persis in the year 330 BCE.

Achaemenid rule ended, at least in western Iran, with the burning of Persepolis and the murder of Darius III. Alexander followed the Persian example in Persis, just as he had done earlier in the western part of the Persian Empire, and behaved like an Achaemenid. This is noticeable in his argumentation, his adoration of Cyrus, his honouring of the dead adversary, his marriage policy etc. The reason for this behaviour was so that he could be recognised as a rival and, later, as a legitimate heir to Darius III. The destruction of Xerxes' palaces and treasuries on the terrace of Persepolis - which can probably be explained by Alexander's unsuccessful attempt to enlist support from the inhabitants of Persis at the beginning of his rule - did not result in his giving up these efforts, nor did the later execution of the satrap Orxines who was seen as a potential rival and adversary. The persophile Peucestas turned out to be a man who was, on the one hand, absolutely loyal to Alexander and, on the other hand, gave the inhabitants of Persis, or rather their nobility, the feeling that everything would remain the way it had been. These endeavours were successful with a large part of the nobility, because Alexander and Peucestas apparently did touch neither the Achaemenid system of local dependencies and local administration, nor the basic ideas of the Persian ideology of kingship. There is no other way to explain the fact that nothing is known about unrest in Persis after Peucestas' appointment, that the new satrap could levy troops there without difficulty, and that a great number of nobles collaborated with Alexander.[3] This kind support from the nobles for their new persophile Macedonian masters continued until the second century BCE, as will be shown later on. This does not mean that there was no opposition at all against Macedonian rule in Fars - the negative image of Alexander in the Zoroastrian part of the Iranian tradition is proof of the hostile attitude of at least parts of the population;[4] however, for a long time, this attitude did not lead to unrest and revolts in Fars.

As far as religious policy is concerned, we can also find signs of Alexander's and Peucestas' efforts to receive recognition in Persis. Here, two historical episodes should be sufficient. Shortly before the defeat of the diadoch Eumenes by Antigonus in 316 BCE, Peucestas arranged a feast in Persepolis. This was certainly to honour Eumenes, but also a demonstration of his own powers (Diod. 19.22.2-3). On or below the terrace the participants to the banquet were grouped according to their rank into four concentric circles around the place of sacrifice. The outer ring was filled with the mercenaries and the allies; the second ring consisted of the Macedonian Silver Shields and those companions who had fought under Alexander; the third group consisted of commanders of lower rank, friends and generals who were unassigned and the cavalry. Finally, there was the inner circle with generals and hipparchs and those Persians who were most highly honoured. It has rightly been pointed out that the sacrificial ceremony and the seating order were in accordance with

Achaemenid custom. The hierarchy of the seating order, which mirrored the proximity to and the distance from the (dead) ruler, reminds us of the "protocol" of the later Persepolitan procession reliefs and the Persian "ideology of the inferiority of the remote".[5]

The second example concerns construction work at Persepolis, and especially the five Greek inscriptions with the names of Zeus Megistos, Athena Basileia, Apollo, Artemis and Helios. These were found in the so-called *frataraka*-temple area below the terrace and probably date from the time of Peucestas. The date seems plausible when we take into account the fact that the style of writing corresponds to that of the "haute époque hellénistique" and that altars for the gods, Alexander and Philip were placed in the centre of the concentric circles at Peucestas' banquet. There is also much evidence in favour of a syncretistic use of the names of the gods: Zeus Megistos instead of Ohrmezd, Apollo and Helios for Mithra, Artemis and Athena Basileia for Anahita.[6]

After Antigonus' victory over Eumenes and a short period of Antigonid rule, during the beginning of which Peucestas was removed against the will of the local Persid nobility, Seleucus soon gained possession of Fars after 312 BCE.[7] The territorial centre of his realm was Babylonia. There is a scholarly dispute about when Seleucid supremacy over Persis ended and when the successors of Alexander in the East lost this province.[8] This question is closely connected with the problem of the rule of the so-called *fratarakā*, i.e. the dynasts who gained a (short) period of independence from the Seleucids for their Persid subjects. At this point it should be mentioned that other readings of this Iranian title in Aramaic writing can sometimes be found - *fratadāra, fratakara*, etc. – but these are not as plausible as *fratarakā*.[9] Since the middle of the nineteenth century, scholars have devoted their attention to the coins of these dynasts and have regarded them as symbols of their political legitimacy and as the most important testimonies of their reign. Only one dynast, Oborzus-Wahbarz, is mentioned in Greek literature (in Polyaenus 7.40). But for a long time the numismatic tradition was unable to guarantee an unequivocal date for the *fratarakā*. A new situation arose during the 1970s, when excavations of the preceding decades gave a new impulse to the studies of Ancient Iran. One thinks of the excavations at Pasargadae, Persepolis and at other sites where post-Achaemenid strata were exposed. In addition, there were also archaeological surveys in Fars, which showed that Persis had remained a fertile and densely populated region even after the rule of Alexander.[10] Lately, successful attempts have been made to rediscover the archaeology of the Hellenistic period on the other side of the Persian Gulf. Here, the most important excavations are those on Failaka and Bahrain.

Thus, in the 1990s, it seemed promising for me to examine anew the post-Achaemenid source material and available archaeological remains in order to shed light upon the so-called "dark centuries" of Persis. This was a light which certainly did not promise to become radiant, but which was illuminating. According to my research,[11] Persis remained relatively quiet for more than a century after Alexander's campaign. An exception was the internal Seleucid Molon conflict in 220 BCE. Some unrest is also mentioned by Polyaenus 7.39, which can probably be dated to the rule of Seleucus I. According to Polyaenus, a Macedonian commander by the name of Seiles had instigated a massacre by his subordinate *katoikoi* of 3,000 insurgent Persians under the pretence that these Iranians should have been his allies in his alleged fight against Seleucus. But this event seems to have remained a single episode.

For a long time, and also recently, some scholars have tried to date the beginning of the *frataraka* coinage to the period around 300 or 280 BCE, and to associate the archaeologically detectable partial destruction of the citadel of Pasargadae, the Tall-i Takht, with a rebellion of the Persians under the first *frataraka*, Baydad.[12] This thesis seems disputable, as numismatic-typological observations indicate a close connection between the coins of the *frataraka* and those of the second century sub-Parthian "kings" of Persis.[13] The literary, epigraphic and archaeological evidence also speaks for a rather late date of the *frataraka* reign. For example, there is no indication whatsoever of a third century loss or reclaiming of Persis by the Seleucids. If a successful Persid revolt had occurred in the first half of the third century BCE, Persis ought to have lost its independence again before the Molon rebellion, for which a Seleucid satrap of Fars, Alexander, is mentioned in the sources (Polyb. 5.40ff). Information about the founding of towns in southwestern Iran by Antiochus I (OGIS 233; Steph. Byz. s.v. Stasis), about the rebellion of Molon, about Persid *katoikoi* at Raphia in 217 BCE (Polyb. 5.79.3-8), and an inscription concerning Antiochus III's remarkable stay at Antioch-in-Persis in the year 205 BCE (OGIS 231) all seem to indicate that Fars had been loyal to the Seleucids in the third century BCE. In addition, the archaeological evidence in the Persian Gulf region, presented by Jean-Francois Salles,[14] leaves no doubt about a clear, continuous and assured military and trading presence of the Seleucids in this region until the end of the reign of Antiochus III. A loss of Persis would have certainly threatened their presence and goals. One should also reflect about the central and important neighbouring provinces of Persis in the west, Babylonia and Elymais/Susiane, which had remained in the safe possession of the Seleucids up to the end of Antiochus' reign. Coin hoards from the area surrounding Persepolis, which contained coins of Seleucus I and the *frataraka*, and which were used to prove a loss of Persis in the third century, do not necessarily point to an immediate succession of the first *frataraka*, Baydad, to the first Seleucid king.[15]

Apart from the close stylistic and iconographic link between the *frataraka* coins and those of their sub-Parthian "successors", the theory of an independent Persis in the second century, presumably immediately before the Parthian conquest, makes sense with regard to the literary evidence. Thus, Livy does not mention any units from Persis in the army of Antiochus III at Magnesia (37.40-41). Even if this could be plausibly explained by factors other than unrest in Fars, such an explanation is not possible for the comment found in Pliny the Elder's *naturalis historia* (6.152). Here, the Seleucid Eparch Numenius is described as being attacked by Persians, presumably after 175 BCE, on land and on water at the Straits of Hurmuz.

Also, Justin's report that Demetrius II had had to turn to southwest Iranian troops for support when fighting the Parthian king Mithradates I in 140 BCE (36.1.4) seems to indicate that Persis was independent. Besides, one should consider the fact that there were attempts to break away from the centre in other Iranian regions of the Seleucid realm as well. According to the excavations on Bahrain and Failaka, the period after 150 BCE was the time when the Seleucid presence in the Persian Gulf region grew weaker and became more endangered. The final loss of Babylonia, Susiane and Characene was not until the reign of Antiochus VII when Seleucid rule in that area came to an irrevocable end.

During my studies on "the dark ages of Persis"[16] I came to the conclusion that of the *frataraka* Baydad, Ardakhshir, Wahbarz and Wadfradad I, who minted tetradrachms, at most probably only two were independent dynasts. Only Wahbarz and Wadfradad I broke away from the Seleucid Empire. A remark by Strabo, which has often been overlooked, points to this. The contemporary Persians were ruled by kings who were subordinates of other kings. In earlier times these were the kings of Macedonia, and, in Strabo's own day, the Parthian kings (15.3.24). Iconographic details of the coins, and, furthermore, the historical comments of Polyaenus and Strabo suggest that the first dynasts who minted coins, Baydad and Ardakhshir, did not rule without the approval of the Seleucids. They were not independent dynasts, as has generally been assumed, irrespective of the question of their dating. The similarity of the images and certain symbols on the early *frataraka* coins to Achaemenid iconography has been emphasised for a long time, and it has been concluded that Baydad must already have broken away from the Seleucids. The images of "ruler on the throne", or "ruler in devotional pose in front of a fire altar" on coins of Baydad and his successors were actually modelled after the so-called treasury-reliefs from Persepolis and the funerary reliefs from Naqsh-i Rustam. Symbols, such as the standard, the throne with arms, the sceptre and the pole are also known from the Achaemenid period. Although such scenes and symbols may indicate that the *frataraka* saw themselves as custodians of the Persian heritage of the Achaemenids, they are not necessarily signs of independent rule. These royal symbols and the royal *ductus* are only similar to, not identical with those of the Achaemenids; Baydad and Ardakhshir hold the Seleucid, not the Achaemenid sceptre. Their coins use the same weight standard as Seleucid coins, and both rulers adopt the title *frataraka*, which is known as that of Achaemenid sub-satraps in Egypt.[17] As we will see, even Wadfradad I, an actually independent *frataraka*, is not totally devoted to the Achaemenids' symbolism and claim to power.

What evidence is there to suggest that Persis did not become independent until after the reigns of Baydad and Ardakhshir? The coins of Wadfradad I show some new details on the reverse. For the first time, the Khvarnah-symbol appears in a similar way as that used by the Achaemenid kings.[18] This is a well-known symbol of charisma and power, which is still occasionally interpreted as

Auramazda.[19] In addition, another coin-type of this dynast shows the wreathing of the ruler by Nike. This gesture clearly imitates Seleucid coins, but also suggests the ruler's independence and his desire to commemorate this achievement. This is not the celebration of a simple military victory.[20]

Apparently, Wadfradad's predecessor Wahbarz, whom Polyaenus calls Oborzus, had already given the impetus to the throwing-off of Seleucid rule. This second century BCE author reports (7.40) that Oborzus, as commander of 3,000 *katoikoi*, had organised the assassination of those military settlers. That he was still a Seleucid representative at the time of the uprising is suggested by the fact that non-Iranian troops would hardly have been under arms in an already independent Persis. Accordingly, Oborzus' deed was probably an attempt to gain total autonomy through the elimination of those potential troublemakers. It is clear from Strabo's comment, quoted above, that no period of independent dynasts was known to him. We can therefore conclude that any period of political independence in Persis can only have been very short. If Wahbarz had attempted a revolt, which might perhaps be connected with the destruction level at the end of Pasargadae's third settlement period,[21] then Wadfradad I was the dynast who proclaimed Persid independence by means of his coins.[22] He was probably the man whom the Seleucid king Demetrius II asked for assistance against the Parthian king Mithradates I in 140 BCE. The immediate successor and namesake of Wadfradad, who was the last to mint tetradrachms, presumably already ruled his subjects on behalf of the Arsacids.

That Mithradates I left the dynasts in office with their right to mint coins is an indication of a sub-Seleucid phase of *fratarakā* rule. One would assume that the Parthians returned to the conditions in existence before Wahbarz rather than granting partial autonomy to the Persis dynasts together with the right to mint coins as something completely new. This is all the more likely as the Arsacids came under heavy pressure from Antiochus VII and the Sacas between 140 and 129 BCE.

The seat of the *fratarakā* in the second century BCE was presumably Persepolis and not yet Stakhr. In any case, there was intense building activity on and below the terrace during their reigns. Artaxerxes III's staircase facade was moved from palace G to Palace H. To the west, a wall was erected, and the crenellated architectural elements, which appear on the *fratarakā* coins, were rebuilt. Below the terrace, there was building activity, as indicated by the find of reliefs of a *fratarakā* and his spouse.[23]

Let us now turn our attention to the religious history of this era. About 150 years of undisputed Seleucid rule in Fars can only be explained by far sighted Macedonian politics and religious policy. This is indicated by the fact that there is no proof of the Seleucid ruler cult in Iranian holy shrines. But were the efforts of the *fratarakā* to gain independence religiously motivated? Could Wahbarz and Wadfradad I have been the exponents of a religious opposition to Hellenism in Fars, or were they perhaps even priestly dynasts or magi themselves, or, as Samuel K. Eddy has suggested, the initiators of an Iranian

FARS UNDER SELEUCID AND PARTHIAN RULE

apocalyptic tradition, hostile to Alexander?[24] In my opinion much can be said against those assumptions:[25]

a) As I have tried to show, the *frataraka* Baydad and Ardakhshir were lords of Persis by order of the Seleucids. Either Wahbarz, or Wadfradad I, was the first dynast to become independent. From the second series of Baydad's coins onwards, and not only after the beginning of their period of independence, the *frataraka* are depicted in a devotional pose in front of a fire altar. The Achaemenid winged man, who can be interpreted as the embodiment of the *Khvarnah* of a famous royal precursor, appears for the first time on Wadfradad's coins. Since the winged man wears the Achaemenid crenellated crown - the ruler himself wears a tiara - the iconography of the coins, as has already been emphasised, reminds us of the triad king/fire altar/winged man on Darius I's tomb facade at Naqsh-i Rustam. This is probably an expression of the new rulers' claim to legitimate succession to the Achaemenid kings in Persis.[26]

b) However, the coin imagery is predominantly political. The *frataraka* wear the so-called "royal" *tiara* (on Baydad's first series)[27] or the *tiara apagês* ("satrap's *tiara*")[28], and not the *tiara orthê* (the "upright tiara") of the Great King or the *tiara* of the magi. The latter is related according to Strabo (15.3.19) to the satrap's *tiara*. The *frataraka* are depicted in an Achaemenid fashion with royal insignia, but these are only partially genuinely Achaemenid. The bow is different (doubly convex instead of arched once), the sceptre is Seleucid. Thus, their royal symbols, their type of diadem, and their title, indicate that the *frataraka* saw themselves as stakeholders of an Achaemenid tradition, but that they did not lay claims to the ideas of universal kingship of the Great Kings. Here, I would like to draw attention to the fact that the diadem tied at the back of the head, which is worn by Baydad and his successors, was not reserved for the king alone in Achaemenid times, but also worn by his *syngeneis*. As it is known today that the *syngeneis* were actual relatives of the Great King, not only bearers of an honorary title, it might be possible that the *frataraka* claimed Achaemenid family ties for themselves.

Thus, we can come to the following conclusions. Although the *frataraka* stressed their close ties to the Achaemenids, and although they recognised the close connection between Persid rule and divine choice and support - they were not magi themselves - nevertheless they did not consider themselves to be Achaemenids and Great Kings. They did not adopt this title, the headgear of the Great King or other symbols of Persian royalty. With their choice of the sub-Achaemenid "satrap's tiara" they did express their claim to regional rule, first as subordinates of the Seleucids, later as independent rulers, but they did not take over the Achaemenid claim to power outside the borders of Persis. Thus, it is not surprising that their rule did not come to an end in the Arsacid era. With their limited goals, the *frataraka* were no serious danger and no obstacle to the

44 THE AGE OF THE PARTHIANS

legitimacy of the Parthians who called themselves "Great Kings" and acted as rulers of an Empire which went beyond the Iranian borders. Presumably, the Seleucids, for their part, had not been afraid of their rule being threatened by these dynasts after a long period of loyalty and peace in Persis.

The Persid and the contemporary Babylonian evidence proves the fact that at least the early Seleucid kings up to Antiochus III - in accord with their Achaemenid predecessors - acted flexibly, wisely and successfully towards their indigenous subjects, and respected and supported local traditions and institutions.[29] Therefore, the Greek ignorance of Persian affairs in Hellenistic times noted by Momigliano should not be mixed up with the actual policy of the Macedonians. On the contrary, the silence of the sources might even reflect the success of this policy. It is not surprising that the previously loyal autochthonous Persian elite did not feel encouraged to break away from Seleucid rule until the general weakness of that rule became apparent around the middle of the second century BCE.

As for religious life in Persis during the early Hellenistic period, contemporary burial practices show that early post-Achaemenid Persis was not completely Zoroastrian. The burials of the "Persepolis Spring Cemetery", the cairn burials and the fact that most *astodans* and ossuaries must be dated to the Sasanian period, point to a religiously mixed southwestern Iran under the *fratarakā*, just as under the Achaemenids.[30]

It is a similarly difficult task to write the history of the kings of Persis under the Parthians.[31] Apart from some – rather late – literary documents about the Sasanians' rise to power in the early third century CE, only a few testimonies for the history and culture of Parthian Persis have come down to us. The most important of these are the coins of the "regional kings", who ruled with the consent of their Parthian overlords.[32] In addition, there are religious documents of a much later date, Christian testimonies of missionary work in Persis, and texts that do no more than attest Parthian rule over that specific region (e.g. Strabo, *Periplous Maris Erythraei*). There are also records that suggest the disappearance of southwestern Iranian historical tradition during that period ("Iranian National History"). The results of archaeological work for the period of 140 BCE to 224 CE do not take us any further either.

As we have already discussed, Persian dynasts (*fratarakā*) had governed Persis on Seleucid instructions and had struck their own coins. This period of Persian history was followed by the rule of an independent dynast, shortly before the arrival of the Parthians in 140 BCE. The coins also testify to the fact that the Parthian model of coinage became generally accepted in Persis from the time of Wadfradad III's second series of coinage onward (i.e. at the beginning of the first century BCE).[33] The coins of Wadfradad II (?), the "Unknown King" and Darew I, as well as the early issues of Wadfradad III are iconographically still related to the coins of the *fratarakā*. The end of the emission of tetradrachms and the establishment of the drachm as the main denomination indicate that they were under Parthian influence. There have been attempts to connect the disappearance of coin legends, i.e. the name and the title of the dynast, under Wadfradad II and the "Unknown King", with "repressive measures of the Arsacid king as a result of a rebellious behaviour of the Persid dynasty".[34] The historical background of such measures could lie in the laborious, but finally successful attempt of the Parthians during the years before 123 BCE to maintain their position against the aspirations of the Seleucid king Antiochus VII and the dynast Hyspaosines of Characene.[35] This means that after the Persian rebellion against the Seleucids under Wahbarz and Wadfradad I, the first Persid dynast to acknowledge Arsacid supremacy must have been Wadfradad II. The Parthian concession to their vassals in Persis of the right to mint coins most probably followed Seleucid models. The reason why indigenous dynasts in southwestern Iran were allowed to remain in office as regional kings must have been that the Parthians did not regard the *fratarakā's* moderate ambitions after their rebellion against the Seleucids as dangerous.

For the pre-Christian era, the coins of the Persid kings with their specific legends ("X, the king, son of Y, the king") are our only source.[36] Persid coinage is clearly based on Arsacid coins, which indicates that the Persid vassals were not trying to distance themselves from their Parthian overlords. Strabo's information that in his, i.e. in Augustan times, the Persid kings were subject to the Parthians (15.3.24; cf. 15.3.3), confirms this assumption.

During the first century CE the coinage of Persis supports the same scenario. However, some scholars have favoured an interpretation of an independent Persis, basing this assumption on the so-called *Periplous Maris Erythraei*. The exact date of this text is disputed, but it is surely a text of the first and not of the third century CE.[37] In chapters 33-37 (ed. Casson) it is mentioned that important parts of the Persian Gulf region, including the ports of Apologus in Characene and Omana near the Straits of Hurmuz, as well as southeastern Arabia, belonged to the *basileia tês Persidos* during this time. Depending on whether this *basileia* referred to the Arsacid or the Persid king and depending on whether it is interpreted as Parthian supremacy over vassals, or supremacy of Persid vassals of the Parthians over those regions, or as independent rule of the kings of Persis, we gain a variety of views of political affairs within the Arsacid empire. I believe that the Persis of the *Periplous* can only be the Parthian empire. By calling Omana a *heteron emporion tês Persidos*, the author of the *Periplous* must have also considered Apologus part of Persis. As there is no evidence to support the rule of the Persid king over Characene, the *basileia tês Persidos* must be the Arsacid empire, as the Parthian sphere of influence must have included Characene, the region of today's Emirates and southeastern Arabia. Nothing points to an independent Persis at that time. If archaeology is unable to detect Parthian features in Fars, and if the classical tradition does not know Fars as a trouble spot, this also speaks in favour of the Arsacids not having to take military and political measures in this part of their empire.

The picture would be rather different if a numismatic discovery of the 1980s had to be related to this period of time and had to be interpreted correspondingly. Some hitherto unknown small silver coins were part of a big find of Persid coins and were, for iconographical and typological reasons, interpreted as being struck by a *kyrios* closely related to the Arsacid royal house in an area within or on the fringes of Persis at the end of the first century CE.[38] If Michael Alram is right with his suggestion that a loyal Arsacid subject had revolted against the indigenous Persid kings,[39] this might point to tensions between the Persid kings and their Parthian overlords. However, these coins are still no proof of an independent period of Persis.

In response to some scholars' opinion that Persis was a rather uneasy Parthian vassal state, one has to make the point that we have only one real piece of evidence for a rebellious Persis in Parthian times. It is part of the Christian-Syrian tradition, the so-called "Chronicle of Arbela". It is said in the chapter on Habel's episcopacy (22ff. Transl. 41 Kawerau) that (the Parthian king) Vologases marched against the Persians, for a long time armed for war, with 120,000 soldiers and defeated them decisively in Khurasan after heavy fighting. However, the value of this piece of information has rightly been questioned.[40]

The coins of the *kyrios* of the late first century CE are also important for the reconstruction of the administrative affairs of Persis. As the early Sasanians increased their status from the *kyrios* Sasan (Middle Persian *MR'HY*, Parthian *hwtwy* to the *basileus* Pabag (ŠKZ mpl25/pal20/grl46 Huyse), the *kyrios* of Parthian times was subordinate to the *MLK'*, i.e. the regional king of Fars. It is tempting to use Tabari's detailed account of the Sasanians' rise to power (1.814ff. de Goeje) for a reconstruction of late Parthian and early Sasanian political history. This text tells us about certain administrative hierarchies and officials and functionaries. It is, however, a very late account of a very early state of affairs. Nevertheless, Tabari's view of the political interdependences in Fars - the king of Istakhr gives orders to the kings of districts and to garrison commanders - and his historical geography of Ardakhshir's early campaigns in the early years of the third century CE might have some plausibility. This is reflected in the coinage of the sub-Parthian *kyrios*.

As the Middle Persian and Parthian bilingual inscription from Bishapur, which gives the beginning of the Sasanian era as 205/6 CE,[41] and Tabari's dating of the rebellion of Ardakhshir to 211/2 CE indicate, the beginning of the Sasanian struggle for independence is closely connected with the Romano-Parthian wars of Severan times and the Parthian struggle for the throne between Vologases VI and his brother Artabanus IV. However, those Sasanian attempts are not a symptom of the political disintegration of the Parthian empire. Artabanus' contemporary successes against Rome (Cass. Dio 78.26.3ff.) and the length of the period of consolidation of the early Sasanian empire speak in favour of the fact that the Parthians, and probably the Sasanians themselves, regarded the affairs in Fars as limited regional clashes over the vassal kingship of Fars. The outcome of the battle of Hurmuzgan in 224 CE between Ardakhshir and Artabanus was inescapable only in retrospect.[42] Most probably, the starting point of the Sasanian era, 205/6 CE, refers to Pabag's appointment as king of Khir, and Ardakhshir's appointment as king of Darabgird. The year 211/2 CE, on the other hand, has to be linked with Ardakhshir's rebellion in Darabgird.

This rebellion would then be contemporaneous with Artabanus' revolt against his elder brother Vologases VI.[43] If we trust the Islamic tradition, Pabag would then have rebelled against Gocihr, the king of Istakhr,[44] and would in vain have asked the Parthian king to crown his son Shapur. The latter, known to us by coins, reigned for only a short period. Ardakhshir, who had disputed his brother's right to the throne, succeeded Shapur who had died in suspicious circumstances. Like his brother, Ardakhshir refers to his father Pabag on his coins.

An interesting piece of evidence of the post-Achaemenid period at Persepolis consists of some graffiti, engraved with very thin lines on the limestone blocks of the Harem of Xerxes and of the Tachara. We cannot be sure about the exact identity of the figures depicted.[45] However, there is every reason to believe that they date to the period of the sub-Parthian kings of Persis. Like their Sasanian counterparts in the third and fourth centuries CE those kings probably regarded Persepolis and Naqsh-i Rustam as "holy places" of their "forebears".[46]

Although our sources are only a few and rather late, it seems Persis had been a loyal vassal kingdom of the Parthians until the very end. All the evidence, including a high degree of Parthian influence on the southwestern Iranian tradition, points not to Persian independence or tense relations between masters and subjects, but on the contrary, to a successful Parthian policy in southwestern Iran. The granting of privileges and rights of autonomy, as well as toleration of cultural independence together, probably, with a harsh control through garrisons and functionaries would have been sufficient to secure Persian loyalty. As in the case of the Seleucids, we should abandon an autonomous and independent role of the Persid *regnum* within the Parthian empire. The history of the early Sasanians confirms this view: they are, apart from their own political and ideological aspirations, Parthian heirs to a high degree.

Notes:

1. Momigliano 1975: 138.
2. Wiesehöfer 1994; 2001a: 105-114; 2001b.
3. The Achaemenid traits of Alexander's ideology and actions were clearly brought out by Briant 2002: 817-871; 2003; 2005; cf. Wiesehöfer 1994: 23-49.
4. Wiesehöfer 1995.
5. Wiesehöfer 1994: 53-54.
6. Wiesehöfer 1994: 72-73; pictures of three of the inscriptions can be found in Rougemont 1999: 6.
7. Wiesehöfer 1994: 55-56.
8. This is the main subject of Wiesehöfer 1994.
9. Wiesehöfer 1994: 105-108.
10. Wiesehöfer 1994: 63.
11. Wiesehöfer 1994: 57ff.
12. Wiesehöfer 1994: 115-117.
13. Cf. Alram 1986: 162-186.
14. Salles 1987.
15. Wiesehöfer 1994: 93-96. 115ff.
16. Wiesehöfer 1994: especially pp. 115-129.
17. Wiesehöfer 1994: 106-108.
18. Wiesehöfer 1994: 110-112.
19. Alram 1986: 168f., pl. 17f., No. 533-543.
20. Alram 1986: 169, pl. 18, No. 544f.
21. Wiesehöfer 1994: 129.
22. The previously unknown two coins that show Wahbarz-Oborzus killing a kneeling Macedonian soldier (first coin: Alram 1987a, pl. 20.7; second coin: Bivar 1998, fig. 26b) are probably fakes (M. Alram, personal communication March 2006).
23. Wiesehöfer 1994: 68-78.
24. Eddy 1961.
25. Wiesehöfer 1994: 129-136.
26. Cf. also Panaino 2003.
27. Alram 1986: 165, pl. 17, No. 511-514.
28. Alram 1986: 165f., pl. 17f., No. 515ff.
29. Wiesehöfer 1996.
30. Wiesehöfer 1994: 83f.
31. For a first attempt cf. Wiesehöfer 1998.
32. Cf. Alram 1987b: 127-130.
33. Alram 1987b: 127-130.
34. Alram 1987b: 128.
35. Cf. Schuol 2000: 291-301.
36. Alram 1987b: 127-130.
37. Wiesehöfer 1998: 427 n. 10.
38. Alram 1987b: 138-140.
39. Alram 1987b: 140.
40. Kettenhofen 1995.
41. Altheim-Stiehl 1978.
42. For the beginnings of Sasanian rule in the light of the coins cf. Alram/Gyselen 2003.
43. Alram and Gyselen 2003: 136f.

44. However, in the coin series of the Persid "kings", a certain Ardakhshir, son of Manuchihr, is Shapur's royal predecessor, see Alram 1986: 184f.
45. Very often they are considered to be the immediate predecessors of the Sasanian kings.
46. Callieri 2003.

4

Friend *and* Foe: the Orient in Rome

Rolf Michael Schneider
(Ludwig-Maximilians University, Munich)

> Yes, and you've never been able to understand the
> suggestiveness of paradox and contradiction.
> That's your problem. You live and breathe paradox
> and contradiction, but you can no more see the beauty
> of them than the fish can see the beauty of water.

> Niels Bohr to Werner Heisenberg in Michael Frayn's play Copenhagen,
> premiered in May 1998

After the Persian Wars a powerful rhetoric surfaced in Classical Athens and became a constant factor in the political thinking of the day, the rhetoric of Orientalism. Since the pioneering but contentious study of Edward Said on *Orientalism: Western Concepts of the Orient*, first published in 1978, this rhetoric has acquired both a new cultural importance and a new political significance.[1] It is interesting to note, however, that little attention has been paid to the counter-phenomenon, the rhetoric of Occidentalism.[2] According to Cicero the division of the world into Orient and Occident was legitimised by the gods. In his book *De natura deorum* (2.164-165), he uses the terms *Oriens* and *Occidens* as the only two metaphors with which to describe the division of the world. The author concludes that the gods care equally for all parts and all people of the world. From the territorial powers of the East and the West he names, however, only four, first Rome, then Athens, Sparta and Rhodes. Rome's claimed supremacy over the Orient as the eastern half of the world marks a cornerstone of Roman Orientalism. My interest in the visual rhetoric of Orientalism has sensitised my view of the extent to which the notions of friend and foe, Orient and Occident, imagery and ideology are coloured by the (opposite) readings of the present political situation, especially in the Near East.[3] These notions are to be found everywhere in contemporary written and visual media. My aim in this paper is to show how, in my own field of Greek and Roman imagery, the image addresses and transforms these notions, and conversely how it is affected by them. In comparison to a text, an

FRIEND *AND* FOE: THE ORIENT IN ROME

image provides different qualities with which it stimulates social communication.[4] The most distinctive quality of the image is its unique power of suggestion. An image can both catch the viewer's attention in a fraction of a second and stamp itself on his mind forever. This power of the image is crucial for my argument. At its core is the issue of how and by whom Roman images of the Oriental were shaped and perceived, and how these images functioned within, and contributed to, the culture of imperial Rome.

However, before I can focus on imperial Rome I need to pose some questions concerning Orientalism today. How do we perceive and deal with the imagery of the Orient(al) in our visual culture? How is this modern imagery shaped, how does it function and what does it mean? These questions affect not only how we behave culturally, think politically and act ideologically, but also how we approach the civilisations and the imageries of the past.

The scope of positive readings of Orientalism in the nineteenth century is epitomized by the self-(re)presentation of the Bavarian prince Otto, King of Greece from 1832 to 1862.[5] A colourised lithograph, printed around 1835 by Gottlieb Bodmer after a model of Dietrich Monten, shows King Otto in what was supposed to be Greek national dress, which was itself a cultural invention strongly based on Orientalised clothes (Fig. 1).[6] A number of other images depict King Otto in the same eastern fashion.[7] Today, however, we are more and more confronted with and controlled by images of the Oriental as a suspicious stranger or an explicit enemy as shown on the title page of *Time Magazine* from 15th December 2003.[8] Despite their obvious disparity both images use the same iconographic strategy to distinguish the Oriental Other: both use clothing as a distinctive marker to refer to a specific cultural body. From antiquity to the present day dress codes have played a key role in visualizing the difference between West and East, friend and foe.[9] The visual Orientalism of the day is based on complex agendas, not only on the economic and political interests of the Christian West but also on its unrivalled hold over the public media.

In today's visual media the Orient(al) is mostly present as an exotic Other, a stranger and foe, whereas the image of the Orient(al) as friend is almost always missing. Uri Avnery's book *My Friend, the Enemy* published in 1986 is a rare exception. This one-sidedness marks a strong prejudice on the part of the West, a prejudice which has also severely biased the view of Classical scholars on Greek and Roman portrayals of the Oriental.[10] It also underlines how much the analysis, perception and evaluation of any image is based on cultural preconceptions. We should keep this in mind when approaching the imagery of the Orient(al) at Rome.

Fig. 1 Coloured lithograph of King Otto of Greece (H 56 cm, W 42 cm). Printed in Munich c. 1835 by Gottlieb Bodmer after a model of Dietrich Monten. Ottobrunn (nr. Munich), König-Otto-von-Griechenland-Museum.

FRIEND *AND* FOE: THE ORIENT IN ROME

53

The culture of imperial Rome was fundamentally related to non-Roman cultures. Rome used victories over non-Romans to legitimise imperial power. Rome claimed to rule the world. Rome integrated a wide range of different civilisations and ethnicities.[11] And Rome communicated with people beyond the *orbis Romanus*.[12] An empire of this diversity could in the long term only survive if it offered discourses of cultural flexibility and symbols of cultural identity capable of being widely adopted.[13] One way to shape cultural identity was to establish images of the cultural Other. A model case of the cultural Other was the visual representation of non-Romans, stereotyped images of peoples living outside the Roman empire. The majority of these images portrayed the Other in the form of two Romanised ethnic costumes, representing the peoples of the North and the East. Images of non-Romans were present in all visual media, every social context and throughout the principate. In Rome the cultural Other was an influential and ambiguous reflection of the self-representation of Rome, or in other words, in contrast to the contemporary non-Roman civilisations the image of the ethnic Other was an essential constituent of Rome's cultural identity. Depending on time, place and function the image of the cultural Other oscillated in Rome between interrelated concepts such as fascination and demarcation, acceptance and contempt, friend and foe. This diversity in Roman visual narratives, however, is rarely reflected in modern scholarship.[14] In general, Roman depictions of non-Romans are still considered to be simply portrayals of the barbarian Other, of peoples who lack the cultural standards of Greece and Rome. This view is deeply rooted in the western tradition of Occidental superiority. It is founded on the assumption that there is a fundamental asymmetry in the relationship between the Classical civilisations of Greece and Rome and the barbarian cultures beyond.[15] In my view, however, the Roman imagery of the Oriental points to the need for a more subtle understanding of the Roman discourse of the non-Roman Other.

My approach to this imagery follows three different points of view. I begin with those Roman portrayals which characterise the Oriental by his distinctive non-Roman features such as posture, dress, physiognomy and hairstyle. This applies especially to the ethnic images of the Parthians. I then turn to Roman portrayals showing the Oriental as a handsome youth distinguished not only by posture and dress but also by a beautiful face and long hair. As this stereotype was used to portray all figures from the East, mythical and historical alike, I focus especially on Parthians, Trojans and Persians. Finally, I read the results of my iconographical research within the social, historical and ideological framework of the time, highlighting the following questions. By whom, how and when were the images of the Oriental conceptualised and set up in Rome? How did the Roman public perceive and deal with this imagery? And how did all this contribute to the shaping of the identity of imperial Rome, and the ideology of Roman Orientalism?

The Parthian: the foe beyond the Roman world

Official relations between Romans and Parthians started late, with a treaty of Roman *amicitia* in 96 BCE.[16] This situation changed when the Roman general Marcus Licinius Crassus attacked the Parthians in the winter of 55/54 BCE without first declaring war. After the defeat of Crassus and the loss of his entire army in 53 BCE, Caesar propagated the ideology of revenge on the Parthians, but did not initiate war.[17] In 20 BCE, by exerting diplomatic and military pressure on Parthia, Augustus succeeded in recovering well over 100 Roman standards and thousands of captive Romans. Although it had been achieved through diplomacy, the so-called settlement of the Parthian question was marked in the public media of Rome as Augustus' greatest victory, as the final legitimation of his new imperial rule.[18] Portrayals throughout the Roman empire propagated the Parthian settlement as the ultimate triumph of the Roman West over the East, and as one of the greatest achievements of Augustan foreign policy. The Augustan poets even introduced a cosmic dimension to the settlement: they construed it as the political prerequisite for the beginning of the Golden Age "heralded" by Augustus in 17 BCE.[19] Consequently, Parthia and later the Sasanian empire constituted the only other (enemy) superpower next to Rome, and was perceived as such.[20]

The first Roman images of the Parthian emerged in the aftermath of this widely adopted self-congratulation.[21] The most famous example is the Prima Porta statue of Augustus named after its provenance just north of Rome in the villa of the emperor's wife Livia (Figs. 2-3).[22] The statue can be dated around 17 BCE. The two main figures of the richly decorated cuirass are depicted in the centre: a Parthian is presenting to a military representative of Rome a (Roman) standard adorned with a legionary eagle and at least two (possibly three) *phalerae*. Surrounded by non-interacting figures of geographic, cosmic and divine nature, they are the only two standing and interacting figures. Both are, however, portrayed in significant asymmetry: on the left, and larger in size, we see the cuirassed representative of Rome from a side view, extending his right hand as if to demand or receive the standard; on the right, the Parthian, smaller in size and mainly viewed from the front, gazes up towards the eagle.[23] This depiction is the most detailed portrayal of a Parthian in Roman art (Fig. 3). Originally he would have been even more emphasized as he would have been distinctively coloured.[24] The head of the Parthian is characterized by irregular curly hair, held in place with a flat ribbon or a diadem, a non-Classical nose, pronounced cheekbones, a moustache and a long beard. He is dressed in long trousers, a belted V-neck tunic with long sleeves and soft shoes. He is shown armed with a bow kept in a combination quiver and bow case (*gorytus*), which was attached to a belt running over his left shoulder.[25]

Fig. 2 Statue of Augustus, wearing a cuirass (H 2.06 m). From the imperial villa of Livia at Prima Porta. Roman, c. 17 BCE. Rome, Musei Vaticani, Braccio Nuovo.

Fig. 3 Statue of Augustus. Detail of the Roman and the Parthian (see Fig. 2).

The dress and physiognomy (but rarely the weapons) of the Parthian became stereotypes deployed by Roman workshops to portray generically the people of the East. Distinctively Parthian is the V-neck tunic, which is widely attested in Parthian art.[26] The bronze statue of a Parthian prince from the Iranian site Shami, usually dated either to the first century BCE or CE, is roughly contemporary with the Parthian of the Prima Porta statue (Fig. 4).[27]

Fig. 4 Bronze statue of a Parthian prince (H 1.94 m). From Shami (southwestern Iran). Parthian, c. first century BCE/CE. Tehran, National Museum of Iran.

The V-neck tunic became a common feature of the Parthian in Roman imagery throughout the principate. Three images may be cited here to convey the ubiquitous reception of this garment in different media, contexts and periods. A fragment of a monumental marble relief in Rome shows the upper part of a fighting Parthian dressed in a V-neck tunic (Fig. 5).[28] On thematic and stylistic grounds, Tonio Hölscher has dated the relief to the time of the Parthian war under Nero, concluded in CE 66. The Parthian and the remains of the shields above him suggest the reconstruction of a major battle between Romans in the upper and Parthians in the lower zone of the relief. It counts in fact as the most important example of a battle scene in early imperial Rome. As for the scale of the monument, the Parthian head implies that the figures measured roughly 2.5 m in height. This would point to an extremely large and important, albeit almost entirely unknown, imperial monument in Rome.

Fig. 5 Fragment of a monumental relief (H 87 cm, W 59 cm). A Parthian fights against Romans (not extant). From Rome. Roman, c. CE 60. Rome, Museo Nazionale Romano.

Fragments of a small ivory frieze found at Ephesus closely follow the visual standards set by the imperial imagery of Rome (Fig. 6).[29] The frieze can be dated around CE 120. It shows bearded Orientals who are identified as Parthians again by their distinctive V-neck tunics. The Parthians are either defeated in battle or brought captive before a Roman general, probably Trajan.[30] If this is correct, the frieze would relate to the Parthian war under Trajan. Unfortunately, we know nothing of either the function or the context of this frieze.

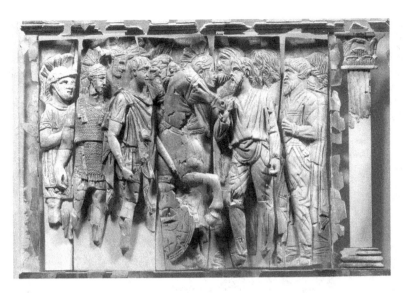

Fig. 6 Ivory frieze (H 20 cm, W 24 cm). Captive Parthians in front of Trajan(?) and Roman soldiers. From Ephesus, Terrace House II (not found in situ). Roman, c. CE 120. Selçulk, Efes Müzesi.

A sculpted limestone fragment now in Trier offers a different context and a different iconography (Fig. 7).[31] It may originally have adorned a grave monument of the later second century CE in Confluentes (Coblenz). A bearded man with beautiful curls stands almost frontally next to a pilaster decorated with abundant scrolls and exotic birds. The figure is wearing the Phrygian cap (without ear-flaps) and a trouser suit with a low V-neck, thus identifying him as a Parthian.[32] The Oriental stranger is depicted in the role of a servant. He offers the viewer a tray, on which are set out several small rectangular objects. In my opinion the most likely interpretation of these objects is that they depict bars of gold, regarded in Rome as symbols of the legendary wealth of the East (Fig. 8).[33] This image of a Parthian with his beautiful curls must have stimulated a more intricate reading than the images discussed so far. The Parthian who proffers gold bars is not necessarily portrayed as an enemy defeated in battle but as a fascinating stranger from the East serving a rich Roman(ised) master in the West. This image of a Parthian, from the edge of the Roman empire, seems to allude to a key ritual of Roman power, the staging of exotic spoils and foreign captives in the context of the triumphal procession.[34]

Roman portrayals of Parthians raise the question of what is known about actual contacts between the Parthians and the people of Rome. Under Augustus at least five Parthian legations are reported to have come to Rome.[35] Eastern kings as well as hostages from the royal family of Parthia living with their Oriental entourages in Rome were regularly paraded in front of the Roman

Fig. 7 Relief of local stone (H 91 cm, W 77 cm). A Parthian proffers gold bars. From Coblenz. Roman, c. CE 170. Trier, Rheinisches Landesmuseum.

Fig. 8 Two bars of gold of Valentian I (524.2 gr. / 520 gr.). From Czófalva, Romania. Roman, CE 367-375. Vienna, Kunsthistorisches Museum.

60 THE AGE OF THE PARTHIANS

public. Suetonius reports on a visit by Augustus to the Circus Maximus: "On the day of one of the shows Augustus made a display of the first Parthian hostages that had ever been sent to Rome, by leading them through the middle of the arena and placing them in the second row above his own seat."[36] It is more than likely that such events encouraged other forms of interactions between Romans and Parthians than the readings promoted by the imperial imagery and ideology of Rome.[37] Such events reveal a further difference in the perception of the Parthian in Rome. Although the general appearance of a Parthian was well known at Rome, the city's workshops and their patrons were not interested in reproducing Parthian dress in authentic or ethnographic detail. Rather, when portraying the peoples from the Orient, Roman workshops followed established Greek models. The result was a conventionalised image of the Parthian adaptable to both the ideological needs of the imperial régime and the cultural preconceptions of the Roman élite. Accordingly, the image of the Parthian was used in public and domestic contexts to portray the Parthian in a variety of significant roles: defeated in battle, captive or as a desirable servant.

In general, we can say that little reliable information about Parthia was available in Rome.[38] The Romans for the most part viewed the Parthians as once the Greek had viewed the Persians. The Achaemenid empire, Alexander the Great and the Seleucid kings provided the Romans with appropriate stereotypes with which they could imagine Parthia. Prominent among these were the lurid details of the Perso-Parthians' brutal despotism, legendary wealth, fantastic luxury, effeminate life-style and excessive sexuality.[39] In these and further extremes the Parthian was Rome's most distinctive cultural Other. The Roman idea of the Other world of the Parthians acquired its fixed form after the return of the standards in 20 BCE. It was a world at a vast distance from Rome, beyond the frontier of the Roman empire. Early imperial writers such as Florus, Pompeius Trogus, Manilius and Tacitus represented the Other world of the Parthians as *alius orbis* and *orbis alter*.[40] This *orbis alter* existed outside the *orbis Romanus* and did not impinge upon the Romans' view of their own supremacy. This Augustan concept of two opposing worlds reflects two apparently incongruent but interconnected issues of Roman imperial ideology, namely the asymmetry between Rome and the East, and Rome's interest in the (Parthian) Orient as her only true cultural counter-pole.

The Oriental: the fascinating Other

The most suggestive manifestation of the Roman perception of the Parthian Other world was the image of the handsome Oriental. This image was introduced into Roman art around the time of the return of the standards in 20 BCE and the first depictions of the Parthian.[41] Initially developed in Classical Athens about 500 BCE, the image became the stereotype of the handsome Other of the East.[42] Finally picked up by workshops in Rome it became the most successful ancient icon of the Orient(al).[43] In contrast to the ethnic stereotype of the Parthian that we have already looked at, the handsome Oriental has a clean-shaven face framed by long coiffured hair and crowned by the Phrygian cap. He usually wears a double-belted tunic with long sleeves, a flowing mantle, long trousers and soft shoes. In short, he is distinguished by youthful beauty, rich dress and intensive colour (Figs. 9, 10, 12, 16, 17, 22-25). The historical – or rather mythical – identity of the Oriental is indicated by his attributes, clothing and/or context.

Such a stereotype made it possible to represent the people of the East as uniform and thus essentially the same: past and present people, ideal images of countries, and cosmic, mythical and divine figures, all could be denoted by the same image. The relation between the image of the handsome Oriental and the ethnic Parthian is shown by a white glass gem in Berlin, a specimen of a popular mass product of the Augustan period (Fig. 9).[44] Two kneeling Orientals, clean-shaven and dressed in trousers and long-sleeved tunics, present Roman standards to Victory. The goddess is placed in the centre, on top of a celestial globe. The eastern dress, the Roman standards and Victory on top of the globe all define the two Orientals as Parthians.

Fig. 9 Glass gem (H 3.5 cm). Two kneeling Parthians present Roman standards to Victory. Roman, c. 20 BCE - CE 20. Berlin, Staatliche Museen zu Berlin, Antikensammlung.

The ambiguity of the handsome Oriental is especially clear in Roman portrayals of Oriental cup bearers, which commonly served as table legs in Roman villas.[45] A fine example is the marble figure found in the Casa del Camillo in Pompeii, and thus made before 79 CE (Fig. 10).[46] The figure portrays a luxury-class slave from the East: young, beautiful, clean-shaven and in Oriental dress. The wine ladle in his *left* hand denotes him as a cup-bearer who is depicted in the act not of serving but of waiting for orders. The popularity of the motif is suggested by a small marble figure from Palmyra (Fig. 11).[47] In this case the cup bearer is portrayed not in stereotypical Oriental dress, but in the actual clothes of the Parthians living nearby in the East. In addition to the wine ladle in his left hand, he also holds a wine jug. The piece highlights both the widespread availability of the motif and its adaptability to local preferences.

Fig. 10 Marble table-leg (H 74 cm). Oriental servant with wine ladle. From Pompeii, Casa del Camillo (VII.12.22-27, room "e"). Roman, c. CE 50-70. Naples, Museo Archeologico Nazionale.

Fig. 11 Stone figure (H 44 cm). Parthian servant with jug and wine ladle. From Palmyra, c. second century CE. Palmyra, Museum.

In an ode dedicated to Agrippa's steward Iccius in 25 BCE, the Augustan poet Horace confirms the desirability of such handsome Oriental cup bearers. The poet refers to the alluring prospect of great wealth and a luxurious life-style when Iccius returns home after his victories over the Arabs, the Parthians – perhaps even over the Chinese:

> What page from (Oriental) court with scented locks will be set to hand your wine cup?[48]

At Rome, the image of the Oriental cup bearer with a wine ladle was closely related to that of Ganymede, the most beautiful cup bearer of all.[49] This prince was associated with both his homeland Troy and neighbouring Phrygia.[50] To show the beauty of his body he was conventionally portrayed naked except for a mantle and Phrygian cap.[51] The Phrygian cap probably alludes to the fact that he was a Trojan, especially as Trojan and Phrygian had been (subtly) interconnected ever since the fifth century BCE.[52] On Roman Republican coins, Roma herself is occasionally depicted with a Phrygian helmet, no doubt in allusion to the city's claimed Trojan origin.[53] The close connection of the Phrygian cap with Troy in early imperial times is confirmed by Juvenal. He describes it as part of the dress of the flamboyantly foreign Galli, the self-castrated attendants of the Mater Magna in Rome and elsewhere.[54] Just like the figures of Oriental cup bearers, sculptures of Ganymede often served in Roman villas as table legs.[55] The handsome Trojan prince is usually accompanied by an eagle, recalling his abduction to Olympus by Zeus and his fate eternally to serve wine to the gods.[56] Zeus' Trojan cup bearer was the mythical archetype of the historical slave cup bearer from the East. Both alike betoken the ability of the Roman élite to command all the resources of the empire in the endlessly enjoyable task of projecting and maintaining their rank.[57]

The Trojan: the Oriental forefather of Rome

The Augustan statue of Ganymede at the stately villa at Sperlonga, on the coast about 70 miles south of Rome, opens up a further discourse regarding the relations between Rome and the Orient (Fig. 12):[58] for it is not only the earliest known Roman representation of the beautiful Trojan boy but also the only one wearing Oriental dress. The statue was erected above the entrance to a cavern, which served as the large villa's dining hall. It was based on a plinth specially fitted into the rock, and so occupied a spectacular setting overlooking the sea (Fig. 13).[59] Giving every appearance of having arrived straight from Olympus, the statue was designed to combine élite workmanship and setting with a new interpretation of Roman Orientalism: Ganymede here is not small but larger than life, he is displayed not indoors but as a landmark outside and appears not naked but in rich Oriental dress. Furthermore, he is made not of monochrome stone but polychrome marble from his Phrygian homeland in contrast to the head and the lost hands of white marble. The exceptional position of the statue must have demanded a specific reading. The statue is in fact the only known depiction of the handsome shepherd as distinctively Trojan.[60] In this way the statue was irrevocably linked to the four major marble groups located inside the grotto, which depicted distinctive incidents from the epic cycle: Aiax' rescue of the dead Achilles, Troy's most deadly enemy; Diomedes' and Odysseus' theft of the sacred Palladium which later secured the primacy of Rome; Odysseus' blinding of the monster Polyphemus; and Odysseus' fight against Scylla's dreadful attack on his ship.[61] The juxtaposition was evident. The ancient viewer would have understood the compelling message(s) of the sculptural dramas loaded with the Augustan ideology of Rome's Trojan descent: the owner of the villa claimed that the epic cycle was a crucial part of Rome's history, and that the selected epic incidents were staged and shaped in a way only the Roman élite was able to achieve.

In Sperlonga the myth of Roman Troy stimulated the production of some of the most remarkable and meaningful narratives related to the Trojan War. As a Trojan, Ganymede was a mythic ancestor of Rome, however, as an Oriental servant on Olympus he was a model to embody the service owed by the East to the Roman élite. The statue at Sperlonga neatly combines the paradoxical themes of friendship and enmity, Roman and Oriental. This makes the Sperlonga statue of Ganymede a case in point regarding the ambivalent aspects of Roman Orientalism.[62] The special relationship between the Roman élite and the Trojan Ganymede

Fig. 12 Statue made of "marmor Phrygium" (H 2.25 m). Ganymede in the clutches of Zeus' eagle. From the villa in Sperlonga. Roman, c. 20 BCE - CE 10. Sperlonga, Museo Archeologico.

Fig. 13 Reconstruction of the grotto at the villa in Sperlonga, showing the statue of Ganymede (see Fig. 12) in its original position over the entrance.

was later propagated by the mint at Ilium: portraits of Hadrian, Marcus Aurelius and Commodus on the obverse were complemented by images of Ganymede with Zeus' eagle on the reverse.[63]

In Augustan imagery Rome's claim to both her Oriental origin and her supremacy over the Orient was pushed even further. Classical scholars have given little attention to the fact that the handsome Oriental was also used to represent the Oriental "half" of Rome's (multi-)cultural identity. This is especially true of the imagery of the most distinguished monuments set up in the early imperial city. A key role in representing Rome's Oriental half was given to the Trojan prince Iulus/Ascanius, the son of Aeneas. Aeneas, the son of Aphrodite, had saved his father Anchises and his son Ascanius when he abandoned burning Troy to contribute to Rome's foundation.[64] The Roman poet Vergil renamed Ascanius in order to relate him by name to Augustus' adoptive family, the Iulii (*Aeneid* I.267-268, 286-289):

> His son Ascanius, whose surname is now Iulus –
> Ilus it was, before the realm of Ilium (= Troy) fell – ...
> From the fair seed of Troy there shall be born a Caesar –
> Iulius, his name derived from great Iulus – whose empire
> Shall reach to the ocean's limits, whose fame shall end in the stars.
> He shall hold the East in fee ...[65]

Iulus/Ascanius, as the youngest Trojan, had passed his Trojan lineage on to Rome. From the Augustan period onwards he was usually portrayed in Oriental dress. One of the first Roman depictions of Iulus/Ascanius occurs on the external frieze to the right of the main (western) entrance of the Ara Pacis Augustae (Fig. 14).[66] Entirely built of marble, the Ara Pacis was commissioned by the Roman senate in 13 BCE to celebrate the victorious return of Augustus to Rome from military campaigns in Spain and Gaul.[67] Outstanding in the richness and subtlety of its sculpted décor, the Ara Pacis portrays the chief concerns of the Augustan order: Roman gods, depictions of sacrificial rituals and public processions, representations of religious symbols and the fecundity of nature as a metaphor of the

Fig. 14 Rome, Ara Pacis Augustae. Relief to the right of the main entrance. Aeneas, behind him Iulus/Ascanius (partly extant). Roman, 13-9 BCE.

Augustan Golden Age.[68] Despite the fragmentary state of the frieze, it is clear that Iulus/Ascanius stands, a grown man, to the right of (that is, behind) his father Aeneas, holding a shepherd's crook. In contrast to the old-fashioned Roman toga of his father, Iulus/Ascanius is shown in a long-sleeved tunic, a mantle and (perhaps) long trousers.[69] His Oriental origin would have been further highlighted by the distinctive (but now lost) colouring of his Trojan dress.

The most crucial Roman portrayal of Iulus/Ascanius, however, was displayed in the Forum Augustum, which was dedicated in 2 BCE (Fig. 15).[70]

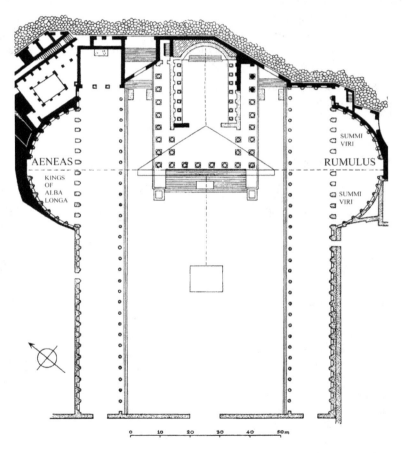

Fig. 15 Rome, plan of the Forum Augustum. The southwestern half is a hypothetical reconstruction (L c. 125 m, W c. 118 m). Dedicated 2 BCE.

The Forum Augustum was a space which transmitted the ideology of the imperial régime in exceptional complexity, workmanship and choice of marble.

Fig. 16 Marble relief (H c. 1.6 m, W c. 1.6 m). Aeneas carrying his father Anchises and holding the hand of his son Iulus/ Ascanius. In the background Aphrodite. From Aphrodisias, Sebasteion. Roman, c. CE 20-60. Aphrodisias, Museum.

The Forum's temple was dedicated to Mars Ultor. Mars was the Roman god most closely associated with the myth(s) of the Oriental origins and the Italic pre-history of Rome. In the Republican period he was supposed to have impregnated Ilia/Rhea Silvia, a direct descendant of the House of Aeneas.[71] He could thus claim to be the father of Romulus and Remus and, hence, an ancestor of all Romans. At the same time Mars was regarded as one of the oldest gods of Rome. Together with Jupiter and Quirinus, he made up the first Capitoline triad said to have been established in Archaic times.[72] Furthermore, Mars' new cognomen *ultor* (= avenger) referred to all the enemies plotting against Rome and her new emperor, with explicit reference to the Parthians.[73] The Forum Augustum itself was extremely rich in imagery.[74] Marble portrayals of the most noble Romans (*summi viri*), historical and mythical, were selected to celebrate the rule of Augustus and to single him out as the embodiment of Rome's legendary history. The climax of the sculptural programme was marked by two colossal images that are considered to have represented the most important mythical ancestors of Rome. They were placed conceptually facing one another in the central niches of the Forum's two large exedrae: to the south, Romulus carrying the emblems of Rome's history (*spolia opima*); to the north, Aeneas carrying his father Anchises out of Troy and leading his son Iulus/Ascanius by the hand. The originals have not survived. Their general appearance is, however, attested by more than a hundred and sixty adaptations, not only in sculpture but also on mosaics, wall paintings, coins, gems and lamps.[75] After a thorough re-examination of the surviving evidence, Martin Spannagel has been able to outline the iconographic concept of the lost originals.[76] A good idea of the appearance of the Trojan group is provided by a relief in the Carian city of Aphrodisias (Fig. 16).[77] The relief embellished the city's Sebasteion, a processional cult complex built roughly between CE 20-60 and dedicated jointly to the city's patron goddess Aphrodite and the Roman emperors. Each of the three Trojans is given a different cultural body: Aeneas is depicted as a Roman general in a Roman cuirass – only his old fashioned beard identifies him as a mythical hero; his father Anchises is shown in a mixture of foreign and Graeco-Roman dress, namely trousers, tunic and mantle; while Aeneas' son Iulus/Ascanius is dressed entirely in Oriental fashion. Behind them is Aeneas' mother Aphrodite. She connotes not only the political bonds between Aphrodisias and Rome but also the magnitude of the Trojan-Julian connection in shaping the identity of imperial Rome.

Another programmatic statement about Rome's Oriental identity is conveyed by the portrayal of Iulus/Ascanius on the Grand Camée de France, the largest surviving cameo from antiquity (Fig. 17).[78] Made of exotic sardonyx and probably carved around CE 23/24, it constitutes an outstanding political manifesto designed for exclusive use at the imperial court in Rome. The Oriental is the only person present in all three panels, which divide the cameo's narrative in vertical hierarchy.[79] The bottom panel is the smallest, and the only one to be rigorously separated from the other two. It depicts the edge of the world populated by defeated barbarians from the East, the West and the North. The middle panel is the largest. It shows a controversially discussed dynastic constellation. Clearly identifiable, however, is the sitting couple at its centre, the emperor Tiberius and his mother Livia. The upper panel emerges immediately from the middle panel and represents deceased members of the imperial family in cosmic space. The most prominent of them is Divus Augustus, who is portrayed at the highest point, in the centre, carried on the back of an Oriental suspended over the current emperor. The Oriental is holding with both hands a celestial sphere, the very symbol of Roman power.[80]

Fig. 17 Grand Camée de France made of sardonyx (H 31 cm, W 26.5 cm). In the centre Tiberius and Livia seated, above them Iulus/Ascanius in Oriental dress carrying Divus Augustus. Roman, c. CE 23-24. Paris, Bibliothèque Nationale.

Recently Luca Giuliani has (re-)read the visual narrative of the cameo and (re-)established that the handsome Oriental must be Iulus/Ascanius. He is, as the Trojan ancestor of Rome's mythical founder(s), the most suitable person to carry Divus Augustus, the founder of imperial Rome.[81]

At Rome images of Trojans can be traced back to the fourth century BCE.[82] However, only in the Augustan period were the myth of Troy and the imagery of the Oriental as Trojan made a cornerstone of Roman imperial ideology.[83] The Orient became a crucial element of Rome's imperial identity, and as such her indisputable property: hence, Rome could claim the East her own. One of the most remarkable statements of this ideology is an epigram attributed to Germanicus, the step-nephew of Augustus. He wrote the poem on his visit to Ilium (built on the site of ancient Troy) in CE 18 on his tour of inspection through the Eastern provinces that ended with his unexpected death.[84] The epigram is addressed to Hector, the greatest Trojan hero, who was killed by Achilles, the greatest Greek hero:[85]

Descendant of Mars, Hector, under the deep(est) earth
(if you can but hear my words),
breathe again, since an avenger has come to you as heir,
who may forever enhance the fame of your fatherland.
Behold! Renowned Ilium rises again, a race inhabits her
inferior to you, Mars, but nevertheless a friend of Mars.
Hector, tell Achilles that all the Myrmidons have perished
and that Thessaly is under the sway of the great descendants of Aeneas.[86]

Hector's avenger is none other than Rome who ultimately avenges the devastation of Troy.[87] Following the death of Hector only Augustus and the people of Rome were considered to be descendants of equally Mars and the Trojans. Hector's newly acquired ancestry from Mars would have underlined the fact that the Trojans and the Romans shared the same descent. According to the poem, Rome has not only revived the legendary power of Troy but has also achieved rule over Greece, Troy's arch-enemy, represented here by the descendants of Achilles' Myrmidons in Thessaly. Such claims emphasise once more the gripping quality of the image of the handsome Oriental that brought together two distinctive aspects of Rome's (Augustan) identity, her actual imperial present and her mythical Trojan past.[88] Only two Trojan princes were portrayed as handsome Orientals in early imperial Rome: Ganymede as the most noble and desirable servant ever, and Iulus/Ascanius as the youngest eastern representative of both Troy and Rome.

Augustan Rome and the Persian Wars

Two further motifs of the handsome Oriental were introduced into the imagery of Augustan Rome: standing (Figs. 21-22) or kneeling (Figs. 18-19) sculptures in the gesture of support.[89] Both statue types are over life-size and mostly made of coloured marble. In the Renaissance, however, hands and faces were often restored suggestively but wrongly in black marble.[90] Originally these parts of the body were carved separately in white marble as shown by the statue of Ganymede in Sperlonga (Fig. 12). In the Augustan period these "support" figures were related to both the Parthians and the Persians. Following a standard set by Cicero, Augustan poets such as Vergil, Propertius, Horace and Ovid usually refer to the Parthians by the name of their historical ancestors, Medes, Persians or Achaemenians.[91] The Persian Wars of the fifth century BCE legitimised not only Alexander's invasion of the Achaemenid empire (335/334 BCE) but also Rome's politics towards Parthia. After the return of the standards in 20 BCE the equation of the Parthians with the Persians became a focal point of imperial ideology.[92]

 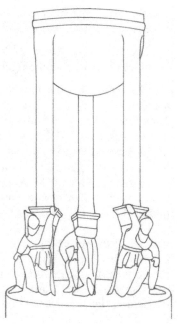

Fig. 18 Statue made of "marmor Phrygium" (H c. 1.70 m). Kneeling Oriental. From Rome. Roman, c. 20-10 BCE. Naples, Museo Archeologico Nazionale.

Fig. 19 Reconstruction of a victory monument (now lost). Originally in Rome and Athens (H at least 4 m). Three kneeling Orientals made of "marmor Phrygium" (see Fig. 18) carrying a bronze tripod. Roman, c. 20-10 BCE.

A visual highlight of this ideology was the grand spectacle of a sea battle, the *naumachia Augusti*, staged to celebrate the dedication of the Forum Augustum in 2 BCE. The battle took place in a specially excavated basin measuring 540 x 360 m (approx. 48 acres!) and was fed by a purpose-built aqueduct. In addition to an unknown number of oarsmen, roughly 3000 fighters were forced to re-enact the victory of the Athenian navy over the Persian (in reality largely the Phoenician) fleet at Salamis in 480 BCE.[93]

A victory monument, now lost, was erected (shortly) after 20 BCE. It can be reconstructed on the basis of two different sources: a brief phrase by the imperial Greek writer Pausanias, and three statues of kneeling Orientals. They form one set as they share not only the same size, motif, Phrygian marble and Augustan workmanship but also the same origin, the city of Rome (Fig. 18).[94]

The precise location of this monument is unknown. Pausanias describes an analogous monument erected in the precinct of the temple of Zeus Olympios at Athens probably around the same time as the monument in Rome:

> There are also statues of Persians made of Phrygian marble supporting a bronze tripod; both the figures and the tripod are worth seeing.[95]

The three Persians in Athens and the three kneeling figures from Rome correspond so closely to each other that we are able to define their function. They must have served to support a large bronze tripod, at least three to four meters high (Fig. 19).[96] Historically, this tripod referred to the tripod dedicated in the sanctuary of Apollo at Delphi by those Greek cities that defeated the Persians at Plataea in 479 BCE (Fig. 20).[97] Politically, however, it referred to two central claims of the Augustan regime: to have "defeated" Parthia and to have restored *pietas,* as a number of similar tripods appear in the Augustan period.[98]

More complex is the discourse which stimulated the reshaping of the standing Oriental in Rome.[99] In the Augustan period the Basilica Aemilia on the northeast side of the Forum Romanum, opposite the Basilica Iulia, was decorated with a gallery of "telamons" all showing standing Orientals; their original location in the basilica is unknown.[100] Fragments (none of them published) of about twenty or more over life-size statues of Orientals in coloured marble have survived (Fig. 21).[101] All are in the same weighted stance and are worked to an exceptional finish. The style links the Orientals to the restoration of the Basilica Aemilia after 14 BCE; since the restoration was paid for by Augustus and the friends of Lucius Aemilius Paullus (Dio Cassius 54.24.3) we may suspect an allusion to the return of the standards in 20 BCE. As the ancient arms of the sculptures are in part lost we need to reconstruct their original pose. The evidence suggests that they were "telamons" with one arm in the gesture of support: the upper arm was outstretched sideways, the lower arm raised upwards and the hand again

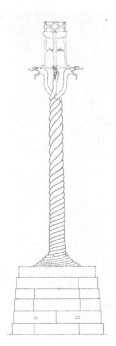

Fig. 20 Reconstruction of the Delphian tripod (H c. 12 m). Dedicated at the sanctuary of Apollo at Delphi by the Greek cities that defeated the Persians at Plataea in 479 BCE.

Fig. 21 Torso made of "marmor Phrygium" (H 1.10 m). Standing Oriental ("telamon") originally shown in the gesture of support (see Fig. 22). From Rome, Basilica Aemilia. Roman, after 14 BCE. Rome, Antiquario Forense.

Fig. 22 Reconstruction of the support gesture of the standing Oriental from the Basilica Aemilia (see Fig. 21).

outstretched to the side (Fig. 22).[102] The weighted stance and the position of the arm highlight a semantic construction of this mannered pose: the standing Oriental virtually embodies the tectonic counter-model of any telamon used to support architecture. The result is a visual combination of an active Oriental servant with the desirable Oriental youth, perhaps related to the ideology of Parthia's "defeat" in 20 BCE. A further reading is suggested by the Latin names recorded for the Orientals: Pliny the Elder calls them *Phryges*.[103] Although imperial texts use *Phryx* occasionally as synonym for Oriental slave, it is tempting to understand Pliny's *Phryges* also as a synonym for the Trojan ancestors of Rome – a synonym especially popular in the early imperial city.[104] This interpretation may be supported by the long frieze, which, together with the gallery of the standing Orientals, decorated the Augustan basilica. The frieze dealt with the (mythical) history of Rome, namely selected

Fig. 23 Marble relief (H 1.95 m, W 3.52 m). Two Oriental "telamons" support the inscription of a Roman magistrate, between them a sella curulis, *next to them two Roman lictors. From Nuceria Alfertana. Roman, c. CE 60. Naples, Museo Archeologico Nazionale.*

narratives of Rome's famous ancestors, Aeneas and Romulus.[105]

However, the standing Orientals of the Basilica Aemilia (Figs. 21-22), like the kneeling Orientals in Athens and Rome (Figs. 18-19), would have stimulated the viewer also to compare the Roman settlement of the Parthian question in 20 BCE with the fifth-century Greek victories over the Persians. The architect Vitruvius, who practised under Caesar and Augustus, confirms the topicality of the standing Oriental as an image referring to the Persian Wars. At the beginning of his ten books on architecture he summarises the essentials an architect ought to know, "the thing signified, and that which gives it significance" (*de architectura* 1.1.3).[106] Vitruvius names only two examples of architectural *ornamenta* the history of which an architect ought to know, first the Caryatides (1.1.5) and then the telamons of Persians (1.1.6):

> the Laconians ... after overcoming with a small force a large army of Persians at Plataea celebrated a glorious triumph with spoils and plunder. And they erected the Persian Stoa from the booty instead of the usual victory memorial for the coming generations to signify the glory and the virtue of the citizens. In this stoa they placed statues of their captives dressed in rich barbaric dress to support the roof – their pride punished by well-merited humiliations. This was done for two reasons: to make their enemies tremble for fear of what Laconian bravery could achieve, and to prompt their fellow-citizens to look at this model of virtue and, encouraged by such glory, to remain ready to defend their freedom. And so from that time many have set up Persian statues to support architraves and their ornaments ...[107]

The only popular Roman statue of a Persian depicted in the form of a telamon is the standing Oriental. It is hardly a coincidence, that both *ornamenta*, the Caryatides and the Persians, selected by Vitruvius to highlight the architect's historical knowledge, were closely related to narratives of Orientalism.[108] Vitruvius' choice is significant as he excluded other *ornamenta* from pre-Augustan architecture, telamons such as Atlantes, Giants, Satyrs and Sileni, and sculpted components such as pediments, metopes and friezes.

The image of the standing Oriental was popular throughout the Roman empire.[109] Of particular interest is a marble relief now in Naples (Fig. 23).[110] It was carved around CE 60 to decorate the front of a prestigious grave monument erected for Marcus Virtius Ceraunus, once *aedilis* and *duumvir* of Nuceria Alfaterna, a Campanian town situated east of Pompeii. Two small standing Orientals look as if they are supporting the inscription that proudly reports Ceraunus' local career. They are dwarfed by two insignia of Roman imperial power, the curule chair (*sella curulis*) in the centre, and the ushers (*lictores*) on either side. Closely attached to the imperial symbols the two Orientals probably provoked ambivalent readings ranging from captive Parthians to "supporting" Trojans and desirable servants.

Friend *and* foe: the Orient in Rome

From the Augustan period onwards ethnic Parthians and handsome Orientals became a distinctive element of Roman imagery. They were widely adopted throughout the Roman empire and not restricted to the periods of actual war between Rome and Parthia.[111] They were continuously popular not only with Roman emperors and members of the Roman *and* non-Roman élite, but also with worshippers of eastern deities like Attis (Fig. 24) and Mithras (Fig. 25). The popularity of these images is further enhanced by the difference between images of the handsome Oriental and those of other non-Romans. In contrast to other portrayals of non-Romans the handsome Oriental combines an allusion to servitude with desirable beauty and all the connotations of coloured marble. In Augustan Rome these features were brought together for the first time and set up as a standard for future generations.

In the context of Augustan Orientalism the new staging of coloured marble acquired specific readings. The over life-size statues of the Oriental were worked in coloured marbles for the first time, and only the most expensive and exclusive varieties were used: the whitish *marmor Phrygium*, and the yellowish *narmor Numidicum*. Though they come from different parts of the Mediterranean, both appear similar as they are reticulated by veins, ranging from crimson to violet. Their exotic colour and high polish gave the Oriental body an intensity and meaning unprecedented in ancient art.[112] The polychrome Orientals granted the East a new presence at Rome as "coloured" embodiments of eastern dress, attitude and luxury. This ideology of ethnicity, marble and colour was further increased as (most of) the polychrome quarries became

76 THE AGE OF THE PARTHIANS

imperial property under Augustus and produced polychromes on a large scale for the first time.

The quarries themselves were situated in distant provinces and required a complex infrastructure to deliver coloured marble to Rome: the imperial polychromes became a unique symbol of the power and cultural accomplishments Rome claimed to have achieved. As a result, the polychrome Orientals represented spoils never before seen at Rome. The display of such remarkable spoils would have reminded the ancient viewer of the Roman triumphal procession.[113] This ritual was a potent demonstration of Rome's relationship to non-Roman cultures: by it foreign people and things were declared in public the property of Rome. By staging and incorporating other cultures Rome legitimised her claim to rule them all.

The complexity of Rome's relationship to non-Roman cultures is highlighted in the image of the handsome Oriental. Through it, Augustan patrons and workshops created a visual metaphor which was able to express very different claims of Rome's relationship to the East. The handsome Oriental embodied every character from the east, and there were many: mythical and religious figures such as Arimaspi, Attis (Fig. 24) with Cautes and Cautopator, Mithras (Fig. 25) and Orpheus; figures belonging to foreign cults in Rome such as the self-castrated Galli; figures of Rome's mythical past such as the attractive Trojan princes Ganymede (Fig. 12), Iulus/Ascanius (Figs. 14,16, 17) and Paris; fascinating Others such as the desirable youth and the beautiful servant (Figs. 10, 21-23); political personifications such as Armenia, Parthia and Mesopotamia; past and current enemies such as the Persians, the Parthians and the Armenians (Figs. 2-3, 5-7, 9, 18, 21-23), and later also the Sasanians.[114] The "Oriental revolution", which according to Warwick Ball represents a crucial factor in the development of the later Roman empire had already happened in Augustan Rome: her "legacy is as much eastern and western, as much oriental as occidental, both to Europe and the world as a whole".[115] However, our modern political notions of friend and foe, of Occident and Orient, based as they are on a Hegelian reading of the bipolarity of force and counterforce, fail to fuse such apparently opposite social and cultural values.

This complexity of the Roman imagery of the handsome Oriental has caused modern scholars a methodological headache. A fine example is the dispute over the identity of the images of two children in foreign dress, one on the south, the other on the north frieze of the Ara Pacis. Both are shown taking part in the procession of selected members of the imperial family.[116] Modern scholars have identified the children either as the two Augustan princes Gaius and Lucius Caesar in the costume of the *lusus Troiae* (an equestrian parade and mock battle staged by élite Roman boys), or as two of the Parthian princes who lived as hostages at the imperial court.[117] On iconographic grounds both readings can stand. The foreign clothing of the two children, whether we interpret them as Gaius and Lucius Caesar in Trojan costume or as two Parthian

Fig. 24 Wall painting. Attis holding a sickle in his right hand. Roman, c. CE 70. Pompeii, Casa di Pinarius Cerialis (III.4.4).

Fig. 25 Wall painting (H 1.80 m, W 2.50 m). Mithras subdues the bull. Roman, c. CE 170. Marino, Mithraeum (in situ).

78 THE AGE OF THE PARTHIANS

or Armenian princes in eastern dress, refers to the Orient as a feature of Rome's cultural identity.[118]

How deeply the concept of the Oriental as friend was imprinted on the cultural identity of imperial Rome is particularly manifest in the widespread popularity of Oriental gods such as Attis and Mithras.[119] Two images highlight the significance of visual narratives in the process of shaping and re-shaping Rome's Oriental identity throughout the principate. The first is a handsome, desirable Oriental on a fresco in a *cubiculum* of the House of Pinarius Cerialis in Pompeii, dated around CE 60 (Fig. 24).[120] Only the sickle in his right hand identifies him as the god Attis. Otherwise the image shows a handsome Oriental dressed in luxurious, diaphanous clothes prompting a range of cultural, religious and gender-related readings. Different issues are at stake in the fresco of the god Mithras found in the Mithraeum at Marino near Rome, painted about CE 170 (Fig. 25). Here the focus is on the handsome image of Mithras in richly decorated, colourful dress, on his power as he subdues the bull, and the implied religious ritual.[121] Modern scholars agree that, whatever its ultimate origin, the cult of Mithras in Rome was strongly based on Roman perceptions.[122] Richard Gordon has recently argued that the cult contributed significantly to the maintenance of Roman socio-political structures, especially those of imperial power.[123] The same is true of the major cult of the "Trojan" Mater Deum Magna Idaea. She had been worshipped in Rome ever since the second century BCE next to some of the city's most venerable sanctuaries, the legendary Hut of Romulus, and what was later the House of Augustus.[124] Named by Vergil mother of the gods, she was not only Aeneas' great-grandmother but also, together with his mother Venus, the foremother of the Romans and Augustus.[125] Ovid let Mater Magna follow Aeneas to Rome and calls him accordingly *Phryx pius* (*fasti* 4.274).[126] This sheds further light on the role of Orientalism in the process of defining Rome's imperial identity and culture. The vibrant role of Rome's Orientalism is also mirrored in her late antique imagery, namely in the three Persian Magi of the Christian portrayal.[127]

In short, the (visual) preoccupation of Augustan (and later) Rome with the Orient was vigorous, perhaps even obsessive. Apart from the Greeks who themselves had been deeply influenced by Oriental cultures since the Archaic period,[128] no other people contributed so profoundly to the shaping of Rome's imperial identity as the civilisations of the East. This is also true of the Oriental cults and their (western) imagery such as Magna Mater, Attis, Mithras and Isis, which were present in Rome almost throughout the principate. However, Augustan ideology had separated the multi-cultural East into two major blocks: on the one side Egypt, on the other side the eastern civilisations, namely the Trojans, Phrygians, Persians, Medes, Achaemenians, Parthians and Armenians (later also the Sasanians). The modes of representation and perception of both blocks in Rome were essentially different. From the Augustan period Egypt had become a distinctive part of Rome's urban imagery as the city became more and more inundated by looted Egyptian obelisks and sculptures; but Roman images of Egyptians themselves were not circulated.[129] In contrast, Rome did not display pillaged artefacts from the other civilisations of the East. Instead she developed and diffused stereotypes of the eastern people, especially images of the ethnic Other and the handsome Oriental.

This focus on selected eastern civilisations in Rome's imperial imagery lent the portrayal of the cultural Other new significance. Here, the image of the handsome Oriental turned out to be a particularly successful icon as it became loaded with a set of different and inconsistent meanings. The image oscillated between Trojan friend, venerated Oriental deity and Parthian enemy, and embodied a strange conceptual overlap between the categories of friend and foe.[130] For Rome, the Oriental as friend and the Oriental as foe were not two opposing poles. On the contrary, the discourse around them was one of the contexts in which Roman identity was defined. For Rome, "Roman" was synonymous with the world: a non-Roman could well become "Roman" but keep at the same time his own cultural identity.[131] In this constantly shifting debate on the Roman and the Foreign, Mary Beard has rightly located the puzzling and contradictory Roman representation of the cult of Mater Magna.[132] The different constructions of the role of the Orient(al) in Rome – ranging from the legitimation of the city's eastern origin at Troy to the condemnation of Rome's most dangerous enemy, the Parthian – amounted to different claims and conflicting counterclaims on how "Roman" was to be defined. The definition of what was "Roman" could be described as a dynamic process driven by the political, religious, social and economic interests of Rome. Such a universal concept of "Romanism" provided imperial Rome with a powerful ideology which aimed at controlling the peoples of non-Roman cultures. The imagery of the handsome Oriental constituted a potent medium of communication which diffused and enhanced the ideology of Roman universalism throughout the Roman empire. This imagery shows perhaps more than any other medium, that the story of Rome is as much the story of the Orient as it is the story of the Occident.[133] Or, in other words, imperial Rome made the Orient(al) as much her friend as her foe.

80 THE AGE OF THE PARTHIANS

Acknowledgments

I warmly thank Vesta Sarkhosh Curtis and Sarah Stewart for their kind invitation to London; my friends Luca Giuliani, Karl-Joachim Hölkeskamp, Susanne Muth and, especially, Richard Gordon for reading the manuscript and for stimulating criticism; Michael Alram, Bert Smith and the following institutions for benevolently providing photographs: Staatliche Museen zu Berlin, Preussischer Kulturbesitz, Antikensammlung, Berlin; Archäologisches Institut der Universität Köln, Forschungsarchiv für Antike Plastik (online photo service Arachne), Cologne; Museum für Abgüsse Klassischer Bildwerke, Munich.

Photo Credits

Fig. 1: Murken (1995), p. 42 fig. 43. – Figs. 2,3, 5, 7-10, 12, 14, 17-23: Museum für Abgüsse Klassischer Bildwerke, Munich. – Fig. 4: Invernizzi (2001), p. 230. – Fig. 6: Dawid (2003), frontispiece. - Fig. 11: Tanabe (1986), pl. 448; Fig. 13: Ulisse (1996), p. 68 fig. 23. – Fig. 16: Bert Smith (Oxford). – Fig. 15: Zanker (1988), p. 194 fig. 149. – Fig. 24: Ghini (1994), p. 55. – Fig. 25: Pugliesi Carratelli (1991), 465 fig. 36b.

Notes:

1. Fisch 1984; Hentsch 1988; Sievernich and Budde 1989; Shichiji 1991; Mackenzie 1995; Said 1995; Osterhammel 1998; Sardar 1999; Kurz 2000; Bohrer 2003. My thanks to Egon Flaig for drawing my attention to Ye'or's 2005 study.
2. For Occidentalism, Carrier 1992; Carrier 1995; Chen 1995; Ball 2000, pp. 448-450; Buruma and Margalit 2005. – For the development of the concept of the West, GoGwit 1995a; GoGwit 1995b.
3. For friend and foe in (modern) European thinking, Hoffmann 1972; Palaver 1997.
4. Mitchell 1986; Brandt 1999; Scholz 2000; Waldenfels 2001; Smith 2002; Giuliani 2003: 9-19.
5. Orientalism and visual culture in the nineteenth century, Sosien 1995; Nochlin 2002; Bohrer 2003.
6. Murken 1995: 42, 44 fig. 43; Baumstark 1999: 414 fig. 258.
7. Murken 1995: 42-44 fig. 43; 47-50, 47-50; 91-92 fig. 83a; 106-107 figs 100c-d; Baumstark 1999: 406-449 ("König Otto und Königin Amalie: Hofstaat und monarchische Repräsentation"). For the eastern and western impacts on the Greek costume, Welters 1995; Papantoniou 1996: 127-133.
8. http://www.time.com/time/coversearch/.
9. Flügel 1930; Eicher 1995.
10. For Orientalism in the field of Classics, Dihle 1994; Schneider 1998; Hauser 2001; Kienlin and Schweizer 2002; Wiesehöfer 2003; Schneider 2006.
11. For foreignness at Rome, Noy 2000.
12. For recent studies on Rome's relationship with non-Romans, Mattern 1999; Ferris 2000; Burns 2003.
13. For this process, see also Beard 1994: 185-187.
14. See, however, Schneider 1998; Landskron 2005; Rose 2005; Schneider 2006.
15. For the Roman imagery of (northern) barbarians, Schneider 1992a; Zanker 2000: 410-419; Heitz 2003; Krierer 2004. – For western categories of cultural asymmetry, Koselleck 1975; see also Stevens 1994: 64-67 on C.G. Jung's concept of "shadow".
16. Timpe 1962; Ziegler 1964: 20-51; Timpe 1975; Schippmann 1980: 31-47; Malitz 1984; Sonnabend 1986: 159-227; Campbell 1993: 213-228; Butscher 1994: 447-453; Wickevoort Crommelin 1995: 24-37; Ball 2000: 8-15; Wheeler 2002; Brosius 2006: 92-101.
17. See below n. 92.
18. Schneider 1986: 29-97, 114-120, 128-130; Sonnabend 1986: 197-221; Zanker 1988: 183-192; Campbell 1993: 220-228; Rich 1998 ; Schneider 1998 ; Landskron 2005: 102-151; Rose 2005.
19. Schneider 1986: 31-32, 36, 71; Wallace-Hadrill 2004.
20. For a comparison of the two superpowers, Howard-Johnston 1995; Winter and Dignas 2001; Wiesehöfer 2003, who is also discussing the ideological preconceptions of such a comparison; Schneider 2006.
21. For potential pre-Augustan images of Parthians in Rome, Schneider 1998: 95.
22. Kähler 1959; Zanker 1988: 188-192; Simon 1990: Boschung 1993: 179-181 no. 171 (bibl.); Schneider 1998: 97-99; Wiesehöfer 2002; Rose 2005: 25-27.
23. Rose 2005: 25-26 has proposed identifying the representative of Rome not as Mars Ultor (*opinio communis*) but as Roma because of the Attic helmet, the "female" strands of hair which escape from the helmet, the "female" anatomy of the body and the dog. The identity of either Mars or Roma, however, is difficult to confirm.

24. Brinkmann and Wünsche 2003: 186-197 (P. Liverani), with a reconstruction of the original colouring of the statue.
25. Calmeyer 1980.
26. For further evidence, Schneider 1998: 98; Landskron 2005: 93-101. See also in this volume, V. S. Curtis: 16.
27. Mathiesen 1992: 166-167 no. 80; Invernizzi 200: 230 colour ill.; Landskron 2005: 95-96.
28. Hölscher 1988: 537-541; La Rocca 1992: 411-414; Schneider 1998: 100.
29. Schneider 1998: 100; Dawid 2003.
30. Dawid 2003: 55-63 pls. 6.19, 10.32a-c.
31. Binsfeld 1983; Schneider 1998: 101-102.
32. For the Phrygian cap, see below n. 51.
33. For Roman bars of gold, Göbl 1978: 145-146 pls. 39 nos. 476-477 (here fig. 8).
34. See below n. 113.
35. Sonnabend 1986: 254-260; Nedergaard 1988; Spawforth 1994: 242.
36. Suetonius, *vita Augusti* 43.4; for the context, Nedergaard 1988: 108-109.
37. Further evidence in Sonnabend 1986: 188, 241; Spawforth 1994: 260-263; Krumeich 2001: 88-92; Rose 2005: 36-37.
38. Sonnabend 1986: 235-246, 264-272, 282-286; Campbell 1993: 216-220; Wiesehöfer 1996: 123-124; Schneider 1998: 103.
39. Paratore 1966: 505-558; Sonnabend 1986: 172, 280-282.
40. Florus, *Epitomae* 1.40.31 (*Sic Pompeio duce populus Romanus totam ... Asiam pervagatus, quam extremam imperii habebat provinciam mediam fecit. Exceptis quippe Parthis ...*); Pompeius Trogus, *Historiae Philippicae* 41.1.1 (*divisione orbis*); Manilius, *Astronomica* 4.674-675 (*orbis alter*; Tacitus, *annales* 2.2.2 (*alio ex orbe*); see, Sonnabend 1986: 202-220.
41. Schneider 1986; Schneider 1998: 104-110; Schneider 2002: 84-86, 433-436 nos. 136-138 (J. Fejfer); Landskron 2003; Landskron 2005: 57-92.
42. For the shaping of this iconography, Vos 1963; Raeck 1983: 10-66; Hall 1988; Miller 1997; Barringer 2004; Ivanchik 2005, questioning the conventional interpretation of the Athenian "Scythomania".
43. For the process of orientalising the Orient(al), see Said 1995: 49-73.
44. Schneider 1986: 39-40; Schneider 1998: 104-105.
45. Schneider 1992b; Schneider 1998: 107-109; Landskron 2005: 65-66.
46. Tran Tam Tinh 1975: 288 fig. 252; Dwyer 1982: 64-65 pl. 21 fig. 80; Schneider 1992b: 303-304 fig. 5; Pugliesi Carratelli 1997: 540-564 (Casa del Camillo, VII.12.22-27, room "e"); Schneider 1998: 107-108.
47. Tanabe 1986: 44 pl. 448.
48. Horace, *carmen* 1.29.7-8: *puer qui ex aula capillis / ad cyathum statuetur unctis ....*
49. Kempter 1980; Sichtermann 1988; Schwarzenberg 2001-02; Turnheim 2004.
50. Kempter 1980: 5; Sichtermann 1988: 154-155; Visser 1998; Schwarzenberg 2001-02: 166; Hertel 2003: 157, 296. – For the genealogy of Ganymede, Scheer (1997), p. 318.
51. For the Phrygian cap, Hinz 1974: 790-792; Seiterle 1985; Schneider 1986: 19-20, 98-99, 123-124; Schneider 1998: 104; Rose 2005: 34-35.
52. Pani 1975: 74; Schneider 1986: 123; Hall 1988; Wilhelm 1988; Rose 2002a: 332; Dench 2005: 248.
53. Crawford 1974: nos. 19.2, 21.1, 22.1, 24.1, 26.4, 27.5, 41.1, 98A.3, 102.2b-c, 269.1, 288.1, 464.3b; Rose 2002a: 331-332 fig. 3.

FRIEND AND FOE: THE ORIENT IN ROME

54. Juvenal, *Saturae* 6.513-516 *semivir* (sc. Gallus) ... *plebeia et Phrygia vestitur bucca tiara*. For the Galli, Graillot 1912: 287-319; Beard 1994: 164-165, 173-183; Roller 1998; Rose 2002a: 332-334. For *semivir*, Vergil, *Aeneid* 4.215, 9.614-620, 12.99: Roller 1998; 129. – For the Phrygian cap see above note 51.
55. Neudecker 1988: 46-47; Schneider 1992b. For imperial cup bearers called Ganymede, Martial, *epigrammata* 9.36; Cain 1993: 86-87.
56. Bremmer 1990: 141.
57. Veblen 1899: 35-67; Bourdieu 1974: 159-201.
58. Schneider 1986: 154 n. 1166; Andreae 1994: 113-120; Andreae 1995: 115-134; Schneider 1998: 108; Schwarzenberg 2001-02: 176.
59. Andreae 1994: 113-120; Andreae 1995: 115-134; Kunze 1996: 159-223; Ulisse 1996: 68 fig. 23; Andreae 1999: 177-223; Grummond and Ridgway 2000: 111-165 (H.A. Weis), 166-190 (P. Green); Andreae 2001: pls. 98-102.
60. For the Roman iconography of Trojans in Oriental garb, Grassinger 1999: 57-63, 207-209 nos 34-40 (the release of Hector); Rose 2005: 34, 44; see also the entries, Aeneas, Alexandros, Askanios, Anchises, Hektor, Paridis Iudicium, Priamos and Troilos, in: *Lexicon Iconographicum Mythologicae Classicae* I-VIII, Zurich / Munich 1981-1997.
61. For the stylistic dating, Kunze 1996: 159-223.
62. The complex visual narratives at Sperlonga do not support Bernhard Andreae's monocausal interpretation of the villa as the property of the emperor Tiberius, and the sculptures as a manifesto of a supposed Tiberian ideology (see above note 59). To my mind the question of the ownership of the villa remains open: there is no justification for fixing on any particular member of the Julio-Claudian family – and the owner may just as easily have been a member of a family closely related to Augustus.
63. Bellinger 1961: 47-63 nos. T136 (Hadrian), T149 (Marcus Aurelius), T186-T187 (Commodus), T209, T211, T213 (without the image of an emperor, second century CE).
64. Zanker 1988: 201-210; Gruen 1992: 6-51; Spannagel 1999: 162-177; Erskine 2001; Mavrogiannis 2003: 15-83; Hölkeskamp 2004: 201-204; Dench 2005: 248-253; Walter 2006.
65. C. Day Lewis, *The Aeneid of Vergil*. New York: Doubleday Anchor Books 1953: 20-21; see, Spannagel 1999: 105-107; Erskin 2001: 22-23.
66. Hardly the Trojan Achates as again supposed by Rose 2005: 44. The shepherd's crook points to Iulus/Ascanius.
67. Torelli 1999; Haselberger 2002: 189 s.v. Pax Augusta, Ara.
68. Wallace-Hadrill 2004.
69. The visible remains, however, do not clarify if Iulus/Ascanius was shown in trousers or not; *contra* Rose 2005: 44n. 127.
70. Zanker 1969; Kockel 1995; Rich 1998: 79-97; Spannagel 1999; La Rocca 2001; Haselberger 2002: 130-131 s.v. Forum Augusti; Ungaro 2002: 109-121; Haselberger and Humphrey 2006: 127-130, 183-190.
71. Simon 1990: 135-145; Spannagel 1999: 162-205.
72. Scholz 1970.
73. Croon 1981; Spannagel 1999: 60-78, 206-224.
74. Zanker 1969; Spannagel 1999.
75. Spannagel 1999: 365-400 (catalogue of the visual evidence).
76. Spannagel 1999: 86-161.
77. Erim 1989: 56 fig. 80; Smith 1987: 132-133 (for the location); Smith 1990: 97-98

fig. 9; Galinsky 1992: 462-463 fig.6; Spannagel 1999: 371 no. A 17.

78. Bernoulli 1886: 277-299; Jucker 1976; Megow 1987: 202-207 no. A 85; Giard 1998; Schneider 1998: 116; Meyer 2000: 11-57; Giuliani 2004.

79. For the visual tradition of such vertical hierarchy, Schneider 1992a: 941.

80. Schneider 1997.

81. Andreae 1995a; Rose 2002a: 341-342; Giuliani 2004. For the best illustration, Giard 1998: pl. VI.

82. Weber 1972 with earlier works; Rose 2002a: 331-342 (who, on p. 339, wrongly confines the Trojan dress to "the old, the young, and the cowardly"); Rose 2005: 34. For the tensions and contradictions of Rome's cultural-ethnic origins in Roman accounts, Dench 2005: 61-69.

83. Zanker 1988: 201-210; Gruen 1992: 6-51; Spannagel 1999: 162-177; Erskine 2001; Mavrogiannis 2003: 15-83; Hölkeskamp 2004: 201-204; Dench 2005: 248-253; Walter 2006.

84. For Ilium in the early empire, Rose 2002b.

85. For Hector's tomb, Erskine 2001: 109; Hertel 2003: 179-180.

86. *Anthologia Latina* 708 (ed. Riese): *Martia progenies, Hector, tellure sub ima / (Fas audire tamen si mea verba tibi) / respira, quoniam vindex tibi contigit heres, / qui patriae famam proferat usque tuae. / Ilios, en surgit rursum inclita, gens colit illam / te Marte inferior, Martis amica tamen. / Myrmidonas periisse omnes dic Hector Achilli, / Thessaliam et magnis esse sub Aeneadis.* Pani (1975), pp. 74-78; Hertel (2003), pp. 280-281; Walter (2006), 89-90.

87. The avenger is Rome, as Richard Gordon orally suggested to me, not Augustus, as claimed by Hertel 2003: 281.

88. For the "cultural" clothing of the Trojans in Roman or Oriental garb as recorded by Vergil, Dench 2005: 276-277.

89. Schneider 1986; Schneider 2002: 84-88, 433-436 nos. 136-138 (J. Fejfer).

90. Schneider 1986: 166-186.

91. Cicero, *Oratio de Domo Sua* 60; Cicero, *Oratio de Haruspicum Responsis* 28. Vergil, *Georgica* 5.211 (*populi Parthorum aut Medus Hydaspes*), 5.290 (*Persidis*); Propertius, *Carmina* 3.3.11 (*Medae*); Horace, *Carmina* 1.2.22 (*Persae*), 1.2.51 (*Medos*), 1.21.15 (*Persas*), 1.27.5 (*Medus*), 1.29.4 (*Medo*), 1.3.1 (*Persicos*), 2.1.31 (*Medis*), 2.9.21 (*Medum*), 2.12.21 (*Achaemenium*), 2.16.6 (*Medi*); 3.3.44 (*Medis*); 3.5.4 (*Persis*); 3.5.9 (*Medo*); 3.8.19 (*Medus*), 3.9.4 (*Persarum*), 4.14.42 (*Medus*), 4.15.23 (*Persae*); Horace, *Carmen Saeculare* 54 (*Medus*); Horace, *Epodi* 13.8 (*Achaemenio*); Ovid, *Ars Amatoria* 1.225 (*Persis*), 1.226 (*Achaemeniis*); Ovid, *Fasti* 1.385 (*Persis*); Ovid, *Metamorphoses* 1.62 (*Persidaque*), 4.212 (*Achaemenias*); Ovid; *Tristia* 5.3.23 (*Persidaque*); see Paratore 1966; Wissemann 1981: 24-26; Sonnabend 1986: 198-199, 244-246, 280-282.

92. Schneider 1986: 58-67; Schneider 1998: 110-113; Spannagel 1999: 75-77, 206-223, 226-230; Rose 2005: 45-53.

93. *Res Gestae Divi Augusti* 23; Schneider 1998: 112-113; Coleman 1993: 51-54; Spannagel 1999: 15; Rose 2005: 45-47. For the naval battle at Salamis, Wallinga 2005.

94. Schneider 1986: 18-97; Schäfer 1998: 67-70; Schneider 2002: 82, 84-85, 433-436 nos. 136-138 (J. Fejfer).

95. Pausanias, *Periegeta*, 1.18.8. For the dating of the monument in Augustan times, Schäfer 1998: 67-70; Schneider 1998: 112 with n.125. – For the Romanisation of Athens in Augustan times, Spawforth 1997; Walker 1997.

96. Schneider 1986: 50-57 pl. 9.

FRIEND *AND* FOE: THE ORIENT IN ROME

85

97. Schneider 1986: 58; for the tripod dedicated to Delphi, Steinhart 1997.
98. Schneider 1986: 67-72; Dräger 1994: 73-96.
99. Schneider 1986: 98-125.
100. Bauer 1993; Haselberger 2002: 66 s.v. Basilica Pauli; Haselberger and Humphrey 2006: 169-173.
101. A preliminary report will be published by Tobias Bitterer, Alfons Neubauer a R. M. Schneider: "Die Orientalenstatuen der Basilica Aemilia, Ein Arbeitsbericht", in: Mitteilungen des Deutschen Archäologischen Instituts, Römische Abteilung 112 (2005).
102. Schneider 1986: 115-125; Schneider 1998: 108-110; Rose 2005: 62-63; *contra* Landwehr 2000: 75-76.
103. Pliny, *naturalis historia* 36.102 *basilicam Pauli columnis et Phrygibus mirabilem* (*est*). For this reading of the text, Schneider 1986: 120-125; Schneider 1998: 109-110.
104. *Phryx* as synonym for slave, Schneider 1986: 123. For the (almost) synonymous use of Phrygian and Trojan, see above n. 52.
105. Schneider 1986: 118; Kränzle 1994.
106. Vitruvius, *de architectura* 1.1.3 ... *quod significatur et quod significant.*
107. Vitruvius, *de architectura* 1.1.6.
108. Vitruvius, *de architectura* 1.1.5-6; Schneider 1986: 103-115.
109. Schneider 1986: 98-135, 200-210 SO 1-68; Castella and Flutsch 1990: 18, 24-25 fig. 9; Schneider 1998: 114-115; Landwehr 2000: 74-85 no. 110.
110. Schneider 1986: 205 SO 29-30; Schäfer 1989: 282-287 no. 22; Schneider 1998: 110.
111. Schneider 1998: 113-116.
112. For polishing, Schneider 1999: 934. For the colouring of Greek sculptures showing Orientals, Brinkmann and Wünsche 2004: 84-98, 166-173 (V. Brinkmann).
113. Östenberg 1999; Östenberg 2003; Flaig 2003: 32-40; Itgenshorst 2005; Hölkeskamp 2007: 20-28. For the spectacular staging of (acclaiming?) Parthians on top of the arch erected after 20 BCE in the Forum Romanum to commemorate the settlement of the Parthian question, Rich 1998: 97-115; Rose 2005: 28-36.
114. For the mythical figures and political personifications, *Lexicon Iconographicum Mythologicae Classicae* I-VIII, Zurich / Munich, 1981-1997. – For the Galli see above note 54.
115. Ball 2000: 7, 450 (quotations); Hingley 2005: 55-56.
116. Simon 1967: 18, 21 pls. 14, 17, 19-21; Rose 1990; Rose 2005: 38-44.
117. See above no. 35.
118. Lately Rose 2005: 38-44, has argued that the two boys are portrayed as foreign princes, the one on the south frieze of Oriental, the one on the north frieze of northern ethnicity, to represent the new peace that had been achieved under Augustus in both east and west.
119. Attis: Schneider 1986, pp. 133-134; Baudy 1997; Lancellotti 2002; Bremmer 2004; Landskron 2005: 59-61. – Mithras: Gordon 2000; Gordon 2001.
120. Pugliesi Carratelli 1991: 435-477, especially 464-465 figs 36a-b (Casa di Pinarius Cerialis, III.4.4).
121. Andreae 1973: pl. 105; Vermaseren 1982; Ghini 1994; Mielsch 2001: 176-177 fig. 209 (dating).
122. Gordon 2000: 288.
123. Gordon 2001.

124. Pensabene 1982; Wiseman 1984; Wilhelm 1988; Beard 1994; Pensabene 1996; Takács 1996; Roller 1999: 261-343; Takács 1999; Bremmer 2004: 557-566; Haselberger and Humphrey 2006: 34-49.
125. Vergil, *Aeneid* 2.788, 6.784-785, 9.82, 10.252. Wilhelm 1988: 86.
126. Ovid, *Fasti* 4.272-274. Wilhelm 1988: 96.
127. Schneider 2006.
128. Hartog 1980; Hall 1989; Burkert 1992; Dihle 1994; Miller 1997; Burkert 2003.
129. Vout 2003; Bol and Kaminski and Maderna 2004: 155-274; Ägypten 2005: 331-450.
130. For recent discussions on Carl Schmitt's political-theological readings of friend and foe, Meier 1994; Palaver 1998.
131. Woolf 1994.
132. Beard 1994, especially 166-167, 183-187.
133. Ball 2000: 446-450.

5

Parthia in China: a Re-examination of the Historical Records

Wang Tao (University College London and School of Oriental and African Studies, University of London)

The Parthian empire lasted from the middle of the third century BCE to the early third century CE, a period of nearly 500 years.[1] It was during this time that China witnessed the turbulent late Warring States period (475-221 BCE), the unification of those states under the Qin in 221 BCE, and the empire-building of the Western and Eastern Han dynasties (206 BCE–CE 220). We now know that, as early as the third millennium BCE, a network already existed in Euroasian steppeland, stretching from the Caspian Sea in the west to the Tarim Basin in the east.[2] However, no written records relating to the early history of Central Asia have survived. It is remarkable, however, that by the end of the first millennium BCE, China was under the most ambitious Han emperor, Wudi (r.140–86 BCE), who adopted an expansionist policy and enjoyed some direct contact with his western neighbours. Among them the Parthian empire was completely dominated by a succession of powerful rulers: Mithadates I (c. 171–138 BCE), Phraates II (c. 138–128 BCE), Artabanus II (c. 128-124 BCE) and Mithradates II (c. 124-87 BCE). It was during this period that China established its official presence in the "Western Regions" (areas west of the Hexi corridor),[3] and began to record information on these places in a fairly systematic way. These early historical records provide very interesting information, and sometimes misinformation, of the emerging Parthian empire in the Iranian highland.

The majority of the relevant early Chinese records are now available in translation in more than one foreign language,[4] to the extent that a historian or archaeologist who has no specialist knowledge of Chinese language can also makes use of them quite easily. However, how much trust can we put into these records? Misinterpretations can arise from uncritical reading of the texts, and the situation is further complicated by the lack of hard evidence from archaeological remains. In this article, I will not aim to cover the vast archaeological evidence - this will be dealt with in a separate paper - but to re-examine the textual references in the Chinese historical sources that are contemporary with, and relevant to, the Parthian empire. I will also offer some interpretations of those references, in the hope that this may help to clarify some misunderstandings and provide a solid ground for the future study of the relationship between ancient Iran and China, as well as the early history of the Silk Road.

The records in the *Shiji, Hanshu* and *Hou Hanshu*

Chinese records relating to the Parthian empire are mainly found in three of the Standard Histories (*zhengshi*): Sima Qian's (*c.* 145–86 BCE) *Shiji*, Ban Gu's (CE 32–92) *Hanshu*, and Fan Ye's (389–445) *Hou Hanshu*. In addition to these, there are references in other books such Yu Huan's (third century) *Weilüe* and Li Daoyuan's (d. 527) *Shuijing zhu*. Before embarking on any textual analysis, it is important to appreciate that there are a number of factors that may affect our understanding of the historical records.

First, it is essential to be aware of the social context in which the records were produced. The *Shiji* was written in the first century BCE, the *Hanshu* in the first century CE, and the *Hou Hanshu* in the fifth century CE. These dates cover a period well over five hundred years, so it is clear these Standard Histories were not produced at the same time. Furthermore, the political climate, as well as the author's personal life and motivation, would have influenced the way in which they approached their writing. For example, Sima Qian (b. 145 BC) was the son of Sima Tan who served as court historian (*taishiling*) to Emperor Wudi. In time, Sima Qian would himself become the court historian in his father's place. Sima Qian began to write the *Shiji* when the Han dynasty was at its peak. His task was therefore not without political ambition. Indeed, it was Wudi's desire that Han influence should extend "for 10,000 *li* into vast domains"[5] and that the name of his empire should be known to all peoples as "the lands within the four seas". During the Han dynasty, massive resources were devoted to the construction of fortifications along the line of the Great Wall and Chinese influence penetrated deep into the Gobi Desert and Tarim Basin. But the most formidable enemy to Wudi's empire building were the Xiongnu tribes, who had controlled the steppes for a long period and were more powerful than the Han. The Han-Xiongnu relationship therefore occupied a significant part of state affairs in the Western Han period. It also impinged on Sima Qian's personal life: acting in defence of Li Ling (an army general who had surrendered to the Xiongnu), Sima Qian offended Wudi. For this he was imprisoned and humiliated with castration. It was intended that this harsh punishment should reflect the severity of his crime. Eventually he was released from prison, and afterwards spent twelve years compiling his monumental work *Shiji*. Fierce anger and a sense of justice drove him to produce this historical narrative, which subsequently became a model for later generations of Chinese historians.

The author of the *Hanshu* had a similar experience. Ban Gu was born into a family of historians in 32 CE. His father Ban Biao wrote a supplement to the *Shiji*, his sister Ban Zhao was a renowned writer of history, and his brother Ban Chao was appointed as Protector General of the Western Regions (*xiyu duhu*) in 91 CE and commanded the Tarim Basin for over 30 years. Given his family connections, it is likely that Ban Gu may have had better access to information about Central Asia. But his life met with tragedy: he was once arrested and charged with the crime of "altering official records"; he assisted Dou Xian's campaign against the Xiongnu, but Dou's failure in military battles also implicated him. He died in prison at the age of sixty. The author of *Hou Hanshu* also ended in tragedy. Fan Ye was accused of participating in a coup and was executed at the age of forty-seven. When reading the *Shiji*, the *Hanshu* or the *Hou Hanshu*, we need to bear in mind the political circumstances, and the personal motivation and experience of the authors.

Second, the textual history of the respective books requires careful scrutiny. There has been a tradition in Chinese historical writing of copying from other sources, and we need to understand that the compiled texts are not necessarily presented in strict chronological order. For example, if we compare records of the Parthians in the *Hanshu* with those in the *Shiji*, it seems that many passages are more or less identical in both books. The *Hanshu* was compiled by Ban Gu in the end of the first century CE, but with late additions by his sister Ban Chao and the scholar Ma Xu. Clearly, the *Hanshu* relied on the *Shiji* as its main source. But there is also the possibility that the version of the *Shiji* that has survived may also contain passages copied from the *Hanshu*, later insertions added during re-editing. So, who copied whom? Was there a single source for the records in the *Shiji* and the *Hanshu*? These are questions that occupy both Chinese and western historians, who must also navigate their way through other issues, such as the corruption of texts and errors by copyists in the transmission of the books.[6] These matters influence how we interpret the meaning of the texts. It can also be helpful to consider of the style of narrative. For example, while we know very little about the author of the *Weilüe*, it is clear that the book represented a private venture, which was criticised by many scholars of the orthodox school.

The *Shiji*

The earliest reference to the Parthian empire is found in the *Shiji*: (*juan* 123) "Dayuan liezhuan" ("Records about Ferghana") which offers several accounts of the countries and peoples of Central and Western Asia. There are two references which refer to Anxi and Tiaozhi. These read:

> Anxi is situated several thousand *li* to the west of the Great Yuezhi. The people are settled on the land and cultivate the fields. They grow rice and wheat, and make wine from grapes. They have walled settlements like the people of Dayuan, and also control several hundred cities of various sizes,

measuring several thousand *li* square. It is by far the largest kingdom. Near the Wei river, there are markets where people who do business and trade use carts and boats, and they travel to neighbouring countries, sometimes journeying several thousand *li*. The coins of the country are made of silver and bear the face of the king. When the king dies, the currency is immediately changed and new coins are issued with the face of his successor. To make records they cut leather and write horizontally. To the west of Anxi lies Tiaozhi, and to the north lies Yancai and Lixuan.

安 息 在 大 月 氏 西 可 數 千 里 。其 俗 土 著 ， 耕 田 ，
田 稻 麥 ， 蒲 陶 酒 。城 邑 如 大 宛 ， 其 屬 小 大 數 百
城 ， 地 方 數 千 里 ， 最 為 大 國 。臨 媯 水 有 市 ， 民
商 賈 用 車 及 船 ， 行 旁 國 或 數 千 里 。以 銀 為 錢 ，
錢 如 其 王 面 ， 王 死 輒 更 錢 ， 效 王 面 焉 。畫 革 旁
行 ， 以 為 書 記 。其 西 則 條 枝 ， 北 有 奄 蔡 ， 黎
軒 。[7]

The description of Tiaozhi also makes a direct reference to Parthia:

Tiaozhi is several thousand *li* west of Anxi, facing the Western Sea. The climate is hot and damp, and people cultivate the fields and grow rice. There is a big bird with eggs like a jar. The population is great, and many places are ruled by petty chiefs, but Anxi has made it her own subject and treats the country as the outer-state. The country is renowned for magicians. The elders in Anxi told tales of the Rui River and the Mother of the West, but no one has seen this.

條 枝 在 安 息 西 數 千 里 ， 臨 西 海 。暑 溼 。 耕 田 ，
田 稻 。 有 大 鳥 ， 卵 如 甕。人 眾 甚 多 ， 往 往 有 小 君
長 ， 而 安 息 役 屬 之 ， 以 為 外 國 。 國 善 眩。安 息
長 老 傳 聞 條 枝 有 弱 水 、 西 王 母 ， 而 未 嘗 見 。[8]

These two accounts offer important clues. As the majority of scholars now agree, "Anxi 安息" refers to Arsaces, the name used by the first king of Parthia and was adopted by all subsequent Parthian rulers. The phonetic reconstruction for Anxi in Early Middle Chinese (EMC) is <*?an-sik,[9] which is probably a transliteration of Arsaces. It was the name by which the Chinese knew Parthia, even after the fall of the Parthian empire. The other name "Bosi 波斯 <*pa-siə" derived from Persia, which appeared in Chinese records after the sixth century CE.

The record also gives information on the climate, local products, currency, transport, and writing system of the Parthians. But, by far the most significant information is the political geography and the various urban settlements of the Parthian empire. We read that Parthia was "several thousand *li*" west of the Da Yuezhi (the Tochari) who had migrated from north-western China to occupy the northern bank of the Wei River (also known as the Oxus, or Amu-darya). It was by far the largest state, with its territory stretching over several thousand square *li*, and several hundreds of walled cities, which were similar in construction to those of Dayuan (Ferghana). To its west was Tiaozhi, but the identification of Tiaozhi is still under debate. Suggested places include Syria, Mesopotamia, even Egypt.[10] An interesting theory has been proposed by the Chinese scholars Sun Yutang and Yu Taishan, namely that "Tiaozhi<*dɛw-tçiǎ" may be an abbreviated transliteration of "[An]tiochi[a]", referring to the former Seleucid kingdom in the northeast of the Mediterranean.[11] The Seleucid kingdom was established after the death of Alexander the Great in 323 BCE, and once controlled a large territory extending from the Mediterranean to the Persian Gulf and Bactria. But, by the second century BCE, it had lost most of its territory to the Parthians; and the Greeks in Bactria had also claimed independence. In 139 BCE, when Parthian solders captured Demetrius, the Parthians became the overlords of Mesopotamia. But, it seems that Mithradates allowed a measure of freedom to the people in the conquered land.[12] This is reflected in the Chinese record: the *Shiji* clearly states that Tiaozhi was then under the rule of the Parthians, but had many petty rulers and was "treated as the outer-state" (*yi wei wai guo* 以為外國).

The text states that to the north of Parthia were Yancai and Lixuan. It is likely that Yancai refers to one of the Scythian kingdoms in the Aral Sea region;[13] however, identification of the latter poses great difficulty.[14] Lixuan<*lɛj-xian (or Lihan<* lɛj-ɣan) is probably an abbreviated transliteration for Alexandria. In later records, such as the *Hanshu*, Lixuan usually refers to Alexandria in Egypt, but this does not accord with it being to the north of Parthia. We can treat this either as a misunderstanding by Sima Qian or as a textual error. Friedrich Hirth, in his translation, tried to avoid the problem by moving the name Lixuan to the beginning of the next sentence, thereby linking Lixuan with Tiaozhi, to the west of Parthia.[15] But, in the third and second century BCE, there were a number of locations called "Alexandria" in Central Asia, including Alexandria Oxiana in Bactria. We should therefore not rule out the possibility that Lixuan in the *Shiji* may refer to one of these Central Asian Alexandria, rather the city of Alexandria in Egypt. It is surprising that the *Shiji* makes no mention of Parthia's southern frontier.

As many scholars have pointed out, the above description of the Parthian empire in the *Shiji* is a bit blurred, and may bear factual errors. For example, it says that Parthia and Tiaozhi both cultivated rice. While rice was indeed cultivated in Babylonia, Susis and in lower Syria, it was not common in Parthia at that time.[16] This error may well reflect the limitations of the information that was available to the author. The source for Sima Qian's description of the Parthian empire came from the reports of the Han envoys, and in particular from Zhang Qian.

In the first half of the second century BCE, the Tochari (Yuezhi) were driven out of north-western China by the Xiongnu, and finally settled in Bactria (Daxia). In 139 BCE, the Han emperor Wudi sought to make an alliance with the Tochari, with the aim of combining forces to defeat the Xiongnu. He sent his envoy Zhang Qian on a journey to Bactria to locate the Tochari. Zhang Qian was captured *en route* and detained twice by the Xiongnu. He managed to escape and in about 130–129 BCE, finally reached the Tochari who had already destroyed the Greek kingdoms and settled north of the Amu-darya. The land west of the Amu-darya was controlled by the Parthians. Zhang Qian spent a year or more in the region, before returning to the Han capital at Chang'an in 126 BCE. Zhang Qian brought back a great deal of information about the countries and peoples in the west. Zhang Qian himself visited only Ferghana (Dayuan), Samarkand (Kangju), Sogdiana (Da Yuezhi) and Bactria (Daxia), but his report suggests that he must have amassed a great deal of information indirectly from people who had been to such places as Parthia and India.[17]

The time of Zhang Qian's travel to Central Asia coincided with a crucial period in the Parthian history. In about 129/128 BCE, the Parthians were fighting on two fronts: the Seleucids in the west, and the Scythians in the east. The Parthian army killed the Seleucid ruler Antiochus VII, but the Parthian king, Phraates II (r. 138–128 BCE), was killed by the Scythians. But in Zhang Qan's account there is no mention at all of this dramatic event. Many scholars assume that it is because that the his main interest was to report to his emperor the location, custom and products of the countries and peoples from this region, but not historical events. Others suggest that he may have left the before the conflict occurred. A third explanation is that Zhang Qian may have had some knowledge of the event, but for some reason it was left out from the present chapter.

In 115 BC, Zhang Qian was sent by the emperor to the Western Regions for the second time. This time he took with him 300 men and a large amount of gold and silk. He arrived in the kingdom of the Wusun who were still in the Ferghana region and engaged in gift-diplomacy with the king of the Wusun. Zhang Qian succeeded in returning to Chang'an with tributes brought from the Wusun. He died a year or so later.

Communication between Central Asia and China did not stop with the death of Zhang Qian. In fact, the opposite was true, and his long journeys led the way to the opening of the "Silk Road" between China and the west. The information collected by Zhang Qian and other envoys was extremely valuable to Wudi as he sought to realise his imperial dream and open up trade with the Western Regions. A journey to the west was soon seen as a personal money spinner for state envoys. The envoys would buy and sell goods along the route, as well as taking rewards from the Han emperor. In the *Shiji*, Sima Qian criticised some of the envoys who had plundered from the lands to which they had travelled. We know too that their reports often failed to meet the emperor's approval. In these circumstances it is quite likely that many envoys may have made up stories to impress the emperor, with scant regard for factual reality.

The *Hanshu*

Knowledge of the Western Regions increased dramatically from Wudi's reign onwards. In the *Hanshu* there are descriptions of the actual routes of the Silk Road, information which may have been provided by the Chinese envoys who travelled on these roads:

> Starting from the Jade Gate and Sunny Barriers there are two routes leading to the Western Regions. The first one goes by Shanshan, north of the southern mountains, following the river westwards until it reaches Shache. This is the southern route. It then heads westwards, crossing the Pamirs and leading to the Dayuezhi and Anxi. The second route starts from the royal court of the Front Cheshi, heads along the northern mountains, and follows the river towards the west, until it reaches Shule. This is the northern route. It then heads towards the west, crossing the Pamirs and leading to Dayan, Kangju and Yancai.

> 自玉門、陽關出西域有兩道。從鄯善傍南山北，波河西行至莎車，為南道；南道西踰葱嶺則出大月氏、安息。自車師前王廷隨北山，波河西行至疏勒，為北道；北道西踰葱嶺則出大宛、康居、奄蔡焉。[18]

Another passage reads:

> Leaving the Jade Gate and the Suuny Barriers, one proceeds by the southern route, passes though Shanshan, travels to the south, then arrives at Wuyishanli. This is the end of the southern route, from where one turns north and then eastwards to reach Parthia.

> 自玉門、陽關出南道，歷鄯善而南行，至烏弋山離，南道極矣。轉北而東得安息。[19]

These descriptions clearly show that the Chinese envoys travelling to Parthia preferred to use the southern route over the Pamirs and then pass through Bactria. The identification of Wuyishanli is very important for understanding the geo-politics of the region. From here, it was a sixty-day journey to the northeast to the seat of the Han Protector-General, more than a hundred day journey to Tiaozhi, and to the west were Lixuan and Tiaozhi.[20]

The name Wuyishanli <*?o-jik-ṣɛːn-li is probably a transliteration of Alexandria, referring to one of the Alexandropolis in Arachosia and Drangiana. However, its exact location is still under dispute. While western sinologists tend to identify it with Herat or Kandahar,[21] many Chinese scholars believe that it refers to Prophthasia (Farah), as a late source gives it a transliterated name Paichi 排持<*bɛːj-dri or Paite 排特< bɛːj-dək.[22] This area was then under the rule of the Saka (Scythians). The text shows that the kingdom of Alexandropolis was independent of the Parthians, and had its own kings,

94 THE AGE OF THE PARTHIANS

palaces and currency. The observation of the coins is surprisingly accurate. The coins of Wuyishanli (and Jibin, modern-day Kashmir[23]) were in the Scythian tradition, with the royal portrait on the obverse and a horse-rider on the reverse.[24]

It is significant that the account of the Parthian empire in the *Hanshu* is much clearer than that in the *Shiji*. The *Hanshu* account reads:

> The king of the Anxi kingdom rules from Fandou. Its distance to Chang'an is 11,600 *li* (*c.* 5,000 km). It is not controlled by the [Han] Protector-General. Its northern border adjoins with Kangju, its eastern border adjoins with Wuyishanli and its western border adjoins with Tiaozhi. The land, weather, products, and customs are similar to those of Wuyi and Jibin. Their coins are also made of silver with the face of the king on the obverse and the face of the queen on the reverse. When the king dies, the currency is immediately changed. The place has some kind of big horse-like birds. There are several hundred cities in Anxi and its territory extends for several thousand square *li*. It is the largest kingdom and is near the Wei River. Its merchants travel by carts and boats to neighbouring countries. To make records they cut pieces of leather on which they write horizontally.

> 安息國，王治番兜城，去長安萬一千六百里；不屬都護。北與康居、東與烏弋山離、西與條支接。土地風氣，物類所有，民俗與烏弋、罽賓同；亦以銀為錢，文獨為王面，幕為夫人面；王死輒更鑄錢。有大馬爵。其屬小大數百城，地方數千里，最大國也。臨媯水，商賈車船行旁國；書革旁行為書記。[25]

The structure and contents of this passage are similar to that in the *Shiji*. However, there are several significant additions. For the first time, the capital of the Parthian empire is given as Fandou. The name "Fandou<*phuan-təw*" is probably a transliteration of "Parthia", but its exact location is uncertain.[26] The starting point of the narrative is much more sino-centric; the account says that the distance between the Parthian capital and Han capital at Chang'an is precisely 11,600 *li* (c. 5000 km),[27] and that Parthia was not under Chinese administration.

In terms of the political geography of the Parthian empire, it also added some new information: its northern border was with Samarkand, its eastern border with Drangiana, and its western border with Antiocheia in Mesopotamia. It reflected the western expansion of the Parthians in the first century CE. There is no mention of Lixuan here at all.

The *Hanshu* account also says that the climate, products, and customs of Parthia were similar to those of Drangiana, Arachosia, and Gandhara. The description of the Parthian coinage is also different from that in the *Shiji* account, by describing the king's portrait on the obverse and the queen's head on the reverse. The majority of Parthian coins are either of the Greek or

Scythian tradition, with royal portraits and divine images. But there is indeed a type of Parthian coinage to match this account, the drachm with a bust of Phraataces and Queen Musa, issued between 2 BCE and 4 CE.[28] The account also accurately noted the coins issued in the Scythian tradition: while the coins had the royal portrait on the front, there was a horse-rider on the obverse. The unusual "horse-like birds", probably ostriches, also attracted the attention of Han writers.

The Chinese records revealed that the Parthians shared many cultural characteristics with the petty kingdoms in the Sogdiana, Bactria, and Ferghana regions. An interesting account of the customs of the peoples who lived in the area between the Parthian empire and the Ferghana region is found in both the *Shiji* and *Hanshu*. It reads:

> From Dayuan heading west towards Anxi the different countries speak different languages, but their customs are largely similar and they can understand each other's speech. The peoples all have deep-set eyes and many men have beards and whiskers. They are good at business and will haggle over a fraction of a cent. Women seem to be held in high respect, and the men make decisions on the advice of their women. These places do not have silk or lacquer. The techniques to cast coins and vessels were previously unknown. Then, some Chinese envoys and soldiers who surrendered to the peoples of the area taught them how to make weapons. Whenever they lay their hands on any Han gold or silver, they make it into vessels and do not use it for money.

自 大 宛 以 西 至 安 息 ， 國 雖 頗 異 言 ， 然 大 同 俗 ，
相 知 言 。 其 人 皆 深 眼 ， 多 鬚 髯， 善 市 賈 ， 爭 分
銖 。 俗 貴 女 子 ， 女 子 所 言 而 丈 夫 乃 決 正。 其 地
皆 無 絲 漆 ， 不 知 鑄 錢 器 . 及 漢 使 亡 卒 降 ， 教 鑄
作 他 兵 器 。 得 漢 黃 白 金 ， 輒 以 為 器 ， 不 用 為
幣 。 [29]

This description seems to have been based on first-hand knowledge and observation. It suggests that the oases between the Pamirs and the Amu-darya were occupied by people who were culturally related to each other, probably all of Iranian stock. The *Hanshu* also describes in detail the location, population, products and customs of many of the Central Asian kingdoms, and some of these are similar to those of the Parthians. For example, the Tochari kingdom in the Amu-darya was closely associated with the Parthians in terms of products, customs, trade and currency; the Samarkand was similar to the Tochari, the Bactria to the Sogdiana, the Ferghana to both the Tochari and the Parthians. The accounts often make comparisons between different places and peoples. It is interesting that the starting point for the comparison was usually the kingdoms in Ferghana, probably because these were the places the Chinese envoys knew best.

The *Hou Hanshu*

By the late Western Han dynasty, and particularly in the Wang Mang period, the Han government suddenly lost control over the Western Regions. It did not regain control for another sixty years, until 73 CE (sixteenth year of the Yongping reign), when the Eastern Han dynasty re-established the post of Protector-General of the Western Regions. The key player was Ban Chao, the historian Ban Gu's brother. He conquered all the petty kingdoms in the Tarim Basin and held power there for nearly thirty years. During this period, Han influence became dominant in the Tarim Basin and beyond. In 97 CE, Ban Chao's envoy Gan Ying tried to reach Da Qin (the Roman Empire), but was stopped by Parthian fisherman.

On the whole, there was more information about the Western Regions available to historians who wanted to write the official history of the Eastern Han dynasty. Ban Chao's son, Ban Yong, played an important role in the Han dominance of the Western Regions and left substantial information for the chapter "Records about the Western Regions" (*Xiyuzhuan*) in the dynastic history, *Hou hanshu*. But the *Hou Hanshu* was not compiled until the first half of the fifth century, more than 200 years after the end of the Eastern Han dynasty. The author Fan Ye had clearly used a number of sources which were written in the third and fourth centuries. One of the most important of these was the *Weilüe*, written by Yu Huan in the third century CE. The original book is no longer in existence, but many of its passages have survived in the commentaries to the *Sanguozhi* (Records of the Three Kingdoms) that was compiled by Chen Shou in the late third century.

In the *Hou Hanshu*, the account of the Parthians reads:

> The kingdom of Anxi is situated at Hedu city, which is 25,000 li from Luoyang, Its northern border adjoins with Kangju, its southern border adjoins with Wuyishanli, and the size of the territory is several thousand square *li*. It has several hundred small cities with a great number of residents and strong soldiers. Mulu city is in its eastern territory, which is also called the Lesser Anxi. The distance from Anxi to Luoyang is 20,000 *li*.

> 安 息 國 居 和 櫝 城 ， 去 洛 陽 二 萬 五 千 里 。 北 與 康
> 居 接 ， 南 與 烏 弋 山 離 接 。 地 方 數 千 里 ， 小 城
> 數 百 ， 戶 口 勝 兵 最 為 殷 盛 。 其 東 界 木 鹿 城 ，
> 號 為 小 安 息 ， 去 洛 陽 二 萬 里 。[30]

Here, the name for the Parthian capital is Hedu<*γwa-dəwk, which, most scholars agree, probably refers to Hekatompylos.[31] There is an interesting challenge here. In the *Hanshu*, the name of the Parthian capital is Fandou. Many scholars have taken this to be Hekatompylos too. But, although their transliterations are similar, we cannot rule out the possibility that they were two different cities. The first capital of the Parthians was Nisa in the province of

Parthia. In about 217 BCE, the Parthian capital was moved to Hekatompylos, which remained as the main capital of the Parthian empire till c. 50 BCE,[32] while Nisa continued to function as an important city. During that period, Rhagae (Rayy), Ecbatana, and Ctesiphon near the river Tigris were also selected as capitals. The name "Hedu" could even be a transliteration of Volog, a trade centre at Vologasia.[33] The Parthians had a multi-capital system, which renders the identification of place names extremely difficult.

In this text, the city of Merv (Mulu) is described as the eastern border of the Parthian empire. As one of the most important Central Asian cities, Merv was under multi-occupation by Greeks, Parthians, Kushans, Sasanians, and Arabs. In the Parthian period, Roman prisoners of war were brought to Merv for construction work.[34] In the *Hou Hanshu*, Merv is called "Lesser Anxi", which may reflect its semi-independent status at that time.

The *Hou Hanshu* records some very important information of the history of Central Asia. For example, it records the emergence of the Kushan empire which took Gandhara and Taxila from the Parthians in the first century CE.[35] In the same chapter, we also read an important description that reflects the geographic and political relationship between the Parthians and the Taiozhi:

> [From Tiaozhi] turn north and then eastwards, another journey on horseback for 60 or so days, then one reaches Parthia. The place was later subjugated by the Tiaozhi who installed a grand general there to watch and supervise all the small cities.

> 轉 北 而 東 ， 復 馬 行 六 十 餘 日 至 安 息; 後 役 屬 條 支 ， 為 置 大 將 ， 監 領 諸 小 城 焉。[36]

This actually contradicts the accounts in the *Shiji* and *Hanshu*, which said that Tiaozhi were to be subjugated by the Parthians (*Anxi yu shu zhi* 安息役 屬之). The account in the *Hou Hanshu* says that Parthia was subsequently subjugated by Tiaozhi (*hou yu shu Tiaozhi* 後役屬條支), and that a governor was installed there to watch over the local population. Yu Taishan thinks that in this case the *Hou Hanshu* text was copied erroneously from the earlier *Shiji* and *Hanshu*; and that the description of the grand general was based purely on the author's imagination rather than on facts.[37] But, the confusion may also arise from later knowledge of the history of Parthia. When Fan Ye compiled the *Hou Hanshu* in the fifth century, the Parthian empire was long gone. During the final stage of the Parthian empire, it had lost the control of the northern part of Mesopotamia. In 164-6 CE, the Romans sacked Seleucia and Ctesiphon, and occupied Dura-Europos. We cannot be sure whether the *Hou Hanshu* text was influenced by the historical fact that the Romans had regained the upper hand in the old territory of Tiaozhi in the second century CE.

The records of the Romans in the *Hou Hanshu* texts present even more problems. In the book, the Roman empire is called Da Qin, but it is also attributed with the old name Likan (or Lixuan), and its location is given in

Haixi or Western Sea. The text gives a very detailed description of the journey from Anxi to Da Qin:

> From Anxi, if you travel 3,400 *li* west, you reach the Kingdom of Aman. Leaving Aman and travelling 3,600 *li*, you reach the Kingdom of Sibin. Leaving Sibin and travelling south you cross a river, then going southwest, you reach the Kingdom of Yuluo after 960 *li*. This is the extreme western frontier of Anxi. Leaving there, and heading south, you embark on the sea and then reach Da Qin. In these territories, there are many precious and marvellous things from Haixi.
>
> 自安息西行三千四百里至阿蠻國。從阿蠻西行三千六百里至斯賓國。從斯賓南行度河，又西南至于羅國九百六十里，安息西界極矣。自此南乘海，乃通大秦。其土多海西珍奇異物焉。[38]

In another passage, a land route from Parthia to the Roman empire is described:

> It is again said, departing from Parthia by the land route, circling around the sea and towards Haixi, you reach Da Qin. The place is densely populated; there is a rest inn every 10 *li*, and a post station every 30 *li*. There is no trouble with bandits and robbers throughout the journey, but on the road are ferocious tigers and lions that are obstacles and bring harm to travellers. Any caravans that do not have over a hundred people and carrying arms could be devoured by the animals.
>
> 又云‘從安息陸道繞海北行出海西至大秦，人庶連屬，十里一亭，三十里一置，終無盜賊寇警。而道多猛虎、師子，遮害行旅，不百餘人，齎兵器，輒為所食’。[39]

Despite these detailed descriptions, it is very difficult to identify all the place names mentioned in the texts. There are a number of different views. The main division is between whether Haixi refers to the Mediterranean Sea or to the Persian Gulf. Hirth first took Da Qin as Syria on the eastern shores of Mediterranean, and argued that Anxi refers to Hecatompylos, Aman to Ecbatana, Sibin to Ctesiphon, and Yuluo to Hatra.[40] This was also the route taken by the Han envoy Gan Ying in his attempt to reach Da Qin. A close reading of the texts that mention Da Qin in the *Hou Hanshu* largely supports this view. Yu Taishan believes that Da Qin actually refers to the Roman empire on the western shores of Mediterranean Sea. The reason that Da Qin is also called Likan is because Egypt was first under the Greek Ptolemaic kingdom, but fell to the Romans in 30 CE. Thus, Chinese authors in the third and fifth century took both names Da Qin and Likan as the same place. The account in the *Weilüe* is even more explicit, and allows us to identify the port city of Angu with Antiochia in Syria.[41]

But this theory is not universally accepted. In fact, as early as 1905, Chavannes first thought that the location of Da Qin, as well as of Tiaozhi, should be sought in the Persian Gulf, or near the mouth of the Euphrates.[42] John Hill has offered a more recent hypothesis:[43] namely that Aman may refer to Herat, Sibin to Susa, Yuluo to Charax Spasinou, and Haixi to the Persian Gulf. This reading fits more readily with the orientations and distances described in the *Hou Hanshu* account, but it cannot solve the problem of how the Da Qin, or Romans, came into contact with China. Judging by the descriptions of Da Qin given in the *Hou Hanshu* and other contemporary or earlier sources, the Chinese of Eastern Han times knew well of the existence of the Roman empire at the other end of the Mediterranean. The *Hou Hanshu* also provides the information relating to the trade of Chinese silks around the Mediterranean:

> The kings of Da Qin always had the desire to send envoys to the Han, but the Parthians wanted to sell them multi-coloured silk made by the Han, and therefore blocked them their way through.

其 王 常 欲 通 使 於 漢 ， 而 安 息 欲 以 漢 繒 綵 與 之 交 市 ， 故 遮 閡 不 得 自 達 。[44]

The question of direct communication between Parthia and China

There is also some textual evidence that relates directly to communication between China and the Parthian empire. When did the first Chinese ever visit Parthia? The *Shiji* ("Dayuan liezhuan") records that during his second trip to Central Asia in 115 BCE, at Wusun, Zhang Qian dispatched his own assistants to a number of kingdoms including Fergana, Samarkand, Sogdiana, Bactria, Parthia, India, and the petty kingdoms in the Tarim Basin. Later, in the same chapter, we read:

> Early on, when the Han envoys visited the kingdom of Anxi, the king of Anxi ordered 20,000 horsemen to meet them on the eastern border of his kingdom. The capital of the kingdom is several thousand *li* from the eastern border. As the envoys travelled to the capital they passed through several dozens of cities inhabited by great numbers of people. When the Han envoys set out again to return to China, the king of Anxi then dispatched his own envoys to come with them to China to see its great breadth and might; they brought with them some ostrich eggs and magicians from Lixuan to the Han court as a gift.

初 ， 漢 使 至 安 息 ， 安 息 王 令 將 二 萬 騎 迎 於 東 界 。 東 界 去 王 都 數 千 里 。 行 比 至 ， 過 數 十 城 ， 人 民 相 屬 甚 多 。 漢 使 還 ， 而 後 發 使 隨 漢 使 來 觀 漢 廣 大 ， 以 大 鳥 卵 及 黎 軒 善 眩 人 獻 于 漢 。[45]

100 THE AGE OF THE PARTHIANS

Many scholars have therefore taken 115 BCE as the date of the first Chinese visit to Parthia, assuming that one of Zhang Qian's assistants may have arrived in Parthia that year. But the text does not mention when the assistant actually arrived there, with the original text stating only "early on" (*chu* 初). Thus, there is no guarantee that 115 BC is the absolute date for the visit described here. The description of the 20,000 horsemen meeting him at the border sounds like an exaggeration.

A close reading of the text suggests that the visit of the Han envoy to Parthia was probably made by a separate envoy at a slighter later date, and not the one sent by Zhang Qian in 115 BCE. In a separate paragraph we read that emperor Wudi sent his ambassadors to "Anxi, Yancai, Lixuan, Tiaozhi and Shendu" which are different locations from Zhang Qian's list. There is no chronological order between these two lists. In the *Hanshu* (*Xiyuzhuan*), it clearly states that it was Wudi who sent the envoys to Anxi. The *Zizhi tongjian*, written by the Song dynasty historian Sima Guang (1019-1086) in the eleventh century, puts the first visit to Anxi by the Han envoy in 105 BC (sixth year of the Yuanfeng reign).[46] The envoy crossed the Pamirs to reach Parthia and came back with a Parthian envoy who brought with him ostrich eggs and magicians. It would seem that Sima Guang's argument is more reasonable.

In the *Hou Hanshu*, we find several accounts of direct exchanges between Parthia and China. For example:

In the first year of the Zhanghe reign [87 CE] of Emperor Zhang, the Parthians dispatched an envoy to offer lions and *fuba*. The *fuba* looks like a unicorn but it does not have a horn. In the ninth year of the Yongyuan reign [97 CE] of Emperor He, the Protector-General Ban Chao dispatched Gan Ying to travel to Da Qin. He reached Tiaozhi next to a large sea. He wanted to cross it, but the sailors of the western border of Anxi said to him: "The ocean is huge. People who make the round trip can do it in three months if the winds are favourable. However, if you encounter winds that delay you, it can take two years. That is why all the sailors prepare food enough for three years. The ocean travel often makes men homesick badly, and a number of them die on the sea." When Gan Ying heard this, he stopped his journey. In the thirteenth year [of the Yongyuan reign, 101 CE], the king of Anxi Manqu again sent in lions, and the big bird from Tiaozhi, which was then named the Anxi bird.

章帝章和元年，遣使獻師子、符拔。符拔形似麟而無角。和帝永元九年，都護班超遣甘英使大秦，抵條支；臨大海欲度，而安息西界船人謂英曰：'海水廣大，往來者逢善風三月乃得度，若遇遲風，亦有二歲者，故入海人皆齎三歲糧．海中善使人思土戀慕，數有死亡者。'英聞之乃止。十三年，安息王滿屈復獻師子及條支大鳥，時謂之安息雀。[47]

PARTHIA IN CHINA 101

Here, we have some very detailed accounts of the exchanges between China and Parthia.[48] First, the gift list is also worth our attention, and includes: *fuba*, which probably refers to Persian gazelle, and the so-called "Anxi bird", or Syrian ostriches, which were also mentioned in the *Shiji* and *Hanshu*. Like lions, these were the animals of the "west" and were particularly favoured by the Chinese emperors, as they represented auspicious omens.

Furthermore, the text names the Parthian king who sent in lions and ostriches as Manqu<*man-khut. We know that the king who ruled Parthia during that period was Pacorus II (c.77–115 CE). But the discrepancy in phonetic reconstruction has led some scholars to propose Manuchihr I of Persis (first half of the second century) as the Parthian king mentioned in the Chinese texts.

Finally, but even more significantly, there is Gan Ying's story. The Chinese envoy Gan Ying's attempt to reach Da Qin from the western frontier of Anxi is probably the first serious attempt by any Chinese to reach the Roman world. But they were stopped by Parthian fishermen. As discussed earlier, many scholars take "the great sea" to be the Persian Gulf, others argue that it could be the Mediterranean. It makes a huge difference in terms of what was over the other side of the sea, if Gan Ying happened to have crossed it.[49]

Concluding Remarks

The Chinese records have been used widely in the study of the history of the Silk Road, as well as the civilization of the Parthians. In a way, it is justified. Together with Greek sources, Chinese records provide the earliest written records about the peoples and civilizations of Central Asia. It is particularly important when we want to understand the complex geographic-political history of the Western Regions and the Parthian empire.

However, there is an absence of eventful historical narrative and no precise chronological information in the Chinese records. The Chinese historical writers were mainly concerned with issues such as climate, local products, trade and the customs or strange behaviour of the local peoples. There was also the practice of copying earlier texts, or mixing information from different periods. As Loewe commented, the information of the alien peoples in the official histories is not for information's sake, but to provide some assistance to the Chinese administration for the purpose of organizing taxation and military services.[50] It is therefore with good reason that we can say that the Chinese records are of limited value for understanding the historical events of Parthia. But, on the other hand, these records provide a starting point for understanding the different historical traditions in the West and in China. To the Chinese historians, history was not only a chain of events, but an environment in which people and objects interacted. In their historical world, foreign countries and alien peoples became meaningful in a special way when the land was measured by its distance to the Chinese capitals, and the peoples came to pay their tributes.

Notes:

1. The commonly accepted date for the Parthian Empire is 247 BCE-CE 227. For a brief history of the Parthians, see Bivar 1983, Koshelenko and Pilipko 1994.
2. For a more recent discussion on the subject, see Kuzmina 1998, and Anthony 1998.
3. For a discussion of the various names given to this region, see Wang 2004: 3.
4. Some early translations appeared in the nineteenth century, but the most important translations that I have consulted are Chavannes 1907, Hirth 1917, Hulsewe 1979, and Hill 2003.
5. The basic unit of measurement *li* in the Han period is approximately 415.8 metres; see Dubs 1955: 160, n. 7. The expression of 10,000 *li* was not literal, but represented a huge number.
6. See Loewe 1979: esp. 11-25 for a textual analysis of the relationship between the *Hanshu* and the *Shiji*.
7. Yu 2005: 16. Whenever the original Chinese texts are quoted hereafter in this paper, I have used this new annotated edition by Yu Taishan.
8. Yu 2005: 17.
9. For phonetic reconstructions hereafter I follow Pulleyblank 1991.
10. See Hulsewe 1979: 113, n. 255.
11. Sun 1995: 385-391, Yu 1992:182-209; and Yu 2005:17, n.79.
12. See Bivar 1983; also Vesta Sarkhosh Curtis's paper in this volume.
13. See Yu 1992: 118-130.
14. For various identifications of the term, see Hulsewe: 117-8, f. 275.
15. Hirth, 1917.
16. See Laufer 1919: 372-373. Yu 2005 follows Laufer's argument. Rice has been found at Susa in the Parthian period, but it is not clear whether it was imported or not. See Simpson 2003.
17. Yu 1995: 203-213.
18. Yu 2005:62-63.
19. Yu 2005: 114-115.
20. Yu 2005: 112.
21. See Hulsewe 1979: 112, n. 250; Hill 2003.
22. Sun 1995: 410-412; Yu 1992:168-181.
23. See Hulsewe 1979: 104, n. 203.
24. Errington and Cribb 1992:49.
25. Yu 2005: 115.
26. Hulsewe 1973: 115, n. 268.
27. Considering the distance from Chang'an to Dayuezhi is 11,600 *li* already, this figure is likely wrong. Yu thinks the number is a mistake, and the real figure should be 16,600 *li*. See Yu 2005: 115-116, n. 289.
28. Koshelenko and Pilipko 1994:142, fig.8.
29. Yu 2005: 39, 136-137.
30. Yu 2005: 272.
31. Hulsewe 1979: 115-116, n. 268.
32. A recent visit to Qumis, between present Semnan and Damqan, has suggested that under the mud-brick ruins might lie the lost city of Hekatompylos. See Wood 1997: 126-127.
33. Hirth once suggested that Hedu was a local name for Hekatompylos, perhaps *Volog; cf. Hulsewe 1979: 115, n. 268.
34. Pliny NH: 46-48

35. See Yu 2005: 283-287.
36. Yu 2005: 271.
37. See Yu 2005: 271, n. 166.
38. Yu 2005: 273.
39. Yu 2005: 279.
40. Hirth 1885.
41. Yu 1992; Yu 2005, pp. 274-281.
42. Chavannes 1905, 1907.
43. Hill 2003.
44. Yu 2005: 278, 342-347.
45. Yu 2005: 37.
46. *Zizi tongjian*, juan 21, p.699.
47. Yu 2005, p.272.
48. Thomas Mallon-McCorgray's communication quoted in Hill 2003.
49. For the contrasting views, see Yu 1995: 214-220, and Hill 2003, esp. Appendix D.
50. Loewe 1979: 5-11.

6

The *Videvdad*: its Ritual-Mythical Significance

P.O. Skjærvø (Harvard University)

The *Videvdad*, or *Vendidad*, is part of the *Avesta*, the holy book of the Zoroastrians.[1] It contains instructions for purification and healing of pollution, how to atone for breaking the purity regulations and other laws, and which penalties to exact. As such, the *Videvdad* is a long text, typical of ancient texts of this kind, whose purpose is to cover all possible real and imagined situations. The text is mostly in the common, but flexible, octo-syllabic Young Avestan metre, since, in an oral tradition, metrical texts are easier to remember than non-metrical texts. Typically, the text contains (metrical and non-metrical) lists of various kinds, sometimes with only one word distinguishing the items, which often rhyme.

The authors of the *Videvdad* have interspersed their technical material, however, with examples from both mythology and what appear to be real life situations, which makes it a treasure trove of archaic lore. It is, for instance, in the *Videvdad* (7.44) that we find the description of three types of surgery (knife, plants, sacred words) that has been shown to be part of Indo-European poetic heritage.[2]

The text is divided into 22 chapters (*karde*s), the first two and last four of which, in particular, recount myths about the origins of pollution and about the first healers. Within this mythical framework, concrete instructions for how to deal with pollution etc., are detailed.

The *Videvdad* is not, however, simply what we might term a "reference book", which the priests could "consult"[3] about matters of pollution and purification, guilt and atonement; it is also an important ritual text and sacred because it is the word of God, Ahura Mazdā, transmitted to Zarathustra, and so imbued with strong powers of healing. It was therefore recited in important purification and healing rituals.[4]

The *Videvdad* has never been seriously studied in its entirety, and modern editions and translations are deficient. Non-specialists still have to turn to Darmesteter's French translation of 1892-93; English translation in 1895) with

106 THE AGE OF THE PARTHIANS

its indispensable introduction and commentary, and Fritz Wolff's 1910 German translation based on Christian Bartholomae's 1904 Avestan dictionary.

The Name

The Young Avestan phrase *dāta- vīdaēuua- dāta- zaraθuštri-* "the law to discard the *daēuua*s, the law of Zarathustra" is commonly thought to refer to the *Videvdad*. The Avestan *daēuua*s correspond to the Old Indic *deva*s, who are beneficent gods, while the Avestan ones are evil, having made the wrong choice in the beginning, allying themselves with the powers of darkness and evil, rather than with Ahura Mazdā.[5] The Avestan word can therefore be rendered as "old god" or "evil god", whereas in the much later Sasanian Zoroastrian literature the Middle Persian word *dēw* probably comes close to what is commonly called a "demon".

It was long assumed that the Avestan term *dāta- vīdaēuua-* meant "the law (for how to fight) *against* the *daēuua*s", and many still use this translation. It was pointed out, however, by Emile Benveniste that the prefix *vī-* does not have the meaning "against", but expresses movement to the sides. Hence the meaning must be "the law discarding the *daēuua*s", which probably implies "the law providing rules for how to keep the *daēuua*s away", that is, for chasing the *daēuua*s, rather than acting *against* them.[6] This is in fact what Zarathustra is said to have done.[7]

The Avestan term was regularly rendered in the Zoroastrian Pahlavi texts as *wīdēw-dād*, spelled variously as ꡯ <wyk-dyw-d't'> or ꡯ <wyk-ŠDYA-d't'> *wī-dēw-dād* and similar. The common name of the text in Pahlavi, however, is *jud-dēw-dād*, "the law (for) keeping the *dēw*s separate", with *ĵud* "separate" rendering *wi-*. The form *vendīdād* is common in western literature and is usually thought to result from a misreading of the Pahlavi graph for *wīdēw-dād*. If we write the two forms in Pahlavi, however, we see that this is not obvious, as we would expect ꡯ <wy-dyw-d't'> or ꡯ <w-dyw-d't'>, but ꡯ or ꡯ <wn-dy-d't'>. Even if we assume an earlier form ꡯ <wn-dyw-d't'>, the <-n-> remains unaccounted for.

I therefore propose that **windē(w)dād* is a secondary, perhaps learned, form, whose prenasalised *-nd-* served the purpose of strengthening, as it were, the *-d-* so that it did not become *-y-*, which was the regular development of intervocalic older **-d-* in Pahlavi. This also happened in the case of Parthian *windār-*, Middle Persian *winnār-* (with *-nn-* < *-nd-*) "set up, arrange", which corresponds to Avestan *viδāraiia-* "hold (up and) out",[8] and *wimand* "border", is the same as Avestan *vimaiδiia-*. Manichean Middle Persian *humbōy-* (Parthian *xumbōy-*) "fragrant" (Avestan *hu-baoiδi-*) similarly avoided the regular development of this old word to **huwōy*.

Pollution and Purification

In the worldview of the ancient Zoroastrians, as reflected in the *Avesta*, pollution results first and foremost from contamination by dead matter (Avestan *nasu*; Pahlavi *nasā*).[9] This includes dead bodies of humans and animals, but also matter that has been secreted or removed from the human body. In this latter category we find blood, above all blood from menstruating women, but also hair clippings and nail parings, which need to be disposed of carefully so that they do not spawn evil things (*Videvdad*, chap. 17).

The rules connected with dead bodies and blood concern not only the spread and extent of pollution, but also the degree of *sin* one incurs (*āstriiete*) by various degrees of contact with these substances, and provide practical ways to cleanse what has become polluted and make it ritually clean (*yaož-dā-*), be it people or objects, such as the fire or ritual utensils.

The rules themselves have been little studied, although comparison with other ancient texts of this kind might lead to interesting discoveries. For instance, dead bodies and menstrual impurity were also the two main sources of impurity according to Jewish purity laws, and among topics that invite comparison are the following (all in chap. 5):

1. If a person uses firewood taken from a tree on which a bird has urinated, defecated, or vomited, is he then guilty? The *Videvdad*'s answer is that he is not, because if such were the case, then all of humanity would already be polluted beyond redemption.
2. Another example: If several persons and dogs lie down together on a bed that has been polluted by a corpse, how far does the pollution reach?
3. And a third: If a man has intercourse with a menstruating woman, what are the rules for the degree of pollution and sinfulness, how can he be cleansed, and how can he atone for the crime?

These situations have parallels in the Jewish world, and the answers to the questions sometimes agree, but at other times differ.[10]

About the textual nature and date of the Avestan corpus

The probable reasons why scholars of Zoroastrianism and of the history of religions in general have not taken more interest in these texts are, on the one hand, the lack of modern editions and translations, and on the other hand, certain attitudes to the texts, among them two in particular:

One is the assumption that the *Videvdad* is a "late text", and so not directly usable as a source for the study of the Zoroastrian "orthodoxy", that is, the assumed religious reform and teachings of Zarathustra, who, according to

108

THE AGE OF THE PARTHIANS

several 19th-20th-century Western scholars, decried such routine and mindless ritual occupations.[11]

Such attitudes were a reaction against the late 18th-century intellectuals' critical and even disparaging reaction to Anquetil Duperron's translations of the *Avesta* in attempts to dissociate the prophet and law-giver Zarathustra and his exalted teachings from what was perceived as the primitive and mindless ritualism of the *Videvdad*.[12]

The other is the notion that texts *without literary merit*, that is, by modern western standards, are not interesting, as they provide the reader with no aesthetical enjoyment.

Both of these views discount the importance of purity rules in the Zoroastrian society, as well as the role of sacred texts and the nature of the *Avesta*.

Chronology of the Avestan texts (Table 2)

The *Avesta* is a collection of texts transmitted orally for centuries and even millennia before they were written down, perhaps, in late Sasanian times, under the Sasanian king Khosrow I (531-579 CE), but perhaps even later.[13] According to the ninth-century Pahlavi *Dēnkard*, at that time, the *Avesta* was divided into 21 books, one of which was the *Videvdad*. Not all of the *Avesta* as described in the *Dēnkard* survives, however. What we have left today is what is contained in the extant manuscripts, the oldest of which go back only to the thirteenth and fourteenth centuries, although most of them are from the sixteenth to nineteenth centuries.

It can also be shown that the parent manuscripts, from which all our manuscripts are descended, existed about 1000 CE. That is, we have no direct evidence for the text from the 400 years before the presumed first manuscript and the ancestor of our manuscripts. Moreover, since the text was transmitted only orally before the first manuscript, there is no direct evidence for the Avestan text at all before *c.* 1000 CE.

Thus, it is obvious that the manuscript text we have cannot be exactly what was "composed" originally in the language that we call (Young) Avestan. Indeed, in an oral tradition, even the notion of "composition" of a text such as the *Avesta* is a vague term and implies the gathering of existing oral traditions into a corpus whose language and contents developed as the corpus was transmitted from generation to generation and as the people who used it moved from place to place.[14]

Originally, this orally transmitted corpus must have been continuously updated linguistically as the spoken language developed. At one point, however, it must have been decided that the text was no longer to be changed, but should be preserved in the linguistic form it had at that time. Arguments for this decision may have been the common one that Avestan was the language in which God had revealed the text or that it was the venerable language of the

The *Videvdad*: Its Ritual-Mythical Significance   109

ancestors. The motivation for the decision may have been, for instance, that the texts were moving out of their homeland and into areas where other languages were spoken.

What we are left with is what in oral literary theory is called a "crystallised" text, that is, an *unchangeable* text, which after a few generations no longer corresponded to the spoken language and was gradually not well understood.[15] It is this "crystallised" version of the text corpus that was then transmitted by the clergy in various places until it was finally written down. The time gap between this final form of the text and the first manuscript is probably at least a thousand years.

Whether there was a canonical text in the sense that certain texts should be included but others excluded we cannot know, since we have no statements to this effect. I am also not certain that we can speak, as Kellens does, about a canonization in the sense of "inclusion of a text in a collection invested with a particular function or dignity", as this must have been what prompted the crystalisation in the first place.[16] We can, however, apply the term "canon" to the corpus of texts selected for writing down.

Since the language was not well understood, translations and commentaries in the spoken languages must have existed at the various times and in the various places where the corpus was used. This auxiliary tradition was eventually gathered in the Pahlavi translations of the Avestan texts.[17]

Place of origin of the *Avesta* and of the *Videvdad*

There are two forms of Avestan, an older and a younger. The corpus therefore falls into two parts, the *Old Avesta* and the *Young(er) Avesta*. The small *Old Avesta* consists of "the five *Gāθā*s (songs) of Zarathustra" and the *Yasna haptaŋhāiti* "the sacrifice in seven sections",[18] while the *Young Avesta* contains the other Avestan texts, among them the *Videvdad* and other texts I shall be referring to in a moment.

We do not know where or when the *Avesta* was actually *composed*, where or when the text was *crystallised* and, later, written down. There are no historical references in the *Avesta*, either to contemporary history or to its own textual history. According to the *Videvdad*, the text was spoken by God to Zarathustra in answer to his questions.[19]

There are, however, several lists of geographical names in the *Avesta*, notably in the *Videvdad*, and these lists contain names of areas in the northeastern Iranian provinces, as we know them from the Achaemenid inscriptions of Darius and Xerxes. The list in the *Videvdad* is as follows:[20]

1. *Airiianam vaējah* "the Aryan *territory"
2. *Gāum yim suɣδō.šaiianəm* "Gawa inhabited by Sogdians" (Old Persian *suguda*)
3. *Mourum sūrəm* "life-giving Margu" (Old Persian *margu*)

110 THE AGE OF THE PARTHIANS

4. *Bāxδīm srīrąm ərəδβō.drafšąm* "Bāxδī (Bactria) the beautiful with uplifted banners" (Old Persian *bāxδī*)
5. *Nisāim yim antarə Mourumca Bāxδīmca* "Nisāya, which is between Margu and Bactria" (Old Persian *nisāya?*)
6. *Harōiiūm yim viš.harəzanəm* "Haraēuua (Herat), the .?." (Old Persian *haraiva*)
7. *Vaēkərətəm yim dužakō.šaiianəm* "Vaikrta, inhabited by hedgehogs(?)"
8. *Uruuąm pouru.vāstrąm* "Urvā, with plentiful pasture"
9. *Xnəntəm yim vəhrkānō.šaiianəm* "Xnanta, inhabited by Hyrcanians" (Old Persian *vąrkāna*)
10. *Harax'aitīm srīrąm* "Arachosia the beautiful" (Old Persian *harauvatī*)
11. *Haētumantəm raēuuantəm x'arənaŋ'hantəm* "Helmand, rich and glorious"
12. *Rayąm θrizaṇtūm* "Raghā of the three tribes" (Old Persian *ragā?*)
13. *Caxrəm sūrəm ašauuanəm* "Caxra the life-giving sustainer of order"
14. *Varənəm yim caθru.gaošəm* "Varna the four-cornered"
15. *yōi hapta həṇdu* "the Seven Rivers" (Old Persian *hindu*)
16. *upa aoδaēšu Raŋhaiiå* "by the *falls of the Raŋhā river"

We see that the list of names in the *Videvdad* begins with the Aryan territory, passes through Sogdiana and Bactria and continues south and southwest to include the Hyrcanians, who gave their name to modern Gurgān southeast of the Caspian Sea, and the Helmand river in southern Afghanistan in the ancient province of Arachosia, modern Qandahar.

Whether the name of Rayā in the *Videvdad* list refers to the famous Ragā, modern Ray south of Tehran, is still being debated, although it is possible. The same holds for Nisāya and Old Persian Nisāya, the location of which is uncertain.

Much effort has been spent on trying to identify the first name, *Airiiana vaējah*, with a known location, sometimes based on the geographical arrangement of the list. In the *Avesta*, however, *Airiiana vaējah* only denotes the mythical locus for all activity that took place from the creation of the world of the living to the coming of Zarathustra, including the birth and activity of Zarathustra himself.[21] Thus, although it is quite likely that the different generations of the "Avestan people" recognised a specific location by this name, it is unlikely to have been more specific originally than, say, Eden.

One possibile interpretation would be to see an allusion to the Aryan space as defined by a *spear-throw* (cf. the proper name *vaēžiiaršti-* "he who throws his spear" in *Yašt* 13.101, 15.48), analogous to the *arrow-shot* of Ǝrəxša, by which the Iranians won back as much territory from the Turanians as the arrow went (see *Yašt* 8.6).[22] Darius, too, measures, as it were, the extent of the lands he commands by how far the Persian man's spear has gone (Darius at Naqš-e Rostam, inscription a [DNa], lines 38-47).

The last two names, the Seven Rivers and the river Raŋhā (Pahlavi Arang) are also likely to be mythical. Thus, in the *Avesta*, the river Raŋhā is the home of the mythical Kara fish:

THE *VIDEVDAD*: ITS RITUAL-MYTHICAL SIGNIFICANCE 111

Yašt 14.29 (cf. *Yašt* 16.7)
ahmāi daθaṯ vərəθraγnō ahuraδātō ərəzōiš xå bāzuuå aojō ...
aomca sūkəm yim baraiti karō masiiō upāpō
yō raŋhaiiå dūraēpāraiiå jafraiiå hazaŋrō.vīraiiå
varəsō.stauuaŋhəm āpō uruuaēsəm māraiieite

Və ꞧ θraγna, set in place by Ahura (Mazdā), gave him the springs of (his)
virility, the strength of (his) arms ...
and that sight that he carries, the Kara fish in the sea,
who, of the water of the Raŋhā with distant shores, deep as (the height of) a
thousand men,
*notices a turn (of the tide?) (even only) as thick as a hair.

According to the *Bundahišn*, the river Arang is in the continent of Sauuah (*Bdh.*
13.34): *nazdist kar māhīg ī araz pad āb ī arang frōd ō sawah šud* "First the Kar
(Araz) fish went down to Sawah by the water of the Arang (river)".

The river Raŋhā is also where the goddess of the heavenly waters, Anāhitā,
received sacrifices from Pāuruua the sailor (*Yašt* 5.61) and from Yōišta of the
Friiānas (*Yašt* 5.81).

The Seven Rivers may have denoted the seven world-rivers, as suggested by
an Avestan fragment in the Pahlavi commentary on *Videvdad* 1.19: *az abestāg
paydāg: haca ušastara hiṇduua auui daošatarəm hiṇdūm* "it is said in the
Avesta: "from the dawn-side river to the evening-side river", as well as a
passage in the hymn to Mithra, where the two *hiṇdu*s "rivers" and the Raŋhā
denote the farthest points of the earth:

Yašt 10.104
miθrəm vouru.gaoiiaoitīm ...
*yeṅhe darəγāciṯ bāzauua fragrəβəṇti *miθrō.aojaŋha*
yaṯciṯ ušastaire hiṇduuō āgəuruuaiieite yaṯciṯ daošataire niγne
yaṯciṯ †sanake raŋhaiiå yaṯciṯ vīmaiδīm aṅhå zəmō

We sacrifice to Mithra...
whose arms, long indeed, reach forth with the strength of Mithra to grab
(the enemy),
both when he is grabbed by the dawn-side river and when by the evening-
side (river)
or when (he is struck down) where the Raŋhā rises,
or when *about the middle of this earth.

We can compare this with the description of Rašnu's movement above the
earth as described in the hymn to him:

112   THE AGE OF THE PARTHIANS

Yašt 12.15-22
yaṯciṯ ahi rašnuuō ašāum <upa> imaṯ karšuuarə yaṯ xᵛaniraθəm *bāmīm ...
yaṯciṯ ... upa zraiiō vouru.kašəm upa auuąm vanąm yąm saēnahe ...
yā hištaite maiδīm zraiiaŋhō vouru.kašahe ....
yaṯciṯ ... upa aoδaēšu raŋhaiiå upa sanake raŋhaiiå ...
yaṯciṯ ... upa karanəm aŋhå zəmō upa vīmaiδiīm aŋhå zəmō upa kuuaciṯ aŋhå zəmō

O Orderly Rašnu, whenever you are over this continent (of) bright Xᵛaniraθa ...
over the Vourukaša Sea, over that tree of the Falcon,
which stands in the middle of the Vourukaša Sea,
over the *falls of the (river) Raŋhā, over the *source of the (river) Raŋhā,
over the border of this earth, over the middle of this earth,
over wherever of this earth,

Compare this with the description of the fashioning of the "good Wind" (*frārōn wād*) in the *Bundahišn* (*Bdh.* 21.1): *pad bunxān ī arang-rōd ī widarg pad ulīh paydāg būd* "it appeared at the source of the river Arang, which is the passageway to up above".

The Arang river is also the location of "the lofty deity" (*burz-yazd*) in the description of the bird Čamrōš (*Bdh.* 24.24): *ēg burz-yazd az ān ī zofr war ī arang abar āyēd* "then Burz-yazd comes up from the deep bay of Arang", which is related to the description found in *Videvdad* 19.42: *nizbaiiemi karō masiiō upāpō būne jafranąm vairiianąm* "I call down the Kara fish living in the waters at the bottom of the deep bays".

It is quite likely, therefore, that the list in *Videvdad* 1 is intended to cover the entire known world, including its mythical limits.

Scholarly opinions about the date of the *Videvdad*

The question of the *date* of the *Avesta* is even more problematic than its location. Suffice it to say here that, in my opinion, the oral "text" of the *Young Avesta* may have been shaped during the first half of the first millennium BCE, that is, before the advent of the Achaemenids, and the version that survives in the manuscripts may well date from about the beginning of the Achaemenids.

This dating is at odds with what is stated in some handbooks, namely that the *Videvdad* is a "late" composition, even post-Achaemenid, that is, Seleucid or Parthian. It is also commonly assumed that, at the time of its composition, Avestan was no longer a spoken language and that the *Videvdad* was actually composed in what was by then a dead language. This would explain, it is thought, the poor grammatical condition of the language of the text.

The late dating of the *Videvdad* goes back to a time in Avestan scholarship when the entire Avesta was dated after 600 BCE. K. F. Geldner, for instance, in *Grundriss*, gave 556 BCE - 379 CE (death of Shapur II) as the earliest and latest

THE *VIDEVDAD*: ITS RITUAL-MYTHICAL SIGNIFICANCE 113

dates, and Antoine Meillet argued for a date of the *Gāθās* close to the traditional date of Zarathustra, that is, in the sixth century BCE.[23]

Throughout the early 20th century, it was also common to ascribe the composition of the *Videvdad* to the Median *magoi*.[24] This thesis was in particular developed by the Wesleyan minister James Hope Moulton, a classicist with an interest in Zoroastrianism and a Christian missionary to the Parsis (1915-16). Moulton was among those convinced that the Zarathustra of the *Young Avesta* and the classical sources, as well as of later Zoroastrianism as practised by the Parsis, was a "mythical", that is, imaginary construct, as far removed from truth as "the ravings of a dangerous lunatic named Nietzsche, who impudently fathered on "Zarathustra" doctrines which have been the undoing of the country from which they came".[25] Moulton dated Zarathustra to about 400 to 500 years before the traditional date of 660-583 BCE (that is, the late second millennium) on the basis of the linguistic archaism of Gathic Avestan[26] and introduced into the discussion of the historical source value of the *Gāθās* P. W. Schmiedel's now out-dated concept of "pillar passages" applied to the New Testament. Such an early date would imply "a gulf of at least five centuries between Zarathushtra and our earliest Greek allusions to him",[27] that is, the same as between the exalted ethical teaching of Zarathustra and the teachings of the *magoi* described by Herodotus. By ascribing the composition of the *Videvdad* to the Median *magoi*, Herodotus', Strabo's, and other classical authors' description of the Median *magoi* as killing animals, exposing dead bodies, and practicing incestuous marriage could be completely severed from Zarathustra's teachings,[28] and Moulton could state categorically that "the ritual portion [of the Avesta], covering nearly all the Vendidad and cognate texts ... cannot possibly be interpreted from sources that give Aryan or Iranian religion"[29] and that "neither science nor religion consents to trace a Prophet's hand in the Vendidad".[30] Moulton's insistence that the ritual described in the *Young Avesta* and the *Videvdad* had nothing to do with Zarathustra's teachings is reflected in modern authors's assessment of the *Gāθās*, as well, as pointed out above.[31]

Moulton's type of arguments survived through the following decades and are reflected, for instance, in Arthur Christensen's essay on Iranian demonology, where he hypothesised that the Medes adopted Zoroastrianism at some indeterminate date and begun using the Avestan language for their own purposes; this resulted in the composition of the *Videvdad*.[32] Similarly, H. S. Nyberg, in his history of Iranian religions, postulated that, "at some point in time, the Zoroastrian mission reached the old Median *magi* in Raga and won them over, and they then shaped Zoroastrianism after their own minds", including composing the *Videvdad* with its ritual prescriptions.[33]

The late date of the *Videvdad* is also found in Arthur Christensen's 1936 book on the Sasanians, according to whom it was composed at the beginning of the Parthian period in Avestan, which by that time was a dead language, and one which they used with difficulty.[34]

Few additional arguments have been offered for this late date, however, and none of them is cogent. One argument was put forth by Walter B. Henning, who, in an article published in 1943,[35] suggested that the units of measure used in the *Videvdad* were the Greco-Roman ones and that the text must therefore be no earlier than Alexander:

> As regards the measures for short distances, the Avestic system, or rather that of the Vendidad and the Nirangistan, so closely resembles the common Greco-Roman system, as a whole and in all details, that its foreign origin can be taken for granted. It was presumably introduced into Persian by the Macedonian conquerors.

The measure system in question is the one based on the measure of body parts, from "finger-breadth" to "fathom",[36] but this is a very common one in antiquity (Egypt, Mesopotamia). The common Greco-Iranian system might even have been inherited from the proto-language. The only non-body measure listed by Henning is that of a "reed", Greek *kálamos*, but that is not yet in Avestan, only Pahlavi.

We should also keep in mind here that this date for the *Videvdad* made sense to Henning, who was convinced Zarathustra had lived in the sixth century BCE.[37]

Thus, although Henning's argument is clearly inconclusive, the premises for these Parthian or post-Alexandrian dates have never, to my knowledge, been re-examined. Instead, as in the case of so many opinions about the *Avesta*, the late date of the *Videvdad* is by now part of the often-cited "common opinion". Thus, Mary Boyce, in volume I of her monumental *History of Zoroastrianism*,[38] published in the prestigious series *Handbuch der Orientalistik*, simply states that "The redaction in which the *Vendidād* survives is late (assigned usually to the Parthian period)", and, in volume III,[39] she repeats Henning's argument, describing the *Videvdad* as follows:

> a composite work which contains matter from various periods; but there is a trace in it of apparent Hellenistic influence in the appearance there, beside traditional Iranian terms for measures of distance, of others for short lengths of measurement which correspond closely to the Greek system.

She then suggests the Seleucid, rather than the Parthian, period:[40]

> It is usual to assign the Vd. purity texts to the Parthian rather than the Seleucid period, which is generally passed over in silence in histories of Zoroastrianism; but purity laws are much more likely to have been a matter for preoccupation in a time of foreign dominance than when Zoroastrians were ruling Iran, cf. their importance in the Persian Rivayats, composed under Islamic government.

THE *VIDEVDAD*: ITS RITUAL-MYTHICAL SIGNIFICANCE

The unsupported suggestion that purity laws preoccupy people under foreign rule, however, leaves completely out of consideration the Zoroastrian world view, which we shall have a look at in a moment. Her idea may be that foreigners are more likely to transgress than locals, but the *Videvdad* does not particularly address non-Mazdayasnians or non-Iranians.[41]

We should also note her use of the term "usual" in this statement, which in Iranian studies in general is the kind of term commonly employed to denote something that was said a long time ago and has not been questioned since, nor been re-examined with regard to its accuracy.

Arguments based on the language and literary quality of the text include one in Ilya Gershevitch's contribution to the chapter on "Old Iranian literature" also in *Handbuch der Orientalistik*:

> Unfortunately the enjoyment in reading [the Videvdad] is marred by two serious flaws: one is the disturbing negligence in respect of what according to older Avestan standards are correct inflectional endings; the other consists in the deadly pedantry which obsesses the authors and leads them to dreary repetitions and hair-splitting classifications.[42]

R. C. Zaehner expressed a similar view:

> It is, then, fair to conclude that it was the Magi who were responsible for the drawing up of the *Vidēvdāt*, the "law against the *daēvas*"; and this would go a long way to account for the appalling grammatical confusion that characterises that not very admirable work.[43]

Again, from the point of view of the Zoroastrian worldview, it is difficult to understand how specialists in Zoroastrianism would brush off the purity regulations as mere pedantry. In fact, it is the *lack* of pedantry in these matters that would be "deadly" to the believers.

The notion of grammatical "standards" is that of written languages and cannot be applied directly to unwritten languages.

Textual history of the *Videvdad* (Table 1)

To understand the nature of the *language* of the *Videvdad,* as we have it, we have to keep in mind the history of the text. We have already seen the tribulations the text must have gone through to get to the stage when it was written down. Let us therefore now take a closer look at the manuscript tradition of the *Videvdad* (Table 1).

This tradition rests on two groups of manuscripts. The manuscripts of the first group contain the text with its Pahlavi (Middle Persian) translation (the Pahlavi Videvdad manuscripts), and among them are the oldest *Videvdad* manuscripts, dating from the fourteenth century.

116   THE AGE OF THE PARTHIANS

The other manuscripts have the text without such a translation and are therefore called *sade*, which means "simple" or "plain". These are much later, the oldest being from the seventeenth century.

Of the fourteenth-century manuscripts, two (K1, L4) are badly damaged and incomplete, although they were copied while they were still intact. Recently, several manuscripts from the Meherji Rana collection in Nawsari have been made known, among them E10, which is a copy of L4.[44] These two are not particularly reliable, however, as we can see from the fact that they differ considerably although ostensibly copied from the same manuscript. The Avestan text of the third (IM) has not yet been collated, and the whereabouts of this manuscript are not known.

The second manuscript group contains two kinds of manuscripts: those written in Iran and those written in India. The three known Persian Videvdad Sade manuscripts go back to an original that dates from about 1500 CE and are overall quite reliable, while the numerous Indian Videvdad Sade manuscripts, dating from the seventeenth to the nineteenth centuries, cannot be stemmatised and are best characterised as *popular* manuscripts.

We have to keep in mind that the *Videvdad* is the book the priests had to refer to for the purity laws. It was therefore much "consulted" and much cited, and the people who cited it and transmitted it over the centuries were not necessarily precise about the text they recited. It also needed frequent *copying*, and it was quite natural that errors would creep in.

The manuscript situation for the *Videvdad* is, therefore, far inferior to that of the *Yasna*. But the fact that the text of the *Videvdad* is, for the most part, as correct as other Young Avestan texts cautions us not to draw conclusions about the history of the text from grammatical errors in it; and we really ought to be amazed that the text is as well preserved as it is.

There is also no reason to believe that the extant text represents the "original text", not even of the first manuscript, let alone of the text that was *crystallised* some time in the first half of the first millennium BCE or what was *composed* even before that.

What is the *Videvdad*?

The *Videvdad* is an Avestan text recited during purification and healing rituals. The text is structured by the myths that underlie it and which go from Ahura Mazdā's creation and ordering of our world, via a relapse into semi-chaos caused by the imperfections introduced by Aŋra Mainiiu, to the final healing of the world. The state of semi-chaos is called the Mixture in the Pahlavi texts and is the time in which we still live.

To understand this situation, we need to look at the Old Iranian cosmological myth in some detail. See Table 3.

According to this myth, in the beginning there were two cosmic principles, Good and Evil, representing light, health, and life, and darkness, illness, and death, respectively. The good God One (Avestan Ahura Mazdā, Pahlavi

THE *VIDEVDAD*: ITS RITUAL-MYTHICAL SIGNIFICANCE

Ohrmazd) began making the world after his evil counterpart had noticed the other's beautiful space and decided to attack, invade, and pollute it. To prevent the Evil One (Avestan Aŋra Maniiu, Pahlavi Ahriman) from achieving his purpose, Ahura Mazdā established the ordered cosmos and all living beings in it as an army to fight evil after the attack.

According to the narrative in the Pahlavi *Bundahišn*, after having overcome Aŋra Mainiiu by reciting his Holy Word (the *Ahuna vairiia* prayer), the first thing Ohrmazd did was to cut out a piece of measured time from eternal time and thus limit the upcoming battle between good and evil to a specific time period.[45]

He then offered a pact with Ahriman, according to which the final showdown between them would come in 9000 years. Of these 9000 years, 3000 years would go according to the will of Ohrmazd; 3000 years would go according to the will of both Ohrmazd and Ahriman; and the last 3000 years would witness the gradual return of Ohrmazd's supremacy.

As his army in the forthcoming battle, Ohrmazd then made numerous divine beings; some he engendered from himself, others he apparently fashioned or brought forth in an unspecified manner. He also made all the common time divisions, years, seasons, months, days, and parts of days to structure the limited time he had just made.

This new world of divine beings is referred to as the "world of thought" in the Avestan texts, which means it cannot be perceived by ordinary human senses, only by thought, and all the divine beings in it were assigned specific functions in the battle between good and evil that was soon to begin.

Ahura Mazdā then made a world containing living beings. This world he first nurtured inside himself as a foetus, until it in due course was born from him as the world of living beings.

All this, we are told, he achieved in a *yasna* ritual, that is, in a divine sacrifice.

Meanwhile, the Evil One produced his own world of thought and filled it with evil beings, and, when Ahura Mazdā brought forth the world of the living from his womb, the Evil One was ready and attacked. He killed the first two living beings, the Lone Cow/Bull (Avestan feminine *gao- aēuuō.dātā-* "the cow established as the [only] one" [*Yašt* 7.0, etc.]; Pahlavi *gāw ī ēw-dād* [*Bundahišn* 1A.12, etc.], masculine because he releases his semen at death) and the first humanoid being, Avestan Gaiia Marətān, Pahlavi Gayōmard, and he then polluted the new world with evil things and afflicted it with darkness, illness, and death.

To re-establish the primordial ordered cosmos in the two worlds, that of thought and that of living beings, somebody had to re-perform — in the world of living beings — Ahura Mazdā's primordial sacrifice in the world of thought. The deliberations of Ahura Mazdā and the other divine beings about whom to appoint to this job are described in an Old Avestan text known as *Yasna* 29.[46]

According to this text, the person chosen was Zarathustra. The Pahlavi texts contain a more detailed account of how Zarathustra's constituents in the world

118   THE AGE OF THE PARTHIANS

of thought were sent down to the world of the living, where they were combined with the elements of the *haoma* ritual, which is part of the *yasna* ritual, and Zarathustra was then conceived and born after his parents drank the *haoma*.

In due course, Zarathustra performed the sacrifice in the world of the living (*Yašt* 13.88-91), which became the proto-typical sacrifice that is still being repeated today as the *yasna* ritual, in which the *Yasna* text is recited, and he was also the first to utter the *dāta- vīdaēuua- dāta-* "the law to discard the *daēuua*s" (*Yašt* 13.90).

The *Yasna*

To understand the special function of the *Videvdad*, we first need to take a look at the function of the *Yasna*.[47]

The *yasna* ritual is a ritual whose function is to reproduce the new day after a period of darkness. Both when it is performed as a part of the *videvdad sade* ritual and when by itself, it is to be timed so that the recital of *Yasna* 62, the hymn to the fire, coincides with sunrise.[48] In the Old Iranian cosmological scheme, its function is to help place Ahura Mazdā back in command of the universe, as expressed, for instance, in *Yasna* 8:

Yasna 8.5-6
vasasca tū ahura mazda uštāca xšaēša hauuanąm dāmanąm
vasō āpō vasō uruuarå vasō vīspa vohū ašaciθra
xšaiiamnəm ašauuanəm dāiiata axšaiiamnəm druuaṇtəm
vasō.xšaθrō hiiāṯ ašauua auuasō.xšaθrō hiiāṯ druuå
gatō hamistō nižbərətō haca spəṇtahe mainiiə̄uš dāmabiiō
varətō auuasō.xšaθrō

May you, O Ahura Mazdā, command at will and wish your own creations! Place at will, O waters, at will, O plants, at will, O all good (things) whose seed is from Order,[49]
the sustainer of Order in command, the one possessed by the Lie one out of command!
May the sustainer of Order have command at will! May one possessed by the Lie not have command at will!
(May he be) gone, discomfited, removed from the Creations of the Life-giving Spirit, restrained, with no command at will.

As is usual with morning and New Year rituals, this process involves the ritual recreation of a microcosmic version of the macrocosm. This recreation process is in turn patterned on the myth of the primordial creation of the world.[50]

The *Yasna* text therefore takes us through this recreation process. It begins with the reconstruction and re-ordering of all the elements in the worlds of

THE *VIDEVDAD*: ITS RITUAL-MYTHICAL SIGNIFICANCE

119

thought and of living beings. The first elements are, as in the beginning, the elements of limited time — from the parts of the day to the seasons and years.

In the *Yasna*, this *re*-ordering process is followed by the story of Zarathustra's birth from the *haoma* ritual and various other texts containing important elements of the primordial sacrifice. It culminates in the preparation and offering of the *haoma* drink, at which point, presumably, Zarathustra is reborn in the persona of the sacrificer and proceeds to recite his *Gāθās*, as perhaps implied in

Yasna 8.7
haxšaiia azəm.ciṯ yō zaraθuštrō fratəmą
nmānanąmca vīsąmca zaṇtunąmca daxʹiiunąmca
aṅhå daēnaiiå anumataiiaēca anuxtaiiaēca anuuarštaiiaēca
yā āhūiriš zaraθuštriš

May I, too, who (am another) Zarathustra, *lead the foremost (people)
of the homes, houses, tribes, and lands
to help this *daēnā* along by (my) thought, speech, and action,[51]
which is that of Ahura Mazdā and Zarathustra.

The *Gāθās* are the holy texts that Zarathustra received from Ahura Mazdā, who had recited them in the beginning in order to cast down the Evil One and which Zarathustra in turn recites with the same effect. The recitation of the holy texts comes to an end with the prayer to Airiiaman, the god of peace and healing (*Yasna* 54.1, see below).

The *Yasna* then continues with a hymn to the great martial deity, Sraoša, who battles and overcomes the powers of darkness. There follow hymns to the fire and the heavenly waters, signifying the rebirth of the sun and the new day.

The *yasna* ritual is therefore a re-ordering ritual, which, when successful, will help Ahura Mazdā re-engender the ordered cosmos, characterised by sunlight, life, and fertility. It complements Ahura Mazdā's efforts in the world of thought, where he fights the evil powers together with his divine helpers.

Of these divine helpers, one of the most important is Sraoša, who, with his fearless club, is the opponent assigned to Wrath with the bloody club. Wrath, in fact, is probably the mythical embodiment of the night sky and the principal representative of the powers of darkness. At sunset, Wrath smites Ahura Mazdā's creation and bathes it in blood, but he is in turn himself struck down and bled by Sraoša.

The other crucial helper is Airiiaman, god of peace and healing.

The result of the *yasna* ritual is thus the re-ordering and rebirth of the cosmos.

120   THE AGE OF THE PARTHIANS

The *Yasna, Vispered,* and *Videvdad sade* (Table 4)

As a ritual text, the *Videvdad* is embedded in a long text called the *Videvdad sade*. The term is misleading, because this is not simply the *Videvdad* without the Pahlavi translation, but a composite text, consisting of the *Yasna* with numerous passages replaced by texts from the so-called *Vispered.*

These three texts, *Yasna, Vispered,* and *Videvdad* all have their separate manuscript traditions, but, while the *Yasna* and *Videvdad* are complete and self-contained texts, the *Vispered* is not a complete text. Rather, it is a collection of the texts substituted for passages of the *Yasna* when the *Yasna* is recited in the *vispered* ritual. This is a ritual performed on various occasions, but specifically at the seasonal festivals, and, in the *Yasna cum Vispered,* the sections concerning the seasons are therefore expanded. But there is no ritual in which the *Vispered* is recited alone.

Similarly, there is no ritual in which the *Videvdad* is recited alone. The text that accompanies the *videvdad sade* ritual is, in fact, the *Yasna cum Vispered,* into which, in different places, are inserted the chapters of the *Videvdad,* and the text then becomes a *Videvdad sade.*[52]

Aside from the insertion of the *Videvdad* chapters, the principal difference between the text of the *Yasna* proper and the text of the *Videvdad sade,* is in the ordering of the times of the day. In the *Yasna,* these are ordered so as to begin with the time periods immediately preceding and following sunrise, as we would expect from a text that brings about the new day.

In the *Yasna cum Vispered,* however, the first two, which always go together, are moved to the end, and their place is occupied by a formula specific to the *Videvdad sade*: "for the Law that comes with the Law, the Law about how to discard the old gods, that of Zarathuštra, sustainer of order, a model of order". The law in question, the *dāta- vīdaēuua-,* is the *Videvdad.*[53]

This substitution occurs for the first time in the *Frauuarānē,* "statement of one's choice" (approximately, "profession of faith") which introduces both the *Yasna* and the *Videvdad sade*:

Yasna 0.1	*Vid. sade 0.4*
frauuarānē mazdaiiasnō zaraθuštriš	=
vīdaēuuō ahura.ṭkaēšō	=
hāuuanə̄e ašaone ašahe raθβe	*dātāi haδa.dātāi vīdaēuuāi*
yasnāica vahmāica	*zaraθuštrāi ašaone ašahe raθβe*
xšnaoθrāica frasastaiiaēca	
sāuuaŋhə̄e vīsiiāica ašaone ašahe raθβe	
yasnāica vahmāica	=
xšnaoθrāica frasastaiiaēca	=

THE *VIDEVDAD*: ITS RITUAL-MYTHICAL SIGNIFICANCE

Yasna
> I shall now choose to sacrifice to Ahura Mazdā in the tradition of
> Zarathuštra,
> discarding the old gods (*daēuua*s) and with Ahura (Mazdā) as my guide,
> *for the Haoma-pressing Hour, sustainer of Order, a model of Order,*
> for (its) sacrifice and hymn
> and satisfaction and glorification,—
> *for the Hour of Life-giving Strength, sustainer of Order ...*
> for (its) sacrifice and hymn and satisfaction and glorification,—

Videvdad Sade
> I shall now choose to sacrifice to Ahura Mazdā in the tradition of
> Zarathustra,
> discarding the old gods (*daēuua*s) and with Ahura (Mazdā) as my guide,
> *for the Law and what comes with the Law,*
> *the Law describing how to discard the old gods, [= the Videvdad]*
> *that of Zarathustra,*[54] *sustainer of order, a model of order.*
> for (its) sacrifice and hymn and satisfaction and glorification,—

This substitution recurs throughout the text and thereby changes its focus and purpose away from being that of a morning ritual to that of *an exorcism ritual*, whose purpose is to exorcise the powers causing pollution and death from Ahura Mazdā's creation and creatures.

Moreover, the *Frauuarānē* is followed in the *Yasna* by a praise of the sun, the heavenly fire, son of Ahura Mazdā, about to be reborn, but, in the *Videvdad sade,* by the praise of Sraoša with the fearless club, whose activity takes place at night:

Yasna 0.2
āθrō ahurahe mazdå puθra
tauua ātarš puθra ahurahe mazdå xšnaoθra
yasnāica vahmāica xšnaoθrāica frasastaiiaēca
tauua ātarš puθra ahurahe mazdå xšnaoθra
yasnāica... frasastaiiaēca

> (and for that) *of the fire,* (you,) O son of Ahura Mazdā,—
> by the satisfaction of you, O fire, O son of Ahura Mazdā,
> for (your) sacrifice and hymn and satisfaction and glorification,—
> by the satisfaction of you, O fire, O son of Ahura Mazdā,
> for (your) sacrifice and hymn and satisfaction and glorification.

Videvdad sade 0.5
sraošahe ašiiehe taxmahe tanumąθrahe
darši.draoš āhūiriiehe

> (and for that) *of Sraoša* with the rewards, the firm one who stretches the
> Holy Word,[55]
> the one with the defiant mace, he the creature of Ahura Mazdā.

122 THE AGE OF THE PARTHIANS

A second difference between the *Yasna* proper and the *Yasna cum Vispered* occurs in the enumeration of the seasons, where the *Yasna cum Vispered* has a more detailed text, which apparently describes the activities of the seasons in greater detail.[56]

The *Videvdad* myth

The myths that underlie the *Videvdad* go from Ahura Mazdā's arrangement of the ordered world of the living to the final healing of the entire cosmos. Within these framing stories, issues of pollution and purification are discussed.

The myth of the *Videvdad* is structurally similar to that of the *Yasna*, but, while the myth of the *Yasna* is about the rebirth of the sun and the ordered cosmos from chaos by the removal of the forces of darkness, the myth of the *Videvdad* is about removing evil from the world of the living and about healing both it and the world of thought.

The first chapter of the *Videvdad* tells the myth about how Ahura Mazdā, as master carpenter, fashioned forth sixteen settlements and how Aŋra Mainiiu, in his amateurish, but nonetheless detrimental way, whittled forth a variety of harmful creatures, speech, actions, bodily defects, and illnesses as adversaries to the good creations.[57] Many of these evils are precisely those discussed in the rest of the *Videvdad*.

The *Videvdad* itself does not say when this event takes place in the cosmic time scheme; however, the first place Ahura Mazdā makes is the Aryan territory, Airiiana Vaējah.

This scenario takes us to a passage in the hymn to the fravashis (Yasht 13), in which Ahura Mazdā is said to have cut out the umbilical cords of the Aryan lands from Gaiia Marətān (Pahlavi Gayōmard), the first living being to be created and to be killed by the Evil One:

Videvdad 1.2
paoirīm asaŋhąmca šōiθranąmca vahištəm
frāθβərəsəm azəm yō ahurō mazdå airiianəm vaējō vaŋhuiiå dāitiiaiiå
āaṭ ahe paitiiārəm frākərəntaṭ aŋrō mainiiuš pouru.mahrkō
ažimca yim raoiðitəm ziiąmca daēuuō.dātəm

As the best of places and settlements
I first fashioned forth, I, Ahura Mazdā, *the Aryan territory of the Good Lawful (river)*.
Then Aŋra Mainiiu full of destruction *whittled forth* as its antagonist
the red dragon and the winter made by the (bad) old gods.

The *Videvdad*: Its Ritual-Mythical Significance

Yasht 13.87

gaiiehe marəθnō ašaonō frauuašīm yazamaide
yō paoiriiō ahurāi mazdāi manasca gušta sāsnåsca
yahmaṯ haca frāθβərəsaṯ *nåfō airiianąm dax́iiunąm*
ciθrəm airiianąm dax́iiunąm
zaraθuštrahe spitāmahe iδa ašaonō ašīmca frauuašīmca yazamaide

We sacrifice to the fravashi of Gaiia Marətān, a sustainer of Order
who was the first to listen to the thought and ordinances of Ahura Mazda,
from whom (Ahura Mazda) fashioned forth the umbilical cords of the
Aryan lands,
the *seed of the Aryan lands.
We sacrifice to the reward and fravashi of Spitama Zarathustra, a sustainer
of Order.

We can therefore assume that, in the first chapter of the *Videvdad*, we find
ourselves at the beginning of the second 3000-year period of the world, shortly
after the deaths of the Lone Bull and Gaiia Martān. These two first living
beings, however, according to the Pahlavi texts, by releasing their semen into
the *Earth* before dying, became the ancestors of the races of men and animals.
Specifically, we are told in the Pahlavi texts that from Gayōmard's semen the
first human couple was born.

After this, two heroes, Haošiiaŋha and Taxma Urupi, fight Evil until the
coming of Yima. About Haošiiaŋha the texts tell us little, but Taxma Urupi
plays an important role in the history of illness and cure, as he features in the
etiological story about the discovery that cow's urine was a potent healing
substance and remover of evils caused by Aŋra Mainiiu.[58]

The same story connects Taxma Urupi with Yima, who succeeds him in the
sequence of mythological sacrificing heroes in the Avesta and to whom the
second chapter of the *Videvdad* is devoted.

The second and third chapters of the *Videvdad* contain the mythical history
of Life-giving Humility (Spəṇtā Ārmaiti), the *Earth*, who is also Ahura
Mazdā's daughter and wife.

In the second chapter, Ahura Mazdā is presented as offering the "religious"
leadership in the world of living beings to Yima, who declines and instead
accepts to become its first ruler. With Yima, the account of the first ages in the
Zoroastrian texts gains substance. Yima's age is the golden age, and under his
kingship men and beasts are immortal, which results in serious overpopulation
of the earth. Yima then expands the earth three times, making her twice as large
as she was at first, but is then unable to expand her further, and the population
is instead reduced by a series of natural catastrophes.

In order to save the living beings from total decimation, Ahura Mazdā
instructs Yima how to build a kind of bunker, in which perfect specimens of
male and female couples of all things in the world of the living are preserved.

It is a matter of some puzzlement how *our* generations of living beings
relate to these events. According to the Pahlavi texts, the population of Yima's

124 THE AGE OF THE PARTHIANS

bunker is being saved for repopulating the earth at the end of time, after a new series of natural catastrophes have *re*-decimated their numbers.[59] It would seem that some living beings *not* kept in Yima's bunker survived the initial catastrophes and kept populating the earth and its seven continents and that it is this population that will be decimated in the final catastrophes and then be supplemented by the population of Yima's bunker. Alternatively, *we* are the ones who are living in Yima's bunker and will emerge in due course. This second alternative is much less probable, however, as that would imply that the genetically perfect population of Yima's bunker would later have been polluted by Evil, after all. The problem is probably insoluble, since we are likely to be dealing with multiple and logically incompatible myths of the origins.[60]

Chapter 3 of the *Videvdad* contains the discussion of the five things that make the earth "happy" and the five things that make the earth "unhappy".[61] This chapter is the first to contain a discussion of how to deal with pollution, especially by corpses.

Of the various unpleasant items in these lists of good and bad things, the place where the earth is most "unhappy" is the entrance to Hell. This feature matches the end of chapter 19, where Zarathuštra's successful sacrifice has chased the evil gods back through the entrance to Hell, and so plays an important structural role in the multiple-ring composition of the *Videvdad*.

The chapters that follow consist mainly of catalogues of the imperfections afflicting living beings, all of which have to be fought by gods and men. The main agent of Aŋra Mainiiu is the cosmic deception, the Druj, or the Lie, who, apparently as its mother, spawns all this evil.

At the other end of the *Videvdad*, in chapter 18, we enter a long discussion of who is a priest or, more precisely, who is not a priest, a discussion that leads to a question:

Videvdad 18.14
pərəsaṯ zaraθuštrō ahurəm mazdąm
ahura mazda mainiiō spə̄ništa dātarə gaēθanąm astuuaitinąm ašāum
kō asti sraošahe ašiiehe taxmahe tanu.mąθrahe darši.draoš āhūiriiehe
sraošāuuarəzō

Zarathuštra asked Ahura Mazdā:
O Ahura Mazdā, O most Life-giving Spirit, O sustrainer of Order, you who have established the living beings with bones!
Who is he, the Auditing priest of Sraoša of the Rewards, the firm one who stretches the Holy Word, the one with the defiant mace, he the creature of Ahura Mazdā?

The question is interesting, because it implies that Sraoša himself is a priest, and, in fact, that is what is implied in the *Avesta*, where Sraoša is said to have been the first in the world of thought to have chanted the five *Gāθā*s of Zarathuštra:

THE *VIDEVDAD*: ITS RITUAL-MYTHICAL SIGNIFICANCE

Yasna 57.7-8
sraošəm ašīm huraoδəm vərəθrājanəm frādaṯ.gaēθəm ašauuanəm ašahe
ratūm yazamaide
yō paoiriiō gāθå frasrāuuaiiaṯ yå paṇca spitāmahe ašaonō zaraθuštrahe

We sacrifice to well-shaped Sraoša of the Rewards, the obstruction-smasher, furtherer of living beings, a sustainer of Order, (as) a model of Order,
who was the first to make heard the *Gāθā*s, the five of Spitama Zarathustra, sustainer of Order.

Moreover, according to the Pahlavi texts, when Ahura Mazdā performs the very last sacrifice in the world of thought to banish evil from the creation for ever, it is Sraoša (Srōš) who is the assistant priest (*rāspīg*).

Bundahišn 34.29-30
ohrmazd ō gētīy šawēd xwad zōd srōš-ahlīy rāspīg ud ēbyāhan pad dast
āwarēd.
ganāg mēnōy ud āz pad ān ī gāhānīg nērang zad abzārīhā wasīyār tar ān
widarg <ī> āsmān <ī> padiš andar dwārist abāz ō tam ud tār

Ohrmazd goes down into the world, himself as officiating priest and Srōš-ahlīy [Avestan *Sraoša ašiia*] as assistant priest, bringing the sacred girdle in his hands.
The Foul Spirit and Āz will be greatly and exceedingly smashed by the magic power of the *Gāθā*s, and <they fall> back to the darkness and gloom through the passage through the sky through which they first rushed in.

But who is Sraoša's *sraošāuuarza*, or auditing priest? Somewhat surprisingly, we are told that this is the rooster, who tells people to get up and perform their religious duties:

Videvdad 18.15-16
āaṯ mraoṯ ahurō mazdå mərəyō yō parō.darš nąma spitama zaraθuštra ...
āaṯ hō mərəyō vācim baraiti upa ušåŋhəm yąm sūrąm
usəhištata mašiiāka staota ašəm yaṯ vahištəm nīsta daēuuū
aēša vō duuaraiti būšiiąsta darəyō.gauua
hā vīspəm ahūm astuuaṇtəm hakaṯ raocaŋhąm *frayāta[62] *nix^v abdaiieiti*
x^v afsa darəyō mašiiāka nōiṯ tē sacaite

Then Ahura Mazdā said: The bird called Fore-seer, O Spitama Zarathustra...
And that bird lifts its voice toward dawn full of life-giving strength.
Get up, men! Praise Order, the best! Scorn the *daēuua*s!
This (lie-demon) Sloth with long hands is running upon you.
She (it is who) puts the entire existence with bones to sleep at once at the coming of the lights (saying):
Sleep long man! (Time) is not passing you by.

126 THE AGE OF THE PARTHIANS

Part of the interest of this text is that it provides an explanation for the appearance in Central Asian and Chinese funeral reliefs of a rooster-shaped priest-deity, who has caused much speculation, but who, I think, is most likely to represent Sraoša and/or his bird.[63] We should also remember that Sraoša enters into Islam as one of the angels at the judgment.

The rooster is in fact an appropriate *sraošāuuarza*, as we see from the listing of the seven priests in the *Vispered* (Vr.3.1), where he is described as *dąhištəm aršuuacastəməm* "most qualified and (speaking) the most correct words", which is precisely what the rooster does according to the *Videvdad*. Moreover, in the *Nirangistan* (N.59 [D.77]), a text containing ritual instructions and explanations, his function is said to be to "oversee" (*aiβiiāxšaiiāṯ*).

This section then leads into the main part of this chapter, where we find our Sraoša in intimate conversation with the Druj, the Lie. He is asking her who her sex partners are, who make her pregnant with evil things, which she in turn explains in detail.

This leads to the question of atonement for somebody who has released his semen into a menstruating woman when they both were aware of what they were doing. If the man to whom the grievous sin accrues from this performs the rites correctly, he will go to the best existence, that is Paradise, but if not "he will fall into the existence that is that of those possessed by the Lie, that is, darkness full of darkness, spawned by darkness":

Videvdad 18.76
yezi azāite təm ahūm paiθiiāite yim ašaonąm
yezi nōiṯ azāite təm ahūm paiθiiāite yim druuatąm
təmaŋhaēnəm təmasciθrəm təmaŋhəm

If he does drive them away, he will fall into the existence of the sustainers of Order.
If he does not drive them away, he will fall into the existence of those possessed by the Lie:
darkness full of darkness, *spawned by darkness.

Zarathuštra Chases the Evil One back to Hell

The prediction of these dim prospects for the one who knowingly indulges in this kind of illicit intercourse (and there are many more) takes us to Hell and its inhabitants, Aŋra Mainiiu and his evil gods, who fight Zarathuštra in chapter 19 of the *Videvdad*.

We are now approaching the end of this text, and we are getting close to the completion of the process of cleansing the world of the pollution caused by the forces of evil and of healing its ailments.

After Zarathuštra has dealt with Aŋra Mainiiu and his minions, he asks Ahura Mazdā how he can make the world safe from the powers of evil and how he can purify those that have already been contaminated.

THE *VIDEVDAD*: ITS RITUAL-MYTHICAL SIGNIFICANCE

127

Ahura Mazdā explains how it should be done, namely, by invoking certain powers, by performing a *haoma* sacrifice, and by applying cow's urine. In other words, Zarathuštra should perform what looks very much like a *videvdad sade* ritual.

The last action is to place Good Thought, here presumably representing a sick body, in the open, so that the heavenly lights may shine on it for nine nights:

Videvdad 19.23
yaoždāta bun vohu manō yaoždāta bun mašiiō
uzgəuruuaiiāt vohu manō hāuuōiia bāzuuō dašinaca dašina bāzuuō hāuuaiiaca
āat vohu manō nidaiδīš sūrō.θβarštanąm raocaŋhąm
yat hē stārąm bayō.dātanąm aiβi.raocaiiåṇti
vīspəm ā ahmāt yat hē nauua xšafna sacåṇte

They shall be purified: Good Thought, they shall be purified: the man.
He shall take up Good Thought with the left arm and the right, with the right arm and the left.
Then you should place Good Thought (under) the lights fashioned rich in life-giving strength
so that the stars established by the (moon) god may shine upon him
until nine nights shall pass for him.

Zarathuštra so does, Good Thought is healed, and Aŋra Mainiiu and his minions are chased back to Hell:

Videvdad 19.47
adāuṇta aduuarəṇta daēuua druuaṇtō duždåŋhō
būnəm aŋhōuš təmaŋhahe yat ərəyatō daožaŋᵛhahe

They chattered, they scattered, the old gods, possessed by the Lie, who give bad gifts,
to the bottom of the existence of darkness, that of *gloomy Hell.

There remains the task of healing *the world of thought*, a task that occupies the last three chapters of the *Videvdad*.

In chapter 20, Zarathuštra asks Ahura Mazdā who the first healer was. Ahura Mazdā tells him who it was (Θrita, father of Kərəsāspa), then goes on to utter the spells needed for the healing, and tells Zarathuštra about the healing plants he brought forth. The chapter ends with the Gathic prayer to Airiiaman, god of healing.

Chapter 21 begins with a homage to the cow and an appeal to the clouds to release the healing waters, which will destroy the illnesses.

This is followed by three successive exhortations to the sun, the moon, and the stars, respectively, to rise and pursue their course, which is, in turn, followed by various rituals and exorcistic spells.

128 THE AGE OF THE PARTHIANS

This procedure is also based on the old cosmogonic myth, as told in the hymn to the fravashis. According to this text, it was the fravashis who first showed their paths to the heavenly waters, the plants, and the heavenly bodies, sun, moon, and stars. The fravashis also assisted Good Thought and the Fire when Aŋra Mainiiu was about to pass into Ahura Mazdā's domain in order to prevent waters from flowing and plants from growing. Instead, waters flowed forth and plants grew up.

This chapter of the *Videvdad*, therefore, alludes to the initial victory over Aŋra Mainiiu and the release of the healing waters and reminds us of Mirçea Eliade's remark: "The idea that life cannot be restored but only-re-created through repetition of the cosmogony is very clearly shown in curative rituals".[64]

The Healing of the Cosmos

In chapter 22, the *Videvdad* comes full circle, when Ahura Mazdā recounts how, when he made his own heavenly dwelling, Aŋra Mainiiu fashioned forth 99,999 illnesses. He now calls upon the Maθra Spəṇta, the life-giving poetic thought, that is, the sacred utterance of his thoughts, to heal *Him*.

The Maθra Spəṇta asks Ahura Mazdā how he is to go about this, and Ahura Mazdā answers by calling upon Nairiia Saŋha, the divine messenger, to go and ask Airiiaman to heal him. Nairiia Saŋha does so.

Airiiaman then quickly goes and fetches sacrificial animals, digs the furrows and the channels needed for the purification ritual, utters the words of exorcism, and so overcomes the illnesses brought on by Aŋra Mainiiu:[65]

Videvdad 22.1-2
mraoṯ ahurō mazdå spitamāi zaraθuštrāi
azəm yō ahurō mazdå azəm yō dāta vaŋhuuąm
yasə taṯ nmānəm ākərənəm srīrəm raoxšnəm frādərəsrəm...
āaṯ mąm mairiiō ākasaṯ āaṯ mąm mairiiō frākərənaoṯ aŋrō mainiiuš
pouru.mahrkō
nauuaca yaskō̄ nauuaitišca nauuaca sata nauuaca hazaŋra nauuasə̄sca
baēuuąn
āaṯ mąm tūm bišaziiōiš mąθrō spəṇtō yō aš.x^varənå

Ahura Mazdā said to Spitama Zarathustra:
I, Ahura Mazdā, the establisher of good things,
I, who made that house, beautiful, luminous, visible...
then the villain looked at me, then the villain made against me, Aŋra Mainiiu full of destruction, 99,999 diseases.
So may you heal me, O Holy Word, you of great munificence![66]

Videvdad 22.19-20

mošu taṭ ās nōiṭ darəγəm yaṭ frāiiataiiaṭ θβaxšəmnō airiiama yō išiiō
gairīm auui spəṇtō.frasnå varəšəm auui spəṇtō.frasnå
nauuanąm aspanąm aršnąm gaonəm baraṭ airiiama yō išiiō
nauuanąm uštranąm aršnąm ... nauuanąm gauuąm aršnąm ...   nauuanąm
anumaiianąm aršnąm ...
nauua vaētaiiō baraṭ nauua karšå frakāraiiaṭ

Quickly that was (done. It was) not long before he, speedy Airiiaman,
*went in haste,
to the mountain Spəṇtō.frasnå, to the forest Spəṇtō.frasnå.
He brought the *boon[67] of nine male horses, speedy Airiiaman.
He brought the *boon of nine male camels, of nine male bulls, of nine male
sheep,
He carried nine strands (of barsom)[68]. He traced nine furrows.

The *Videvdad*, therefore, has two endings, as it were. The first ending is
Zarathuštra's battle in the World of the Living, culminating in his victory over
Aŋra Mainiiu and the old gods and the healing of Good Thought. The second
ending is in the World of Thought, namely, the healing of the ailing cosmos, in
fact of Ahura Mazdā himself, through the administrations of his holy utterance,
the Mąθra Spəṇta.

The first ending and the actions of Zarathustra show that we are at what, in
the Pahlavi texts, is the end of the second 3000-year period, which was when
Zarathustra was born, 30 years before the beginning of the third and last 3000-
year period. Then, when he was 30 years old, he had his first meeting with
Good Thought and Ohrmazd. Here, he accepted to bring Ohrmazd's word to
the world and was appointed principal fighter of Evil.

It is therefore clear that the time frame of the *Videvdad* is the second 3000
years of the pact, the Mixture.

The *Videvdad* and the *Gāθā*s (Table 4)

To conclude this survey of the *Videvdad*, we need to consider the position
of its chapters in the *Yasna cum Vispered* text. The arrangement is the one in
Table 4, from which we see that the *Yasna cum Vispered* text differs from the
Yasna proper only up to the Young Avestan text concluding the recitation of
the *Gāθā*s.

In the *Videvdad sade*, the chapters of the *Videvdad* are distributed before,
between, and after the Old Avestan texts. We can of course look at this the
other way around, as well, and say that the Old Avestan texts and the additions
from the *Vispered* are inserted between the chapters of the *Videvdad*. In either
case, this means that, as the *Videvdad* is recited, with its powerful exorcism, it
joins forces with the intrinsically powerful *Old Avesta*, god's holy utterance, to
annihilate the forces of evil.

130 THE AGE OF THE PARTHIANS

I should say straightaway that there is no obvious correlation between the *Videvdad* chapters and the parts of the *Gāθā*s they are close to, with two exceptions.

One is a general agreement between the two texts in that they both start with myths of the origins, the *Videvdad* with the making of the lands and the myth of Yima, the *Gāθā*s with the myths of the installation of Zarathuštra as first sacrificer in *Yasna* 29 and the myth of the two Spirits, and the participation of the sacrificers in the struggle against the Lie in *Yasna* 30.

The other correlation is between the endings of the two texts, and here the correlations are much stronger.

The V*ahištōištī gāθā* (*Yasna* 53-54.1)

Yasna 53, the last of the five *Gāθā*s, is a difficult text, but its general contents are clear.

It begins with the affirmation that Zarathuštra's sacrifice was the best, in the sense that it brought about the desired effect. Anybody who wishes to achieve the same should therefore imitate Zarathuštra's sacrifice:

Yasna 53.1
vahištā īštiš srāuuī zaraθuštrahē
spitāmahiiā yezī hōi dāt̰ āiiaptā
aṣ̌āt̰ hacā ahurō mazdå yauuōi vīspāi.å huuaŋhəuuīm
yaēcā hōi dabən saš̌ə̄ncā daēnaiiå vaŋhuiiå uxδā š́iiaoθanācā

The best ritual is (thus) renowned as that of Zarathustra
Spitama. For when Ahura Mazdā shall give to him as prizes
in accordance with (its?) Order the possession of a good new existence for an entire life span,
(but) also (that of those) who fashion and master the utterances and actions of *his* good vision-soul.

The participants in whatever goes on in *Yasna* 53 are asked to find, by their vision-souls *(daēnā*s), the existence that is that of Good Thought:

Yasna 53.5-6a
sāx^və̄nī vaziiamnābiiō kainibiiō mraomī
xšmaibiiācā vadəmnō mə̄ncā ī mə̨zdazdūm
vaēdō.dūm daēnābīš abiiascā ahūm yə̄ vaŋhə̄uš manaŋhō
aṣ̌ā və̄ aniiō ainim vīuuaŋghatū tat̰ zī hōi huš̌ə̄nəm aŋhat̰
iθā ī haiθiiā narō aθā jə̄naiiō ...

I am speaking to (you), the young women who are about to be conveyed (away) [or: carried (off)], two instructions,[69]
— and to you (young men(?)) — those) of the singer. And pay attention to them!

THE *VIDEVDAD*: ITS RITUAL-MYTHICAL SIGNIFICANCE 131

(The first:) Keep finding for yourselves by (your) vision-souls and for these our women the existence which is that of Good Thought!
(The second: When going) through (the sunlit spaces of) Order let each (of you) illuminate [or: try to overcome] the other! For that shall be a good gain for him!
In this way (mark) them (well as) true, O men! In that way[70] (mark them well as true), O women! ...

Yasna 53 then ends with imprecations and curses against those possessed by the Lie, hoping they may be dragged off to Hell by the fetter of death, while the sustainers of order will bring peace to the habitations:

Yasna 53.8
anāiš ā dužuuarəšnaŋhō   dafšniiā hə̄ntū
zax'iiācā vīspåŋhō   xraosəṇtąm upā
huxšaθrāiš jə̄narąm xrūnərąmcā   rāmąmcā āiš dadātū   šiieitibiiō vīžibiiō
īratū īš duuafšō huuō   dərəzā mərəθiiaoš mazištō   mošucā astū

On account of those (performances) of theirs let them be there (at the judgement, as men) of bad virility, dupes,
and ridiculed all (of them)! Let *them* be howled upon (= booed)!
By those who have good commands let *them* be smashed and bled!
—And let (*this one*?) give peace by these (performances of ours) to the settled towns!—
Let torment huddle *them* off as their greatest (share?), the one with the fetter of death, and let it be soon!

Correspondingly, in *Videvdad* 19, we have further details about Zarathuštra's successful sacrifice, how it is structured and what its effects are, namely, to heal Good Thought and to chase Aŋra Mainiiu back to Hell.
The chapter also contains the description of the meeting, after death, of the soul and the *daēnā*.
Videvdad 20 contains spells to remove the Lie and the illnesses brought over mankind by Aŋra Mainiiu.
Yasna 54.1, which is the concluding strophe of this *Gāθā*, contains a prayer to Airiiaman to come to support the poet's people and Zarathuštra's Good Thought and a prayer for rewards for his *daēnā*:

Yasna 54.1
ā airiiə̄mā išiiō   rafəδrāi jaṇtū
nərəbiiascā nāiribiiascā   zaraθuštrahē
vaŋhə̄uš rafəδrāi manaŋhō   yā daēnā vairīm   hanāt mīždəm
ašahiiā yāsā ašīm   yąm išiiąm ahurō   masatā mazdå

Let speedy Airiiaman come here for support
for (our) men and women, for the support of Zarathustra's
Good Thought, whereby (his) vision-soul may gain a worthy fee.

132 THE AGE OF THE PARTHIANS

I am now asking for the reward of/for Order, which Ahura Mazdā shall
*deem worthy of being sped (hither).

Correspondingly, in *Videvdad* 22: Airiiaman heals Ahura Mazdā of the
diseases made by Aŋra Mainiiu. The effect of the healing by the *Airiiaman
Ishiya* is described in several Avestan fragments as follows:

Fragment Westergaard 4.1[71]

*airiiamanəm te išīm mazištəm mraomi spitama vīspanąm ərəzuuō
srauuaŋhąm
təm zī vīspanąm srauuaŋhąm uparō.kairīm fradaθąm yim airiianəm išīm
təm arå̊nti saošiiaņtō*

I tell you, O Spitama, that the *Airiiaman Ishiya* is the greatest, O upright
(Zarathustra), of all words.
For I brought it forth as of work superior to all words, the *Airiiaman Ishiya*.
The Revitalisers shall impel it.

Fragment Westergaard 4.2
*ahe *framruiti[a] spitama xšaiieni hauuanąm dāmanąm azəm yō ahurō mazdå̊
naēciš xšaiiåt̰ dužḍaēnō aŋrō mainiiuš zaraθuštra xᵛaēšu dāmōhu spitama*
    a. Mss. *framraomi*.

*When it is said forth, O Spitama, I shall rule over my own creations, I,
Ahura Mazdā.
Not at all shall the one of evil *daēnā* rule, Aŋra Mainiiu, O Zarathustra,
among his own creations, O Spitama.

Fragment Westergaard 4.3 (cf. *Yasna* 9.15, *Yašt* 19.81)
*zəmargūzō bauuåt̰ aŋrō mainiiuš zəmargūzō bauuåņti daēuua
us irista paiti arå̊nti vī juuåhu[a] paiti tanušu
astuuå gaiiō dāraiiåņti*
    a. Mss. *vīzuuåhu*.
Aŋra Mainiiu will hide in the earth, the *daēuua*s will hide in the earth.
They will raise the dead again.
In return for living bodies they shall spread out and uphold the life with
bones.[72]

A Pahlavi version is also found:

Dēnkard 9.46[73]
*ērmān-xwāhišnīh ō tō mahist gōwam spitāmān az harwistīn srawān abēzag
pad hāwand abestāgīh ēn weh čē-m ān az harwistīn srawān abargārtar frāz
dād kē ērmān xwāhišnīh awēšān ēw ōšmurēnd kē sūdōmand kē hēnd*

I say to you, O Spitama, that "seeking *ērmān*" (*airiiamā išiiō*) is the greatest
of all pure words, like something out of the Avesta. This is the best, because
I made that one superior to all words, "seeking *ērmān*". Let them recite it
who are beneficial (among) those who are.

THE *VIDEVDAD*: ITS RITUAL-MYTHICAL SIGNIFICANCE

pad ān ī ōy frāz ōšmurišnīh spitāmān pādaxšāy bawam andar ān ī xwēš dām man kē ohrmazd ham u nē pad čiš pādaxšāy bawēd ān ī dušdēn ganāg mēnōy zarduxšt andar ān ī xwēš dām spitāmān

By its being recited, O Spitama, I shall be ruler in my own creation, I, who am Ohrmazd. And he shall not be ruler over anything, he, the Foul Spirit, O Zarathustra, in his own creation, O Spitama.

zamīg-nigān bawēd ganāg mēnōy andar zamīg nigān kē dēw hēnd kū-šan kālbod bē škīhēd ud ul rist pad ān ārāyīhēd pad ayārīh ī ōy bē zīndagīh ō tan abāz dahēnd ud tanōmand jān dārēnd

The Foul Spirit will be enterred in the earth. Enterred in the earth those who are the *dēw*s, i.e., their frame will be broken. And the dead will thereby be (re)arranged, (i.e.) by his help. They will give life back to the body, and those who have a body will have a soul.

In light of the preceding, we see that *Yasna* 53-54.1 and *Videvdad* 19-22 correspond as follows:

Yasna 53-54.1	*Videvdad* 19-22
Zarathuštra's sacrifice is the best	Zarathuštra's sacrifice is successful
his followers find the existence of Good Thought	he heals Good Thought
the losers are cursed to Hell	myth of the *daēnā*
Airiiaman comes to support the poet's people	Aŋra Mainiiu and his minions are chased back to Hell
and Zarathuštra's Good Thought prayer for rewards for his *daēnā*	Airiiaman heals the diseases made by Aŋra Mainiiu

The relationship between the *Gāθā*s and the accompanying *Videvdad* in the *Videvdad sade* is therefore quite clear: The first chapters of the *Videvdad* set the stage for and anticipate the *Gāθā*s, while the last chapters strengthen them with additional spells and curses.

Notes:

1. Complete editions of the *Videvdad*: Brockhaus 1850, Westergaard 1852-54, Spiegel 1853-58 (text), 1852-63 (translation), and Geldner 1886-95. Jamasp 1907, in his edition of the Avestan and Pahlavi texts of the *Videvdad*, reproduces Geldner's text but, unfortunately, gives no further readings from manuscripts available to him, such as the second half of K1 in the Cama Oriental Institute. Also the manuscript IM which, apparently, is descended from a branch of the tradition parallel to K1 and L4 (Jamasp 1907: xxiv-xxxi), and DJJ, a descendent of K1 in a different branch than the other known descendants (Jamasp 1907: x-xvii). See Table 1.
2. First noticed by James Darmesteter 1877: 293 and discussed most recently by Watkins 1995, chap. 58.
3. The entire Avesta was transmitted orally for centuries before it was written down, so that "consulting" would consist of *recalling* from one's own or others' memories the text in question, rather than *reading* it.
4. See the overview in Stausberg, vol. III, 2004: 337-41.
5. *Yasna* 30.6 *aiiå nōiṯ ərəš vīšiiātā daēuuācinā hiiaṯ īš dəbaomā / pərəsmanə̄ŋg upā.jasaṯ hiiaṯ vərənātā acištəm manō / aṯ aēšəməm hə̄ṇduuarə̄ṇtā yā bąnaiiən ahūm marətānō* "Between these two (*mainiius* = spirits, inspirations) the *daēuua*s, however, have not chosen correctly, because deception came upon them as they were consulting, so that they chose the worst thought. And so they keep running together to Wrath, with which the mortals sicken (this) existence".
6. Benveniste 1970.
7. See *Yasna* 9.12-15, *Yašt* 17.18-20, *Yašt* 19.79-81, *Videvdad* 19.2-4.
8. E.g., *Bundahišn* 1A.8 *sidīgar az āb zamīg dād gird dūr-widarg ... mayān ī ēn āsmān bē winnārd* "third, (Ohrmazd) made the earth from water—round, with passages in the distance—he set it up in the middle of this [spherical] sky", cf. *Yašt* 13.9 *vīδāraēm zaraθuštra ząm pərəθβīm ahuraδātąm yąm masīmca paθanąmca* "I held (up and) out the broad earth, set in place by (Ahura) Mazdā, large and wide". See Bailey 1961: 89-90.
9. See, for instance, Choksy 1989.
10. My colleague Yaakov Elman of Yeshiva University, New York, says, "The Babylonian rabbis would have found what I find: the Zoroastrian system is tantalizingly familiar, though frustratingly (but interestingly) different".
11. See, e.g., Gershevitch 1968: 12: "Gāθic texts on the whole represent what has been called "Zaraθuštrianism", the pure doctrine of the founder, whereas the Younger Avesta is the scripture of a mixed religion, for which we may reserve the term "Zoroastrianism" and (p. 18): "Zoroastrianism" opened the gates to a flood of heterogeneous religious, mythical, ritual, and other elements, which partly occur, ill-defined, only in the Avesta"; for the rejection of the study of the *Gāθā*s as ritual texts, see, e.g., Insler 1975: 22: "I have tried to emphasize ... the moral and ethical character of Zarathustra's teaching, which, to my mind, has been seriously neglected in the recent misplaced fascination with the ritualistic background of these exalted lyrics".
12. See, e.g., see Browne 1900: 44-57. The French encyclopedists, Diderot and Voltaire, were quite disappointed at the dryness and lack of spiritual exaltation of Zarathustra (see Duchesne-Guillemin 1962: 387-88); Voltaire, in his *Dictionnaire philosophique* (under), dismissed the Zoroastrian scriptures as an abominable hodgepodge. The founder of the Asiatic Society at Calcutta, William Jones, refused to believe that the texts were genuine on the grounds that they contained platitudes and sheer nonsense

THE *VIDEVDAD*: ITS RITUAL-MYTHICAL SIGNIFICANCE

135

that could not possibly be ascribed to Zarathustra, the great legislator: either Zarathustra was devoid of common sense, or he did not write the books (Jones 1771: 38, 45; 1799, IV: 605, 609).

13. See Kellens 1998: 482-3.
14. See Skjærvø 2003-2004 and 2006-2007.
15. The phenomenon by which an orally composed text, from being constantly *recomposed in performance*, at some stage, for some reason, is no longer *recomposed* but *fixed in (re)performance*, see Nagy 1996: 108-9; Bakker 1997: 21 n. 12. On the *crystallization* of the Avesta, see Skjærvø 1994: 207-8, 240-41; Kellens 1998-99: 686.
16. Kellens1998: 490-1.
17. See Skjærvø 1999: 8-9; Cantera 2004: chap. 4.
18. *Yasna* 57.8 *yō paoiriiō gāθå frasrāuuaiiaṯ yå paṇca spitāmahe aṣaonō zaraθuštrahe* "(the divine Sraoša,) who was the first to perform the five songs of Zarathustra Spitāma, sustainer of order".
19. *Videvdad* 1.1 *mraoṯ ahurō mazdå spitamāi zaraθuštrāi* "Ahura Mazdā said to Zarathustra Spitāma"; *Videvdad* 2.1 *pərəsaṯ zaraθuštrō ahurəm mazdąm* "Zarathustra asked Ahura Mazdā"; *Videvdad* 2.2 *āaṯ mraoṯ ahurō mazdå* "then Ahura Mazdā said".
20. For various interpretations of the list, see Christensen: 1943; Gnoli 1980: 60-68; Gnoli 1987; Witzel 2000; Grenet 2005.
21. The exact meaning of *vaējah* is debated. See Kellens 1984: 106-7 n. 26 with refs.; Mayrhofer 1986-2001: II/18, 577. Kellens 1997-1998: 761 renders *airiiana vaējah vaŋhuiiå dāitiiaiiå* as "espace appartenant aux Iraniens où tourbillonne la (rivière) bonne/divine (et) adéquate", which, elsewhere (e.g., 1999-2000: 736), he shortens to "le tourbillon iranien de la rivière bonne (et) adéquate".
22. For the later sources, see Tafazzoli 1986.
23. Geldner 1896: 37; Meillet 1925: 27. Haug (1890: 264) had argued for a much earlier date for the "larger portion of the Vendidad at about B.C. 1000-900".
24. For a recent evaluation of the contribution of the Magi, see de Jong 2005.
25. Moulton 1917: 5.
26. Moulton 1917: 10-11. Thus also Bartholomae: much earlier than the traditional date of 660 BCE (1904:1675).
27. Moulton 1917: 13.
28. Thus Zaehner 1961: 162.
29. Moulton 1913: 183.
30. Moulton 1917: 225.
31. Haug 1890: 226: "the greater bulk of the [*Videvdad*] contains (like the Talmud) too minute a description of certain ceremonies and observances to allow a modern critic to trace it to the prophet, or even to one of his diciples"; p. 261: "From [Zarathustra's] never mentioning the ceremonies enjoined in the Vendidad, it undoubtedly follows that, though he might know them, he did not attach much weight to their observance"; Moulton 1913: 301 n. 1: "My main contention is that the *ritual* of the Vendidad was alien to Zarathushtra, who, as I understand him, had nothing of the ritual or the saerdotal in his system".
32. Christensen 1941: 28-9.
33. Nyberg 1937: 378.
34. Christensen 1936: 33. More recently also Hintze 2000: 75: "wohl in der Arsakidenzeit".
35. On the astronomical chapter of the Pahlavi *Bundahišn* see Henning 1943: 235-236.

136 THE AGE OF THE PARTHIANS

36. Avestan measures: "finger(-width)" (*dišti-*; *Videvdad* 17.5), "span" (*vītasti-* = 12 fingers), "long span" (*fratarə.vītasti-*; *Videvdad* 8.76), "ell" (*frārāθni-*; *Videvdad* 7.29; cf. Old Persian *arašni* "ell"), "fathom" (*vī.bāzu-*; *Videvdad* 9.2), "arm('s length)" (*frabāzu-*), "foot" (°*paδa-*; *Videvdad* 9.8), "step(s)" (°*gāiia-*; *Videvdad* 17.4), "league" (*hāθra-*), "16 leagues" (*yujiiasti-*; *Herbedestan* 8), "(length of a race) course" (*carətu-*; *Videvdad* 2.25).
37. See, for instance, Henning 1951.
38. Boyce 1975: 95.
39. Boyce 1991: 68.
40. Boyce 1991: n. 78.
41. Non-Iranians are mentioned only in *Videvdad* 1.17. In *Videvdad* 18.62, the prostitute is blamed for mingling the semen of the (religiously) qualified (*dahma*) with that of the unqualified, of those who sacrifice to the *daēuua*s with that of those who do not, and of those who have forfeited their body with that of those who have not.
42. Gershevitch 1968: 27.
43. Zaehner 1961: 162.
44. E10 in the Meherji Rana library at Nawsari, not used by Geldner, is accessible on Alberto Cantera's website videvdad.com. Onthis manuscript see Cantera forthcoming.
45. The Avestan terms are *θβaršta* "cut (out)" and *aθβaršta* "not cut", see Kellens 2000.
46. For discussion, see Skjærvø 2003: 170-1.
47. For details, see Skjærvø 2006.
48. Stausberg 2004: 338.
49. Or: who shine with the brilliance of Order (i.e., like the sunlit sky).
50. See, for instance, Eliade 1991, chapter 2.
51. This is what I think the three verbs *anu.man-*, *anu.vac-*, and *anu.varz-* imply. The preverb *anu-* appears to indicate "follow along". Traditionally, the three terms are translated as "think, etc., according to the *daēnā*", which also makes sense, since the *daēnā* is the totality of a person's thoughts, etc.
52. In the *Hōmāst* ritual, performed to expiate for the legal infringements committed by a menstruating woman, the *Videvdad* is added to the *Yasna*, but not inserted into it. See Darmesteter 1892-93: vol. I, LXVIII-LXIX. In the *Vištāsp Yašt sade* ritual, the *Vištāsp Yašt* in inserted into the *Yasna cum Vispered* instead of the *videvdad*. See Darmesteter 1892-93: II, 603.
53. We do not understand fully the meaning of the expression *dāta- haδa.dāta-* "the Law that comes with the Law".
54. In the vocative, accusative and genitive, the formula has forms of *zaraθuštri-*, not *of zaraθuštra-*. The dative should therefore have been *zaraθuštrōe*.
55. The thoughts of the poet transformed into and performed as sacred utterances. Sraoša, apparently, conveys the sacred utterances of Ahura Mazdā down to the sacrificer and, perhaps, those of the sacrificer to Ahura Mazdā. The traditional translation as "he who has the manthra in his body" makes no immediate sense (thus, for instance, Grenet 2003: 134, who sees a possible reference to this epithet in the representation in a wall painting from Penjikent of a book placed in front of a figure who could be Sroš). Cf. Ahura Madā's threat/promise to "stretch" someone's soul (*uruuan*) away from the good/bad existence (*Yasna* 19.7, 71.15), keeping in mind that, according to *Yasna* 28.4, the *uruuan* is also the breath on which the songs are conveyed.
56. We may therefore well ask: which of the two versions of the *Yasna* is the older? It is of course not obvious that the *Vispered* version is the later just because its variants from the *Yasna* have been collected separately. On the contrary, the fact that the

THE *VIDEVDAD*: ITS RITUAL-MYTHICAL SIGNIFICANCE

Vispered version contains details closely related to practical matters, such as the work that is done in the different seasons, might suggest *it* is the older version and that the *Yasna* is a clerical reworking of the original *Vispered*. Such a scenario would be similar to that of the creation story in Genesis, where the "official" or "priestly" version, as it were, is the later, while the older, and more "popular" version, one might say, is relegated to a secondary position in the transmitted text.

57. The verb used to describe the action is a verb that means "to cut forth/out" (*fra-θβərəsa-*). For Aŋra Mainiiu's activity, another verb with similar meaning is used (*fra-kərəŋta-*) which, presumably, refers to an inferior execution of the craft. Elsewhere, Ahura Mazdā's creative activity is expressed by *dā-* "place, put in its proper place" and *fra-dā-*, literally, "place forth".

58. See Dhabhar (ed.) 1932: 295-6.

59. As told, for instance, in the *Bundahišn* 33.30.

60. See Kellens 2002-2003: 818-25.

61. We may note that the word *śā-* "happy" also has sexual undertones, see Kellens 1995: 34-6.

62. The manuscripts have *raocaŋhąm frayrātō*, see Skjærvø 2005: 200.

63. Note the spur seen clearly on the Xi'an tomb (Grenet 2004: 276).

64. Eliade 1991: 81.

65. Cf. the resume of *Videvdad* 22 in *Dēnkard*, book 8: *ud xwēškārīh ī ērman pad bēzašagīh ī gēhān* "and the duty of Airiiaman in the healing of (all) living beings", cited by Darmesteter 1892-93, II: 276.

66. The function of the *x^varənah* in the Zoroastrian cosmogonical and cosmological scheme is unclear, but it appears it is involved in conception and birth, hence also rebirth.

67. Elsewhere *gaona* is used about the "boon" a man gives a woman when sleeping with her: *Videvdad* 3.25 *yō imąm ząm aiβi.vərəziieiti ... upa hē gaonəm baraiti mąnaiiən ahe yaθa nā friiō friiāi vaṇtauue starəta gātuš saiiamanō puθrəm vā gaonəm vā auui auua.baraiti* "One who works this earth ... he brings a boon to it, just like a loving man a loving wife, lying on a spread-out bed. He brings her a son or (some other) 'boon'". Etymologically, *gaona* ought to mean "increase", or similar.

68. Cf. *Nirangistan* 72 (Darmesteter no. 90) *cuuaṭ nā nitəma barəsmana ratufriš θriš *uruuarå *caiiå vaēitiš aētaiiå uruuaraiiå aŋhən tarō dənānō varəsō.stauuaŋhō āaṭ upəma aēšō.drājaŋha yauuō.fraθaŋha* "*How much (is) the minimum barsom with which a man satisfies the models? —Three plants. — Which shall the *strands of this plant be? — Exceeding a ... (and) the thickness of a hair. But the maximum (with which he satisfies the models) should be the length of a plough and the width of a yoke" (see Skjærvø 1997, 116-7).

69. If < **sāh-wan/r-* < **sāh-*, as in *sāsnā-* "ordinance, commandment" and *sīša-* "teach".

70. The opposition *iθā ~ aθā* seems to indicate that the poet is standing with the men, at a distance from the women.

71. Westergaard 1852-54: 332; Darmesteter, 1892-93, vol. I: CIV, vol. III: 4-5.

72. Kellens 1974: 221. The passage may be parsed differently as: "They will raise the dead again in living bodies".

73. See Darmesteter 1892-93, vol. I: CIV; Molé, 1963: 144-5.

Table 1.

ONE POSSIBLE CHRONOLOGY OF THE AVESTAN CORPUS

TIME TEXTS	SPOKEN LANGUAGES
1500-1000 BCE Old Avestan oral traditions	Old Avestan
± 1000 BCE crystalisation of Old Avestan texts	
1000-500 BCE Young Avestan oral traditions	Young Avestan
520 BCE DARIUS'S BISOTUN INSCRIPTION	OLD PERSIAN
± 500 BCE crystalisation of Young Avestan texts	
??? canonisation of the *Avesta*	Old Persian
500 BCE - 550 CE oral transmission of the entire corpus	Old ⇒ Middle Persian
± 600 CE WRITING DOWN OF THE ENTIRE CORPUS	MIDDLE PERSIAN
6th-19th centuries copying of manuscripts, development of variant readings	
Arab conquest	Middle/modern Persian
650-1000 CE loss of manuscripts, deterioration of the tradition	
± 1000 CE one manuscript of each part of the *Avesta*	
13TH-14TH CENTS OLDEST EXTANT MANUSCRIPTS	MODERN PERSIAN

Table 2.
Chronology of the Avestan texts

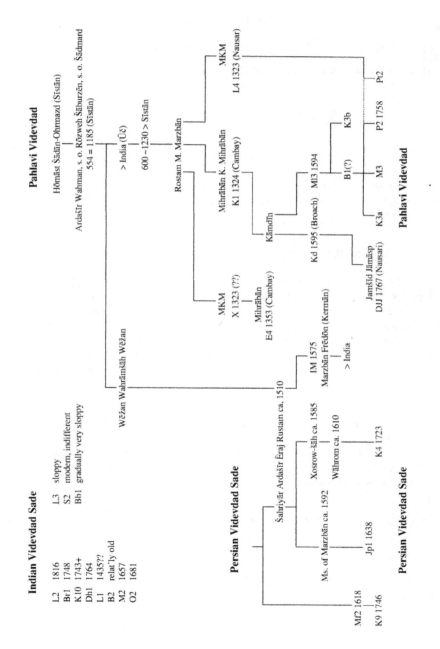

140   THE AGE OF THE PARTHIANS

Table 3. Cosmic time

DURATION OF THE PACT: 3 x 3000 YEARS:

I. THE WORLD OF THOUGHT: 3000 YEARS

Pahlavi Videvdad: the creation being in the world of thought

Bundahishn: the creation being in the world of thought

II. THE WORLD OF LIVING BEINGS IN THE WORLD OF THOUGHT:
3000 YEARS

Pahlavi Videvdad: the creation being in the world of living beings without the Adversary
Bundahishn: creation of the world of living beings in world of thought, unthinking, unmoving, intangible; with Opposition but according to the will of Ohrmazd

III. THE WORLD OF LIVING BEINGS (MYTHICAL ERAS): 3000 YEARS

Pahlavi Videvdad: from the coming of the Adversary to the coming of the Dēn *Bundahishn*: with opposition, according to the will of both	—ENTRY OF THE ADVERSARY —birth of first two humans —Haošiiaŋha/Hōšang —Taxma Urupi/Taxmōraf —YIMA/JAM —Reign of Dahāg —Reigns of Frēdōn and the Kayanids THE BIRTH OF ZARATHUSTRA.

IV. MILLENNIA OF ZARATHUSTRA AND THE REVITALISERS (SAOŠIIANTS)

Pahlavi Videvdad: from the coming of the Dên to the Final Body *Bundahishn*: Ahrimen is undone	ZARATHUSTRA'S REVELATION The Achaemenids, etc. millennium of Ušēdar millennium of Ušēdarmāh coming of the last Sōšāns

THE *VIDEVDAD*: ITS RITUAL-MYTHICAL SIGNIFICANCE

TABLE 4.

THE CORRESPONDENCES BETWEEN THE *YASNA, VISPERED, AND VIDEVDAD SADE*

VIDEVDAD SADE	*YASNA + VISPERED*		*VIDEVDAD S.*	*YASNA + VISPERED*
VS.0.1-3	Y.0.4-06		VS.35/41A.1-5	**Vr.15.1-5**
VS.0.4	~ Y.0.7		VS.35/41A.6-9	
VS.0.5	(Y.3.20)		VS.35-41	**YH**.35-41
VS.0.6-8	Y.0.13-15		VS.35/41B-C	
VS.1A.1-3	Y.1.1-3		VS.42	Y.42
VS.1A.4	~ Y.1.7		VS.42A.1-7	**Vr.16.0-4**
VS.1A.5-8	Y.1.3-6		VS.42B.1-3	**Vr.17.1**
VS.1A.9-10	Y.1.7-8		VS.42C-D	**VIDEVDAD 9-10**
VS.1.B1-9	**Vr.1.1-9**			
VS.1C.1-7	Y.1.10-16		VS.43-46	2.43-46
VS.1C.8	~ Y.1.17		VS.43/46A.1-10	**Vr.18.0-3**
VS.1C.9-10	Y.1.18-19		VS.43/46B-C	**VIDEVDAD 11-12**
VS.1C.11	~ Y.1.20			
VS.2A.1-2	Y.2.1-2		VS.47-50	3.47-50
VS.2A.3	~ Y.2.7		VS.47/50A	**Vr.19**
VS.2A.5-8	Y.2.3-6		VS.47/50B-C	**VIDEVDAD 13-14**
VS.2B.1-11	**Vr.2.1-11**			
VS.2C.1-9	Y.2.10-18		VS.51	4.51
VS.3.1	~ Y.3.1		VS.51A	**Vr.20**
...			VS.51B-C	**VIDEVDAD 15-16**
VS.11A.1-7	Y.11.1-7		VS.52A	**Vr.21**
VS.11B.1-5	**Vr.3.1-5**		VS.52B.1-7	**Vr.21 = *YH.35-41***
VS.11C.1-6	Y.11.9-15		VS.52B.8-9	**Vr.21.0**
VS.11D.1-2	**Vr.3.6-7**		VS.52C-D	**Vr.21-22**
VS.11E.0-6	**Vr.4.0**		VS.52E-F	**VIDEVDAD 17-18**
VS.11E.7-9	**Vr.4.1-4**		VS.52G.1	Y.52
VS.11F.1	~ Y.11.16			
VS.11F.2-4	Y.11.17-19		VS.53	5.53
...			VS.53A	**Vr.23**
VS.27A.1-6	Y.27.1-6		VS.53B-C	**VIDEVDAD 19-20**
VS.27A.7-8			VS.54	Y.54
VS.27B.1-5	**Vr.12.1-5**		VS.54A	**Vr.24**
VS.27C	Y.27.8-12		VS.54B-C	**VIDEVDAD 21-22**
VS.27D-G	**VIDEVDAD 1-4**		VS.55-56	Y.55-56
			VS.57A	Y.57
VS.28-30	1.28-30		VS.57B	
VS.28/30A.1-7	**Vr.13.0-3**		VS.58	Y.58
VS.28/30B-C	**VIDEVDAD 5-6**		VS.59A	Y.59
			VS.59B-M	
VS.31-34	1.31-34		VS.60-62	Y.60-62
VS.31/34A.1-6	**Vr.14.0-4**			
VS.31/34B-6	**VIDEVDAD 7-8**			**SUNRISE**
VS.31/34E.1-3				
			VS.6r-72	Y.63-72

Abbreviations:

Dk, DkM	*Denkard*
GBd	*Greter Bundahishn*
RV	*Rigveda*
Y	*Yasna*
Yt	*Yasht*

Bibliographical Abbreviations:

AAASH	*Acta Antiqua Academiae Scientiarum Hungaricae*
AfO	*Archiv für Orientforschung*
AIr	*Acta Iranica*
AJA	*American Journal of Archaeology*
AMI(T)	*Archäologische Mitteilungen aus Iran (und Turan)*
AOAT	*Alter Orient und Altes Testament*
ArO	*Archiv Orientální*
AS	*Anatolian Studies*
BAI	*Bulletin of the Asia Institute*
BiOr	*Bibliotheca Orientalis*
BSOAS	*Bulletin of the School of Oriental and African Studies*
CHIr	*Cambridge History of Iran*
CAH	*Cambridge Ancient History*
CUP	*Cambridge University Press*
DAFI	*Délégation archéologique française en Iran*
EncIr	*Encyclopaedia Iranica*
IrAnt	*Iranica Antiqua*
JNES	*Journal of Near Eastern Studies*
JA	*Journal Asiatique*
JRAS	*Journal of the Royal Asiatic Studies*
JSAI	*Jerusalem Studies in Arabic and Islam*
OIP	*Oriental Institute Publications*
RE	*Pauly's Real-Encyclopädie der klassischen Alter-tumswissenschaften*
SEL	*Studi Epigrafici e Linguistici sul Vicino Oriente*
St Ir	*Studia Iranica*
ZDMG	*Zeitschrift der deutschen morgenländischen Gesellschaft*

Bibliography:

Abgarians, M. and Sellwood, D. (1971). "A Hoard of Early Parthian Drachms", *NC*: 103- 119.

Ägypten (2005). *Ägypten Griechenland Rom: Abwehr und Berührung*, Städ; sches Kunstinstitut und Städtische Galerie, Frankfurt am Main, 26. November 2005 – 26. February 2006, Tübingen.

Alram, M. (1987). "Die Vorbildwirkung der arsakidischen Münzprägung", *Litterae Numismaticae Vindobonenses*: 117- 146.

— (1986). *Nomina Propria Iranica in Nummis (Iranisches Personen-namenbuch IV)*, Vienna.

— (1987)a. "Eine neue Drachme des Vahbarz (Oborzos) aus der Persis?, *Litterae Numismaticae Vindobonenses* 3: 147-155.

— (1987b). "Die Vorbildwirkung der arsakidischen Münzprägung", *Litterae Numismaticae Vindobonenses* 3:117-146.

Alram, M. and Gyselen, R. (2003). *Sylloge Nummorum Sasanidarum Paris – Berlin – Wien, Bd. I: Ardashir I. – Shapur I*, Vienna.

Altheim-Stiehl, R. (1978). "Das früheste Datum der sasanidischen Geschichte, vermittelt durch die Zeitangabe der mittelpersisch-parthischen Inschrift aus Bīšāpūr", *AMI*, N.F. 11: 113-116.

Andreae, B. (1973). *Römische Kunst*. Freiburg im Breisgau, Basel,Vienna.

— (1994), *Praetorium Speluncae: Tiberius und Ovid in Sperlonga*, Akademie der Wissenschaften und der Literatur Mainz, Abhandlungen der Geistes- und Sozialwissenschaftlichen Klasse 12, Stuttgart.

— (1995a), "Aeneas oder Julus in Sperlonga", in: Rößler, D. and Stürmer, V. (eds.), *Est modus in rebus: Gedenkschrift für Wolfgang Schindler*, Berlin: 93-95.

— (1995b), *Praetorium Speluncae: L'antro di Tiberio a Sperlonga ed Ovidio*, Soveria Mannelli.

— (1999), *Odysseus: Mythos und Erinnerung*, Haus der Kunst München, 1.October 1999 - 9.January 2000, Mainz am Rhein.

— (2001), *Skulptur des Hellenismus: Aufnahmen Albert Hirmer und Irmgard Ernstmeier-Hirmer*, Munich.

Anthony, D. W. (1998). "The opening of the Euroasian steppe at 2000 BCE", in Mair, V.H.(ed.) *The Bronze Age and Early Iron Age People of Eastern Central Asia*, Washington D.C. and Philadelphia: 94-113.

Assar, G. R. F. (2006a). "History and coinage of Elymais during 150/149 – 122/121BC", in *Nāmeh-ye Irān-e Bāstān. The International Journal of Iranian Studies*, IV/2 (March): 27-91.

— (2006b). "A revised Parthian chronology of the period 165-91 BC", *Electrum* 11, Krakow: 88-158.

Augé, C., Curiel, R. and Le Rider, G. (1979). *Terrasses sacrée de Bard-è Néchandeh et Masjid-i Solaiman, les trouvailles monétaires*, MDAI XLIV, Paris.

Avnery, U. (1986). *My Friend, the Enemy*, London.

Bahar, Malik al-Shu'ara (ed.) *Tārikh-i Sistān*, Tehran 1314/1935.

Bailey, H. W. (1961). *Indo-Scythian Studies being Khotanese Texts Volume IV*, Cambridge.

Bakker, E. J. (1997). *Poetry in Speech. Orality and Homeric Discourse*, Ithaca and London.

Ball, W. (2000). *Rome in the East: The Transformation of an Empire*, London.

Barringer, J.M. (2004). "Scythian hunters on Attic vases", in Marconi, C. (ed.), *Greek Vases: Images, Contexts and Controversies*, Proceedings of the Conference sponsored by The Center for Ancient Mediterranean at Columbia University, 23-24 March 2002, Leiden: 13-25.

Bartholomae, C. (1904). *Altiranisches Wörterbuch*, Strassburg.

Bauer, H. (1993). "Basilica Pauli", in: M. Steinby (ed.), *Lexicon Topographicum Urbis Romae: A-C* I. Rome: 183-187.

Baumstark, R. (ed.) (1999). *Das neue Hellas: Griechen und Bayern zur Zeit Ludwigs I.*, Katalog zur Ausstellung des Bayerischen Nationalmuseums München, 9. November 1999 – 13. February 2000, Munich.

Baudy, G. (1997). "Attis", *Der Neue Pauly* 2, Stuttgart, Weimar: 247-248.

Beard, M. (1994)."The Roman and the foreign: the cult of the 'Great Mother' in Imperial Rome", in Thomas, N. and Humphrey, C. (eds.), *Shamanism, History and the State*, Ann Arbor: 164-190.

Bellinger, A.R. (1961). *Troy: The Coins*, Troy Supplementary Monograph, 2, Princeton.

Benveniste, E. (1970). "Que signifie *Vidēvdāt*?", in Boyce, M. and Gershevitch, I. (eds.), *W. B. Henning Memorial Volume*, London: 37-42.

Bernard, P., "Philostrate et Taxila" in Bernard, P., Grenet, F. and Rapin, C. (eds.), *De Bactres ... Taxila: nouvelles données de géographie historique. Topoi*, 6, fascicle 2: 457-530.

Bernoulli, J.J. (1886). *Römische Ikonographie* II.1: *Das julisch-claudische Herrscherhaus*, Berlin, Stuttgart.

Binsfeld, W. (1983). "Grabmalquader", in *Die Römer an Mosel und Saar: Zeugnisse der Römerzeit in Lothringen, in Luxemburg, im Raum Trier und im Saarland*, Ausstellung Rolandseck bei Bonn, 12. bis 28. September 1983 (second edition), Mainz am Rhein: 177 Nr. 116.

Bivar, A.D.H. (1983). "Iran under the Arsacids", *CHIr* 3 (1), *The Seleucid, Parthian and Sasanian Period* : 21-99.

— (1998). *The Personalities of Mithra in Archaeology and Literature* (Biennial Yarshater Lecture Series, 1), New York.

Bohrer, F.N. (2003). *Orientalism and Visual Culture: Imagining Mesopotamia in Nineteenth-Century Europe*, Cambridge.

BIBLIOGRAPHY

Bol, P.C., Kaminiski, G. and Maderna, C. (2004). *Fremdheit – Eigenheit: Ägypten, Griechenland und Rom, Austausch und Verständnis*, Städel-Jahrbuch, Neue Folge 19, Stuttgart.

Bopearachchi, O. (1991). *Monnaies gréco-bactriennes et indo-grecques*, Paris.

Boschung, D. (1993). *Die Bildnisse des Augustus, Das römische Herrscherbild*, I. Abteilung, Berlin.

Bourdieu, P. (1974). *Zur Soziologie der symbolischen Formen*, Frankfurt am Main (first published 1970).

Boyce, M. (1957). "The Parthians *gošan* and Iranian minstrel tradition", in *JRAS*: 10-45.

— (1975). *A History of Zoroastrianism*, I, Leiden, Cologne.

Boyce, M, and Grenet, F. (1991). *A History of Zoroastrianism III, Zoroastrianism under Macedonian and Roman Rule*, Leiden, Cologne.

Brandt, R. (1999). *Die Wirklichkeit des Bildes,* Munich.

Bremmer, J. N. (1990), "Adolescents, symposion, and pederasty", in Murray, O. (ed.), *Sympotica: A Symposium on the 'Symposion'*, Oxford: 135-148.

— (2004). "Attis: a Greek god in Anatolian Pessinous and Catullan Rome", *Mnemosyne* 57: 534-573.

Briant, P. (2002). *From Cyrus to Alexander the Great. A History of the Persian Empire*, Winona Lake.

— 2003. *Darius dans l'ombre d'Alexandre*, Paris.

— 2005. *Alexandre le Grand*, Paris.

Brockhaus, H. (1850). *Vendidad sade. Die heiligen Schriften Zoroaster's Yaçna, Vispered und Vendidad. Nach den litographierten Ausgaben von Paris und Bombay mit Index und Glossar*, Leipzig (repr. Hildesheim, New York, 1990).

Brosius, M. (2006). *The Persians: An Introduction*, London, New York.

Browne, E. G. (1900). *A Literary History of Persia*, vol. 1, London.

Burkert, W. (1992). *The Orientalizing Revolution: Near Eastern Influence on Greek Culture in the Early Archaic Age*, Cambridge, Massachusetts.

— (2003). *Die Griechen und der Orient: Von Homer bis zu den Magiern*, Munich.

Burns, T. S. (2003). *Rome and the Barbarians, 100 B.C. – A.D. 400*, Baltimore, London.

Buruma, I., Margalit, A. (2005). *Occidentalism: The West in the Eyes of Its Enemies*, New York.

Cain, P. (1993). *Männerbildnisse neronisch-flavischer Zeit*, Munich.

Callieri, P. (2003). "At the roots of the Sasanian royal imagery: the Persepolis graffiti", in Compareti, M., Raffetta, P., Scarcia, G. (eds.), *Ērān ud Anērān. Studies presented to Boris Ilich Marshak on the Occasion of His 70th Birthday (Webfestschrift)*: http://www.transoxiana.org/Eran/Articles/callieri.html.

Calmeyer, P. (1980). "Köcher. B. Archäologisch", in *Reallexikon für Assyriologie und Vorderasiatische Archäologie* VI. Berlin: 45-51.

146 THE AGE OF THE PARTHIANS

Campbell, B. (1993). "War and diplomacy: Rome and Parthia, 31 BC - AD 235", in Rich, J. and Shipley, G. (eds.), *War and Society in the Roman World*, London: 213-240.

Cantera, A. (2004). Studien zur Pahlavi-Übersetzung des Avesta, Wiesbaden.

— (forthcoming). "The Pahlavi Vīdēvdād Manuscripts of the Meherji Rana Library (Nawsari, India)".

Carrier, J. G. (1992). "Occidentalism: The world turned upside down", *American Ethnologist* 19.2: 195-212.

Carrier, J.G. *et al.* (eds.) (1995). *Occidentalism: Images of the West*, Oxford.

Casson, L. (1989). *The Periplus Maris Erythraei*, Princeton.

Castella, D. and Flutsch, L. (1990). "Sanctuaires et monuments funeraires à Avenches – en Chaplix VD", *Archäologie der Schweiz* 13: 2-30.

Chavannes, E. (1905). "Les pays d'occident d'après le *Wei-lio*", *T'oung Pao* 6: 519-571.

— (1907). "Les pays d'occident d'après le *Heou Han chou*", *T'oung Pao* 8: 149-234.

Chen, X. (1995). *Occidentalism: A Theory of Counter Discourse in Post-Mao China*. New York.

Choksy, J. K. (1989). *Purity and Pollution in Zoroastrianism: Triumph over Evil*, Austin, Texas.

Christensen, A. (1936). *L'Iran sous les Sassanides*, Copenhagen, Paris.

— (1941). *Essai sur la démonologie iranienne*, Copenhagen.

— (1943). *Le premier chapitre du Vendidad et l'histoire primitive des tribus iraniennes*, Copenhagen.

Coleman, K.M (1993). "Launching into history: aquatic displays in the early empire", *JRS* 83: 48-74.

Colledge, M.A.R. (1977). *Parthian Art*, London.

Crawford, M. (1974). *Roman Republican Coinage* 1-2, Cambridge.

Croon, J.H. (1981). "Die Ideologie des Marskultes unter dem Principat und ihre Vorgeschichte", in Temporini, H. and Hase, W. (eds.), *Aufstieg und Niedergang der römischen Welt* II: *Principat, Religion* 17.1, Berlin: 246-275.

Curtis, V.S. (1988). *The Parthian Costume: Origin and Distribution*, unpublished PhD thesis, University of London.

— (1994). More Parthian finds from ancient Elymais in southwestern Iran, *IA* 29: 201- 210, pls. I-V.

— (1998). "The Parthian costume and headdress", in Wiesehöfer, J. (ed.), *Das Partherreich und seine Zeugnisse,* Historia Einzelschriften 122, Stuttgart: 61-67.

— (2000). "Parthian culture and costume", in Curtis, J. (ed.), *Mesopotamia and Iran in the Parthian and Sasanian periods. Rejection and Revival c. 238 BC – AD 642*, London: 23 - 34.

— (2004). "Parther. Parthian Art", *RLA*: 346- 350.

— (in press). "Religious iconography on ancient Iranian coins", in Cribb, J. and Herrmann, G. (eds.), *Central Asia from Alexander to Islam*, London.

BIBLIOGRAPHY 147

— (forthcoming). "Kings of Persis: bridging the gap between Achaemenid and Sasanian Persia", in Curtis, J. *et al.* (eds.) *Proceedings of the Achaemenid Conference,* London.

Darmesteter, J. (1877). *Ormazd et Ahriman, leurs origines et leur histoire,* Paris.

— (1892-93). *Le Zend-Avesta,* 3 vols., Paris (reprinted Paris, 1960).

— (1895). *The Zend-Avesta,* The Sacred Books of the East, vol. 4, (second edition), Oxford.

Dawid, M. (2003). *Die Elfenbeinplastiken aus dem Hanghaus 2 in Ephesos: Räume SR 18 und SR 28,* Forschungen in Ephesos VIII/5, Österreichisches Archäologisches Institut in Wien,Vienna.

De Jong, A. (2005). "The contribution of the magi", in Curtis, V. S. and Stewart, S. (eds.), *Birth of the Persian Empire,* London, New York: 85-99.

Dench, E. (2005). *Romulus' Asylum: Roman Identities from the Age of Alexander to the Age of Hadrian,* Oxford.

Dhabhar, B. N. (ed.) (1932). *The Persian Rivayats of Hormazyar Framarz and Others. Their Versions with Introduction and Notes,* Bombay.

Dihle, A. (1994). *Die Griechen und die Fremden,* Munich.

Doerner, F.K. and Goell, T. (1963). *Arsameia am Nymphaios. Die Ausgrabungen im Hierothesion des Mithradates,* Berlin.

Dräger, O. (1994). *Religionem significare: Studien zu reich verzierten römischen Altären und Basen aus Marmor,* Mitteilungen des Deutschen Archäologischen Instituts, Römische Abteilung, 33, Ergänzungsheft, Mainz am Rhein.

Drijvers, J. W. (1998). „Strabo on Parthia and Parthians", in Wiesehöfer, J. (ed.), *Das Partherreich und seine Zeugnisse,* Historia Einzelschriften 122, Stuttgart: 279-293.

Duchesne-Guillemin, J. (1962). *La religion de l'Iran ancien,* Paris.

Dubs, H. H. (1955). *The History of the Former Han Dynasty by Pan Ku,* Ithaca, New York.

Dwyer, E. J. (1982). *Pompeian Domestic Sculpture: A Study of Five Pompeian Houses and their Contents,* Rome.

Eddy, S. K. (1961). *The King is Dead. Studies in Near Eastern Resistance to Hellenism (334-31 BCE),* Lincoln.

Eicher, J. B. (ed.) (1995). *Dress and Ethnicity: Change Across Space and Time,* Berg Ethnicity and Identity Series, Oxford.

Eliade, M. (1991). *The Myth of the Eternal Return. Or, Cosmos and History,* Princeton (French orig. *Le Mythe de l'éternel retour: archétypes et répétition,* Paris, 1969).

Erim, K. T. (1989). *Aphrodisias: Ein Führer durch die antike Stadt und das Museum,* Istanbul.

Errington, E. and Cribb, J. (1992). *The Crossroads of Asia: Transformation in Image and Symbol in the Art of Ancient Afghanistan and Pakistan,* Cambridge.

148 THE AGE OF THE PARTHIANS

Erskine, A. (2001). *Troy between Greece and Rome: Local Tradition and Imperial Power*, Oxford.

Ferris, M.I. (2000). *Enemies of Rome: Barbarians through Roman Eyes*, Stroud.

Fisch, J. (1984). "Der märchenhafte Orient: Die Umwertung einer Tradition von Marco Polo bis Macaulay", *Saeculum: Jahrbuch für Universalgeschichte* 35: 246-266.

Flaig, E. (2003). *Ritualisierte Politik: Zeichen, Gesten und Herrschaft im Alten Rom*, Historische Semantik 1, Göttingen.

Flügel, J. C. (1930). *The Psychology of Clothes*, London.

Frayne, M. (1998).*Copenhagen*. London.

Fuller, M. and Bivar, A. D .H. (1996). "Parthian ostraca from the Syrian Jazira" *Bulletin of the Asia Institute* (Studies in Honor of Vladimir A. Livshits) 10: 25-31.

Galinsky, A. (1992). "Venus, Polysemy, and the Ara Pacis Augustae", *AJA* 96: 457-475.

Geldner, K. F. (1886-95). *Avesta the Sacred Book of the Parsis*, 3 vols., Stuttgart.

Gershevitch, I. (1968). "Old Iranian literature", in *Handbuch der Orientalistik* I/IV, 2/1, *Literatur*: 1-30.

Ghini, G, (1994). "Il mitreo di Marino: considerazioni sul culto e sull'iconografia", in Devoti, L. (ed.), *Il Mitreo di Marino*, Marino: 51-84.

Ghirshman, R. (1962). *Iran. Parthes et Sassanides*, Paris.

— (1974). "Un tetradrachm d'Andragoras de la collection de M. Foroughi", in Kouymijan, D. K. (ed.), *Near Eastern Numismatics, Iconography, Epigraphy and History, Studies in Honor of George C. Miles*, Beirut: 1-8.

— (1976). Terrasses sacrées de Bard-è Néchandeh et Masjid-i Solaiman, MDAI XLV, Leiden.

Giard, J.B. (1998). *Le Grand Camée de France*, Paris.

Giuliani, L. (2003). *Bild und Mythos: Geschichte der Bilderzählung in der griechischen Kunst*, Munich.

— (2004). *Leggere un'immagine: Il Grand Camée de France e la successione di Tiberio*, Paper at the Dipartimento di discipline storiche dell'Università di Bologna, 27th September 2004, see: http://www.storicamente.org/ 01_fonti/ immagini/giuliani.htm.

Gnoli, G. (1980). *Zoroaster's Time and Homeland*, Naples.

— (1987). "Avestan Geography", in *EncIr* III/1: 44-47.

Göbl, R. (1978). *Antike Numismatik* 1-2, Munich.

GoGwilt, C. (1995a). *The Invention of the West: Joseph Conrad and the Double Mapping of Europe and Empire*, Stanford.

— (1995b), "True West: The Changing Idea of the West from 1880s to the 1920s", in Federici, S. (ed.), *Enduring Western Civilization: The Construction of the Concept of Western Civilization and its "Others"*, Connecticut, London: 37-62.

BIBLIOGRAPHY

Gordon, R. (2000). "Mithras", *Der Neue Pauly* 8, Stuttgart, Weimar: 287-291.
— (2001). "Ritual and hierarchy in the mysteries of Mithras, *ARYS, Antigüedad: Religiones y Sociedades* 4 : 245-274.
Graillot, H. (1912). *Le culte de Cybèle mère des dieux à Rome et dans l'empire romaine*, Bibliothèque des Écoles françaises d'Athènes et de Rome, 107, Paris.
Grassinger, D. (1999). *Die mythologischen Sarkophage,* 1. Teil: *Achill – Adonis – Aeneas – Aktaion – Alkestis – Amazonen*, Die antiken Sarkophagreliefs 12.1, Berlin.
Grenet, F. (2003). "Note additionelle", in de la Vaissière E. and Pénélope Riboud, D. "Les livres des Sogdiens", *St Ir* 32: 127-136.
— (2004). "Zoroastrian scenes on a newly discovered Sogdian tomb in Xi'an, northern China", *St Ir* 33: 273-284.
— (2005). "An archaeologist's approach to Avestan geography", in Curtis, V. S. and Stewart, S. (eds.), *Birth of the Persian Empire*, London, New York: 29-51.
Grenet, F and Bopearachchi, O. (1996). "Une monnaie en or du souverain indoparthe Abdagases II", *St Ir* 25, 2: 219-231.
— (1999), " Une nouvelle monnaie en or d'Abdagases II", *St Ir* 28, 1:73-82.
Gruen, E.S. (1992). *Culture and National Identity in Republican Rome*, Cornell Studies in Classical Philology, 52, Ithaca.
Grummond, N.T. De and Ridgway, B.S. (2000). *From Pergamon to Sperlonga: Sculpture and Context*, Berkeley, Los Angeles.
Hall, E. (1988). "When did the Trojans turn into Phrygians? Alcaeus 42.15", *Zeitschrift für Papyrologie und Epigraphik* 73: 15-18.
— (1989), *Inventing the Barbarian: Greek Self-Definition through Trage-dy*, Oxford.
Hansman, J. (1992). "Characene and Charax", *EncIr* V: 363-365.
Hartog, F. (1980). *Le miroir d'Hérodote: essai sur la représentation de l'autre*, Paris.
Haselberger, L. *et. al.* (2002). *Mapping Augustan Rome*, Journal of Roman Archaeology, Supplementary Series 50, Portsmouth, Rhode Island.
Haselberger, L. and Humphrey, J. (eds.) (2006). *Imaging Ancient Rome: Documentation – Vizualization – Imagination,* Proceedings of the Third Williams Symposium on Classical Architecture held at the American Academy in Rome, the British School at Rome, and the Deutsches Archäologisches Institut, Rom, on May 20-23, 2004, Journal of Roman Archaeology, Supplementary Series 61. Portsmouth, Rhode Island.
Haug, M. (1890). *The Sacred Language, Writings, and Religion of the Parsis*, (third edition, edited and enlarged by E.W. West), London.
Hauser, S.R. (2001). "Orientalismus", *Der Neue Pauly*, vol. 15,1, Stuttgart Weimar: 1233-1243.

150 THE AGE OF THE PARTHIANS

Heitz, C. (2003). *Nördliche 'Barbaren' in der römischen Bildkunst: die Guten, die Bösen und die Häßlichen*, unpublished Ph.D.thesis, Seminar für Klassische Archäologie, Institut für Altertumswissenschaften, Ruprecht-Karls-Universität Heidelberg.

Henning, W. B. (1943). "An Astronomical Chapter of the Bundahishn", *JRAS*: 229-48.

— (1951). *Zoroaster. Politician or Witch-Doctor?* Ratanbai Katrak Lectures, London.

Hentsch, T. (1988). *L'orient imaginaire: la vision politique occidentale de l'est méditerranéen*, Paris.

Herrmann, G.(1977). *The Iranian Revival*, Oxford.

Hertel, D. (2003). *Die Mauern von Troia: Mythos und Geschichte im antiken Ilion*, Munich.

Herzfeld, E. (1941) *Iran in the Ancient East*, Oxford.

Hill, G. (1922). British *Museum Catalogue of Greek Coins of Arabia, Mesopotamia and Persia,* London.

Hill, J. (2003). *The Western Regions according to the Hou Hanshu,* available on the Silk Road Seattle website: http://depts.washington.edu/uwch/silkroad/texts/hhshu.

Hintze, A. (2000). "Zur Überlieferung der ältesten Zeugnisse indoiranischer Sprachen", in Yoko Nishina (ed.), *Europa et Asia polyglotta. Sprachen und Kulturen. Festschrift für Robert Schmitt-Brandt zum 70. Geburtstag*, ed. Dettelbach, 2000: 67-85.

Hinz, W. (1973). *Neue Wege im Altpersischen*, Wiesbaden.

— (1974). "Tiara", in *Paulys Realencyclopädie der Classischen Altertumswissenschaft*, Supplementband XIV, Munich: 786-796.

Hirth, F. (1885). *China and Roman Orient: Research into their Ancient and Medieval Relations as Presented in Old Chinese Records*, Leipzig and Shanghai.

— (1917). "The story of Chang K'ien, China's pioneer in Western Asia", *Journal of the American Oriental Society* 37: 89-152.

Hoffmann, H. (1972). "Freund/Feind", in J. Ritter (ed.), *Historisches Wörterbuch der Philosophie* 2, Darmstadt: 1104-1105.

Hölkeskamp, K. J. (2004)."Römische *gentes* und griechische Genealogien", in id., *SENATVS POPVLVSQVE ROMANVS: Die politische Kultur der Republik – Dimensionen und Deutungen*, Stuttgart: 199-217. First published in Vogt-Spira, G. and / Rommel, B. (eds.), *Rezeption und Identität: Die kulturelle Auseinandersetzung Roms mit Griechenland als europäisches Paradigma*. Stuttgart: 3-21.

— (2007). "Hierarchie und Konsens: 'Pompae' in der politis-chen Kultur der römischen Republik", in. A.H. Arweiler (ed.), *Machtfra-gen: Zur kulturellen Repräsentation und Konstruktion von Macht*, Interdis-ziplinäres Kolloquium in Kiel, 3.-5. November 2005, aus Anlaß des 65. Geburtstages von Konrad Heldmann, Stuttgart.

BIBLIOGRAPHY

Hölscher, T. (1988). "Beobachtungen zu römischen historischen Denkmälern III", in *AA*: 523-541.

Houghton, A. and Lorber, C. (2002): *Seleucid Coins. A Comprehensive Catalogue. Seleucus I through Antiochus III*, Lancaster, P.A., New York.

Howard-Johnston, J. (1995) "The Two Great Powers in Late Antiquity: a Comparison", in Cameron, A. (ed.), *The Byzantine and Early Islamic Near East* 3: *States, Resources and Armies*, Princeton, N.J: 157-226.

Hulsewe, A.F.P. (1979). *China in Central Asia: The Early Stage 125 B.C. – A.D. 23: An Annotated Translation of Chapters 61 and 96 of the History of the Former Han Dynasty*, Leiden.

Humann, K. and Puchstein, O. (1890). *Reise in Kleinasien und Nord- Syrien*, Berlin.

Huyse, Ph. (1999). *Die dreisprachige Inschrift Šābuhrs I. an der Ka'ba-i Zardušt (ŠKZ)* (CII, pt. III, vol. 1, texts I), vol. 1-2, London.

Insler, S. (1975). *The Gāthās of Zarathustra*, Tehran, Liège.

Invernizzi, A. (2001a). "Die Kunst der Partherzeit", in Seipel, W. (ed.), *7000 Jahre persische Kunst: Meisterwerke aus dem Iranischen Nationalmuseum in Teheran*, Milan.

— (2001b). "Arsacid Dynastic Art", *Parthica* 3: 133- 157, pls. I- IV.

Itgenshorst, T. (2005). *Tota illa pompa: Der Triumph in der römischen Republik*, Hypomnemata 161, Göttingen.

Ivanchik, A.I. (2005). "Who were the 'Scythians' archers on archaic Attic vases? ", in Braund, D. (ed.), *Scythians and Greeks: Cultural Interactions in Scythia, Athens and the Early Roman Empire (sixth century BCE – first century AD)*, Exeter: 100-113.

Jamasp, H. (1907). *Vendidâd. Avesta Text with Pahlavi Translation and Commentary and Glossarial Index*, 2 vols., Bombay.

Jenkins, G. K. (1955). "Indo-Scythic mints", *Journal of the Numismatic Society of India* 17.

Jones, W. (1771). *Lettre à Monsieur A du P, dans laquelle est compris l'examen de sa traduction des Livres attribués à Zoroastre*, London (repr. in *The Works of Sir William Jones*, London 1799, IV: 583-613).

Jucker, H. (1976). "Der große Pariser Kameo: Eine Huldigung an Agrippina, Claudius und Nero", *Jahrbuch des Deutschen Archäologischen Instituts* 91: 211-250.

Kähler, H. (1959). *Die Augustusstatue von Primaporta*, Cologne.

Keall, E.J. (1974). "Some thoughts on the early eyvan".in Kouymjian, D.K. (ed.), *Near Eastern Numismatics, Iconography, Epigraphy and History, Studies in Honor of George C. Miles*, Beirut: 123-130.

— (1977). "Political, Ecomomic and Social Factors in the Parthian Landscape of Mesopotamia and western Iran: evidence from two case studies", in Levine, L. D. and Young, T. C., Jr. (eds.) *Mountains and Lowlands: Essays in the Archaeology of Greater Mesopotamia*, Malibu: 81-89.

Kellens, J. (1974). *Les noms-racines de l'Avesta*, Wiesbaden.

— (1984). *Le verbe avestique*, Wiesbaden.

152   THE AGE OF THE PARTHIANS

— (1995). "L'âme entre le cadavre et le paradis", *JA* 283: 19-56.

— (1998). "Considérations sur l'histoire de l'Avesta", *JA* 286: 451-519.

— (1997-1998). "De la naissance des montagnes à la fin du temps: le Yašt 19. Résumé des cours et travaux de la chaire de langues et religions indo-iraniennes", *Annuaire du Collège de France 1997-1998*: 737-65.

— (1998-99). "Langues et religions indo-iraniennes," *Annuaire du Collège de France 1998-1999*: 685-705.

— (1999-2000). "Langues et religions indo-iraniennes", *Annuaire du Collège de France 1999-2000*: 721-51.

— (2000). "L'ellipse du temps", in Hintze, A. and Tichy, E. (eds.), *Anusantatyai. Festschrift für Johanna Narten zum 70. Geburtstag*, Dettelbach, 127-31.

— (2002-2003). "Langues et religions indo-iraniennes", *Annuaire du Collège de France 2002-2003*: 815-45.

Kempter, G. (1980). *Ganymed: Studien zur Typologie, Ikonographie und Ikonologie*, Dissertationen zur Kunstgeschichte 12. Cologne, Vienna.

Kent, R.G. (1953). *Old Persian Grammar. Texts, Lexicon*, second rev. edition, New Haven, Connecticut.

Kettenhofen, E. 1995b. "Die Chronik von Arbela in der Sicht der Althistorie", in Criscuolo, L., Geraci, G., Salvaterra, C. (eds.), *Simblos. Scritti di storia antica*, Bologna, 287-319.

Kienlin, T.L. and Schweizer, B. (2002). "Der Orient als Gegenbild Europas: zur Konstruktion kultureller Einheiten", in Aslan, R., Blum, S, Kastl , G., Schweizer, F. and Thumm, D. (eds.), *Mauerschau: Festschrift für Manfred Korfmann* 1, Remshalden-Grunbach: 191-220.

Kockel, V. (1995). "Forum Augustum", in Steinby, M. (ed.), *Lexicon Topographicum Urbis Romae: D-G* II, Rome: 289-295.

Konow, S. (1929). *Kharoshthī inscriptions with the exception of those of Aśoka*, Calcutta.

Koselleck, R. (1975). "Zur historisch-politischen Semantik asymmetrischer Gegenbegriffe", in Weinreich, H. (ed.), *Positionen der Negativität, Poetik und Hermenutik* 6 Munich: 65-104 (re-published in Koselleck, R., *Vergangene Zukunft: Zur Semantik geschichtlicher Zeiten*, Frankfurt, 1989: 211-259.

Koshelenko, G. A. and Pilipko, V. N. (1994). "Parthia", in J. Harmatta (ed.), *History of Civilizations of Central Asia, vol. 2: The Development of Sedentary and Nomadic Civilizations: 700 B. C. to A. D. 250*, Paris: 131-150.

Kränzle, P. (1994). "Der Fries der Basilica Aemilia", in Borbein, A. H. (ed.), *Antike Plastik* 23, Munich: 93-130.

Krierer, K.R. (2004). *Antike Germanenbilder*, Österreichische Akademie der Wissenschaften, Philosophisch-Historische Klasse 318, Vienna.

Krumeich, R. (2001). "Dokumente orientalischen Selbstbewusstseins in Rom: Die Weihreliefs des Iuppiter Dolichenus-Priesters parthischer Herkunft M. Ulpius Chresimus", *Bonner Jahrbücher* 201: 69-92.

BIBLIOGRAPHY

Kunze, C. (1996). "Zur Datierung des Laokoon und der Skyllagruppe aus Sperlonga", *Jahrbuch des deutschen Archäologischen Instituts* 111: 139-223.

Kurz, I. (2000). *Vom Umgang mit dem Anderen: Die Orientalismus-Debatte zwischen Alteritätsdiskurs und interkultureller Kommunikation*, Bibliotheca Academica 5, Würzburg.

Kuttner, A.L. (1999). "Hellenistic images of spectacle, from Alexander to Augustus", in Bergmann, B. and Kondoleon, C. (eds.), *The Art of Ancient Spectacle*, New Haven: 96-123.

Kuzmina, E. E. (1998). "Cultural connections of the Tarim Basin people and pastoralists of the Asian Steppes in the Bronze Age", in Mair, V. H. (ed.) *The Bronze Age and Early Iron Age People of Eastern Central Asia*, Washington D. C., Philadephia: 63-93.

Lancellotti, M. G. (2002). *Attis: Between Myth and History, King, Priest and God*, Leiden.

Landskron, A. (2003). "Ein tanzender Orientale in Tarragona", *Jahreshefte des Österreichischen Archäologischen Instituts in Wien* 27: 141-148.

Landskron, A. (2005). *Parther und Sasaniden: Das Bild der Orientalen in der römischen Kaiserzeit*, Wiener Forschungen zur Archäologie 7, Vienna.

Landwehr, C. (2000). *Die römischen Skulpturen von Caesarea Mauretaniae II, Idealplastik: Männliche Figuren*, Mainz am Rhein.

La Rocca, E. (1992)."'Disiecta membra Neroniana': L'arco partico di Nerone sul Campidoglio", in Froning, H., Hölscher, T. and Mielsch, H. (eds.), *Kotinos: Festschrift für Erika Simon*, Mainz am Rhein: 400-414.

La Rocca, E, (2001). "La nuova immagine dei fori Imperiali", in *Mitteilungen des Deutschen Archäologischen Instituts, Römische Abteilung* 108: 171-213.

Laufer, B. (1919). *Sino-Iranica: Chinese Contribution to the History of Civilization in Ancient Iran,* Chicago.

Loewe, M. A. N. (1979). "Introduction", in Hulsewe, A. F. P. *China in Central Asia: The Early Stage 125 B.C. – A.D. 23: An Annotated Translation of Chapters 61 and 96 of the History of the Former Han dynasty*, Leiden: 1-70.

MacDowall, D. W.(1965). "The Dynasty of the later Indo-Parthians", *NC*: 137-148.

Mackenzie, J. (1995). *Orientalism: History, Theory and the Arts*. Manchester, New York.

Malitz, J. (1984). "Caesars Partherkrieg", *Historia* 23: 21-59.

Marshall, J. *Taxila,* (1951). 3 vols., Cambridge.

Mathiesen, H. E. (1992). *Sculpture in the Parthian Empire: A Study in Chronology*, Aarhus.

Mattern, S. P. (1999). *Rome and the Enemy: Imperial Strategy in the Principate*, Berkeley, Los Angeles, London.

Mavrogiannis, T. (2003). *Aeneas und Euander: Mythische Vergangenheit und Politik im Rom vom 6. Jh. v. Chr. bis zur Zeit des Augustus*, Naples.

154 THE AGE OF THE PARTHIANS

Mayrhofer, M. (1986-2001). *Etymologisches Wörterbuch des Altindoarischen*, 3 vols., Heidelberg.

Megow, W. R. (1987). *Kameen von Augustus bis Alexander Severus*, Antike Münzen und geschnittene Steine 11, Berlin.

Mehrkiyan, J. (1381/2003). "Negār-kand-e elīmayi algi", in *Nāmeh-ye pazhūheshgāh-e mirās-e farhangī*, 1, winter 1381/2003: 81-86 (English summary: 11).

Meier, H. (1994). *Die Lehre Carl Schmitts: Vier Kapitel zur Unterscheidung Politischer Theologie und Politischer Philosophie*, Stuttgart.

Messina, V. (2003). "More Gentis Parthicae. Ritratti barbutti di Demetrio II sulle impronte di sigillo da Seleuci al Tigri, *Parthica* 5: 21-36.

Meyer, H. (2000). *Prunkkameen und Staatsdenkmäler römischer Kaiser: Neue Perspektiven zur Kunst der frühen Prinzipatszeit*, Munich.

Mielsch, H. (2001). *Römische Wandmalerei*, Darmstadt.

Millar, F. (1993). *The Roman Near East: 31 B.C – A.D. 337*, Cambridge, Mass.

Miller, M.C. (1997). *Athens and Persia in the Fifth Century BCE: A Study in Cultural Receptivity*, Cambridge.

Molé, M. (1963). *Culte, mythe et cosmologie dans l'Iran ancien*, Paris.

Momigliano, A. (1975). *Alien Wisdom*, Cambridge.

Mørkholm, O. (1991). *Early Hellenistic Coinage*, Cambridge, New York.

Moulton, J. H. (1913). *Early Zoroastrianism: Lectures delivered at Oxford and in London, February to May 1912*, London.

— (1917). *The Treasure of the Magi: A study of modern Zoroastrianism*, London, New York.

Murken, J, *et al.* (1995). *König-Otto-von-Griechenland-Museum der Gemeinde von Ottobrunn*, Bayerische Museen 22, Munich.

Nagy, G. (1996). *Poetry as Performance. Homer and Beyond*, Cambridge.

Nedergaard, E. (1988). "The four sons of Phraates IV in Rome", in Fischer-Hansen, T. (ed.), *East and West: Cultural Relations in the Ancient World*, Danish Studies in Classical Archaeology: Acta Hyperborea 1, Copenhagen: 102-115.

Neudecker, R. (1988). *Die Skulpturenausstattung römischer Villen in Italien*, Beiträge zur Erschließung hellenistischer und kaiserzeitlicher Skulptur und Architektur 9, Mainz am Rhein.

Nikitin, A. K. (1994). "Coins of the last Indo-Parthian King of Sakastan (A farewell to Ardamitra) ", *South Asian Studies* 10: 67-9.

Nochlin, L. (2002). "The Imaginary Orient", in Pinder, K. N (ed.), *Race-ing Art History: Critical Readings in Race and Art History*, New York, London: 69-85.

Nöldeke, Th. (1878). *Geschichte der Perser und Araber zur Zeit der Sasaniden*, Leiden.

Noy, D. (2000). *Foreigners at Rome: Citizens and Strangers*, London.

Nyberg, H. S. (1937). *Irans forntidiga religioner*, Stockholm.

BIBLIOGRAPHY

155

Östenberg, I. (1999). "Demonstrating the conquest of the world: the procession of peoples and rvers on the shield of Aeneas and the triple triumph of Octavian in 29 B.C. (Aen. 8.722-728)", in *Opuscula Romana: Annual of the Swedish Institute in Rome* 24: 155-162.

— (2003). *Staging the World: Rome and the Other in the Triumphal Procession*, Lund.

Osterhammel, J. (1998). *Die Entzauberung Asiens: Europa und die asiatischen Reiche im 18. Jahrhundert*, Munich.

Palaver, W. (1997). *Die mythischen Quellen des Politischen: Carl Schmitts Freind-Feind-Theorie*, Beiträge zur Friedensethik 27, Stuttgart, Berlin, Cologne.

Panaino, A. (2003). "The bayān of the Fratarakas: gods or 'Divine'Kings?", in Cereti, C.G., Maggi, M. and Provasi, E. (eds.), *Religious Themes and Texts of Pre-Islamic Iran and Central Asia. Studies in Honour of Prof. Gherardo Gnoli on the Occasion of His 65th Birthday on 6th December 2002* (Beiträge zur Iranistik, 24), Wiesbaden: 265-288.

Pani, M. (1975). "Troia resurgens: Mito troiano e ideologia del principato", in *Annali della Facoltà di lettere e filosofia, Università degli studi, Bari* 18: 63-85.

Papantoniou, I. (1996). *Greek Regional Costumes*, Nafplion.

Paratore, E. (1966). "La Persia nella letteratura latina", in. *La Persia e il mondo greco-romano: Atti del covegno, Roma 11-14 aprile 1965*, Accademia Nazionale dei Lincei, Quaderno 76, Rome: 505-558.

Pensabene, P. (1982). "Nuove indagini nell'area del tempo di Cibile sul Palatino", in Bianchi, U., Vermaseren, M. J. (eds.). *La soteriologia dei culti orientali nell'impero romano: Atti del Colloquio Internazionale su La Soteriologia dei culti orientali nell'Impero Romano, Roma 24-28 Settembre 1979*, Leiden: 68-108.

Pensabene, P. (1996). "Magna Mater, Aedes", in Steinby, M. (ed.), *Lexicon Topographicum Urbis Romae: H-O* III, Rome: 206-208.

Philostratus, Life of Apollonius of Tyana, 2, 17.

Plutarch, Crassus.

Pompeius Trogus Fragmenta, Seel, O. (ed.) Leipzig (1956). Prologue 42, p. 180.

Price, M.J. (1991). *The Coinage in the Name of Alexander the Great and Philip Arrhidaeus*, 2 vols., Zurich, London.

Pugliesi Carratelli, G. (ed.) (1991). *Pompei: Pitture e Mosaici* III, Rome.

— (ed.) (1997). *Pompei: Pitture e Mosaici* VII, Rome.

Pulleyblank G. E. (1991). *Lexicon of Reconstructed Pronunciation in Early Middle Chinese, Late Middle Chinese, and Early Mandarin*, Vancouver.

Raeck, W. (1981). *Zum Barbarenbild in der Kunst Athens im 6. und 5. Jahrhundert v. Chr.*, Habelts Dissertationsdrucke, Reihe Klassische Archäologie 14, Bonn.

Rich, J.W. (1998). "Augustus's Parthian honours, the Temple of Mars Ultor, and the arch in the Forum Romanum", in *Papers of the British School at Rome* 66: 71-128.

Robert, L. (1960). "Inscription héllénistique d'Iran", *Hellenica* 11-12: 85-91.

Roller, L. E. (1998). "The ideology of the Eunuch priest", in Wyke, M. (ed.), *Gender and the Body in the Ancient Mediterranean*, Oxford: 118-135.

— (1999). *In Search of God the Mother: The Cult of Anatolian Cybele*, Berkeley.

Rose, C. B. (1990). "'Princes' and Barbarians on the Ara Pacis", *AJA* 94: 453-467.

— (2002a). "Bilingual Trojan iconography", in Aslan, R., Blum, S., Kastl, G., Schweizer, F. and Thumm, D. (eds.), *Mauerschau: Festschrift für Manfred Korfmann* 1, Remshalden-Grunbach: 329-350.

— (2002b). "Ilion in the early empire", in Berns, C., von Hesberg, H., Vandeput, L. and Waelkens, M. (eds.), *Patris und Imperium: Kulturelle und politische Identität in den Städten der römischen Provinzen Kleinasiens in der frühen Kaiserzeit,* Kolloquium Köln, November 1998, Bulletin antieke beschaving, Supplement 8. Leuven , Paris, Dudley MA: 33-47.

— (2005). "The Parthians in Augustan Rome", *AJA* 109: 21-75.

Rosenfield, J. M. (1967). *The Dynastic Art of the Kushans*, Berkeley, Los Angeles.

Rostovtzeff, M. (1935). *Iranians and Greeks in South Russia*, Oxford.

— (1935). "Dura and the problem of Parthian art", Yale classical Studies V, New Haven: 157-304.

Rougemont, G. (1999. "Inscriptions grecques d'Iran", *Empires perses d'Alexandre aux Sassanides* (Dossiers d'Archéologie, 243), Dijon: 6-7.

Safar, F. and Mustafa, M.A. (1974). *Hatra, the City of the Sun God*, Baghdad.

Said, E. W. (1995), *Orientalism: Western Conceptions of the Orient*, second edition. London (first edition published 1978).

Salles, J.-F. (1987), "The Arab-Persian Gulf under the Seleucids", in Kuhrt, A. and Sherwin-White, S. (eds.), *Hellenism in the East*, London: 75-109.

Sardar, Z. (1999). *Orientalism*, Buckingham.

Schäfer, T. (1989). *Imperii Insignia: Sella Curulis und Fasces, Zur Repräsentation römischer Magistrate*, Mitteilungen des Deutschen Archäologischen Instituts, Römische Abteilung, 29, Ergänzungsheft, Mainz am Rhein.

— (1998), *Spolia et signa: Baupolitik und Reichskultur nach dem Panthererfolg des Augustus*, Nachrichten der Akademie der Wissenschaften in Göttingen, I. Philologisch-Historische Klasse 2, Göttingen.

Scheer, T. (1997). "Darnaidai", in *Der Neue Pauly* 3, Stuttgart, Weimar: 318-319.

Schmitt, R. (1990). "Der Name Hyspasines (samt Varianten)" , *Bulletin of the Asia Institute* 4: 245- 249.

BIBLIOGRAPHY 157

— (1998). "Parthische Sprach und Nebenüberlieferungen aus arsakidi-scher Zeit", in Wiesehöfer, J. (ed.), *Das Partherreich und seine Zeugnisse*, Beiträge des internationalen Colloquiums, Eutin 27.-30. Juni 1996, Historia Einzelschriften 122, Stuttgar: 163-204.

Schneider, R.M. (1986). *Bunte Barbaren, Orientalenstatuen aus farbigem Marmor in der römischen Repräsentationskunst*, Worms.

— (1992a). "Barbar II (ikonographisch)", *Reallexikon für Antike und Christentum*, Supplement I, Stuttgart: 895-962.

— (1992b). "Orientalische Tischdiener als römische Tischfüsse", *AA*: 295-305.

— (1997), "Roma Aeterna – Aurea Roma: Der Himmelsglobus als Zeitzeichen und Machtsymbol", in Assmann, J. and Hess-Lüttich, E. W. B. (eds.), *Kult, Kalender und Geschichte. Semiotisierung von Zeit als kulturelle Konstruktion*, Special Issue of Kodikas/Code, an International Journal of Semiotics 20.1-2, Tübingen: 103-133.

— (1998). "Die Faszination des Feindes: Bilder der Parther und des Orients in Rom", in Wiesehöfer, J. (ed.), *Das Partherreich und seine Zeugnisse,* Beiträge des internationalen Colloquiums, Eutin 27.-30. Juni 1996, Historia Einzelschriften 122. Stuttgart: 95-146.

— (1999), "Marmor", *Der Neue Pauly* 7, Stuttgart, Weimar: 928-938.

— (2001). "Coloured marble: the splendour and power of imperial Rome", *Apollo. The International Magazine of the Arts* (July): 3-10.

— (2002). "Nuove immagini del potere romano: sculture in marmo colorato nell'impero romano", in De Nuccio, M. and Ungaro, L. (eds.), *I marmi colorati della Roma imperiale: Roma, Mercati di Traiano, 28 settembre 2002 – 19 gennaio 2003*, Venice: 82-105.

— (2006). "Orientalism in late antiquity: the oriental in Imperial and Christian imagery" in Huyse, P. and Wiesehöfer, J. (eds.), *Ērān ud Anērān: Beiträge des Internationalen Colloquiums, Eutin 7.– 9. Juni 2000*, (Oriens et Occidens, 13), Stuttgart: 241-278.

Scholz, R. O. R. (2000). "Bild", in Barck, K., Fontinus, M., Schlenstedt, D., Steinwachs, B. and Wolfzettel, F. (eds.), *Ästhetische Grundbegriffe* 1. Stuttgart, Weimar: 618-669.

Scholz, U.W. (1970), *Studien zum altitalischen und altrömischen Marskult und Marsmythos*, Bibliothek der klassischen Altertumswissenschaften, Neue Folge, 2, Reihe 35, Heidelberg.

Schuol, M. (1998). "Die Zeugnisse zur Geschichte und Kultur der parthischen Charakene", in J. Wiesehöfer (ed.), *Das Partherreich und seine Zeugnisse*, Historia Einzelschriften 122, Stuttgart: 407-415.

— (2000). *Die Charakene. Ein mesopotamisches Königreich in hellenistisch-parthischer Zeit* (Oriens et Occidens, 1), Stuttgart.

Schwarzenberg, E. (2001-2), "Ganymède", in *Hephaistos. Kritische Zeitschrift zu Theorie und Praxis der Archäologie und angrenzender Gebiete* 19-20: 159-201.

Seiterle, G. (1985). "Die Urform der phrygischen Mütze", in *Antike Welt. Zeitschrift für Archäologie und Kulturgeschichte* 16, no. 3: 2-13.

158 THE AGE OF THE PARTHIANS

Sellwood, D. (1980). *An Introduction to the Coinage of Parthia*, London.
— (1983). "Minor states in southern Iran", *CHIr* 3(1), Cambridge, London, New Yorke, Sidney and Melbourne: 299 – 321.
Shahbazi, A.S. (1987). "Arsacids. I. Origin". *EnIr.* II: 525.
— (1991). *Ferdowsi: a Critical Biography*, Costa Mesa, California.
Shayegan, R. (forthcoming). *The Antecendents of Early Sasanian Political Ideology*.
Shichiji Y. (ed.) (1991). "Orientalismus, Exotismus, koloniale Diskurse", in Iwasaki, E. (ed.), *Begegnung mit dem , Fremden': Grenzen - Traditionen – Vergleiche*, Akten des VIII. internationalen Germanisten-Kongresses, Tokyo 1990, Munich: 253-502.
Sichtermann, H. (1988). "Ganymedes", in *Lexicon Iconographicum Mythologicae Classicae* IV, Zurich, Munich: 154-169.
Sievernich, G. and Budde, H. (eds.) (1989). *Europa und der Orient: 800-1900, Berliner Festspiele, 4. Festivals der Weltkulturen Horizonte '89 im Martin-Gropius-Bau Berlin*, Gütersloh, Munich.
Simon, E. (1967). *Ara Pacis Augustae*, Tübingen.
— (1990). *Die Götter der Römer*, Munich.
— (2001). "Rom und Troia: Der Mythos von den Anfängen bis in die römische Kaiserzeit", in Korfmann, M. (ed.), *Troia – Traum und Wirklichkeit: Begleitband zur Ausstellung, 17. März bis 17. Juni 2001*, Stuttgart, Archäologisches Landesmuseum Baden-Württemberg: 154-173.
Simpson, St. J. (2003). "From Mesopotomia to Merv: reconstructing patterns of consumption in Sasanian household", in Potts, T., Roaf, M. D. and Stein, D. (eds.). Culture though Objects: Ancient Near Easern Studies in Honour of P. R. S. Moorey, Oxford: 347-375.
Skjærvø, P. O. (1994). "Hymnic Composition in the Avesta", *Die Sprache* 36: 199-243.
— (1997). "Avestica II. Yokes and spades and remnants of the 'Tripartite Ideology'", *MSS* 57: 115-128.
— (1999). "Avestan quotations in Old Persian?" in Shaked, S. and Netzer, A. (eds.), *Irano-Judaica* IV, Jerusalem: 1-64.
— (2003). "Zarathustra: first poet-sacrificer", in Adhami, S. (ed.), *Paitimāna. Essays in Iranian, Indian, and Indo-European Studies in Honor of Hanns-Peter Schmidt*, vols. I-II in one, Costa Mesa: 157-94.
— (2003-2004). "The antiquity of Old Avestan", *Nāme-ye Irān-e Bāstān. The International Journal of Ancient Iranian Studies* 3/2: 15-41.
— (2005 [pub. 2006]). "Avestica III. Four notes on Avestan morphology," in Weber, D. (ed.), *Languages of Iran: Past and Present. Iranian Studies in Memoriam David Neil MacKenzie*, Wiesbaden: 197-206.
— (2006). "The Avestan Yasna: Ritual and Myth", in F. Vahman and C. V. Pedersen (ed.), *Religious Texts in Iranian Languages. Symposium held in Copenhagen May Month 2002*, Det Kongelige Danske Videnskabernes Selskab, Copenhagen: pp. 53-80.

BIBLIOGRAPHY 159

— (2006-2007). "The importance of orality for the study of Old Iranian literature and myth", *Nāme-ye Irān-e Bāstān. The International Journal of Ancient Iranian Studies*.

Smith, R. R. R. (1987). "The Imperial Reliefs from the Sebasteion at Aphrodisias", *JRS* 77: 88-138.

— (1990). "Myth and allegory in the Sebasteion", in Roueché, C. and Erim, K. T. (eds.), *Aphrodisias Papers: Recent Works on Architecture and Sculpture, Including the Papers given at the Second International Aphrodisias Colloquium held at King's College London on 14 November 1987*, Journal of Roman Archaeology, Supplement Series 1, Ann Arbor: 89-100.

Sonnabend, H. (1986). *Fremdenbild und Politik: Vorstellungen der Römer von Ägypten und dem Partherreich in der späten Republik und frühen Kaiserzeit*, Frankfurt am Main, Bern, New York.

Sosien, B. (1995). "Horace Vernet en Orient", in Moureau, F. (ed.), *L'oil aux aguets ou L'artiste en voyage*, études réunies, Paris: 79-88.

Spannagel, M. (1999). *Exemplaria Principis: Untersuchungen zu Entstehung und Ausstattung des Augustusforums*, Heidelberg.

Spawforth, A. (1994). "Symbol of unity? The Persian-wars tradition in the Roman empire", in. Hornblower, S. (ed.), *Greek Historiography*, Oxford: 233-269.

— (1997). "The early reception of the imperial cult in Athens: prob-lems and ambiguities", in Hoff, M. C. and Rotroff, S. I. (eds.), *The Roma-nization of Athens: Proceedings of an International Conference held at Lincoln, Nebraska (April 1996)*, Oxbow Monograph 94, Oxford: 183-201.

Spiegel, F. (1853-58). *Avesta, die heiligen Schriften der Parsen, zum ersten Male im Grundtexte sammt der Huzvâresch Uebersetzung herausgegeben*, 2 vols., Vienna.

— (1852-63). *Avesta, die heiligen Schriften der Parsen, aus dem Grundtexte übersetzt mit steter Berücksicht auf die Tradition*, 3 vols., Leipzig, 1852, 1859, 1863.

Stausberg, M. (2004). *Die Religion Zarathustras. Geschichte — Gegenwart — Rituale*, III, Stuttgart.

Steinhart, M. (1997). "Bemerkungen zu Rekonstruktion, Ikonographie und Inschrift des platäischen Weihgeschenks", *Bulletin de Correspondance Hellénique* 121: 33-69.

Stevens, A. (1994). *Jung: A Very Short Introduction*, Oxford.

Sun, Yutang (1995). *Sun Yutang xueshu lunwenji*, Beijing.

Syme, R. (1989). "Janus and Parthia in Horace", in Diggle, J., Hall, J.B. and Jocelyn, H.D (eds.), *Studies in Latin Literature and Its Tradition in Honour of C.O. Brink*, The Cambridge Philological Society, Supplementary Vol. 15, Cambridge: 113-124.

Tafazzoli, A. (1986). "Āraš", *EncIr* II: 266-7.

Takács, S. A. (1996). "Magna Deum Mater Idaea, Cybele, and Catullus' Attis", in Lane, E. M. (ed.), *Cybele, Attis and Related Cults: Essays in Memory of M. J. Vermaseren*, Leiden, New York, Köln: 367-386.

160 THE AGE OF THE PARTHIANS

— (1999). "Mater Magna", in *Der Neue Pauly* 7, Stuttgart,Weimar: 998-1000.

Tanabe; K. (ed.) (1986). *Sculptures of Palmyra* I, Tokyo.

Timpe, D. (1962)."Die Bedeutung der Schlacht von Carrhae", *Museum Helveticum* 19: 104-129.

— (1975). "Zur augusteischen Partherpolitik zwischen 30 und 20 v.Chr. ", in *Würzburger Jahrbücher für Altertumswissenschaft*, Neue Folge 1: 155-169.

Torelli, M. (1999). "Pax Augusta, Ara", in Steinby, M. (ed.), *Lexicon Topographicum Urbis Romae: P-S* IV, Rome: 70-74.

Tran Tam Tinh, V. (1975), "Les problèmes du culte de Cybèle et Attis à Pompéi", in Andreae, B. and Kyrieleis, H. (eds.), *Neue Forschungen in Pompeji und den anderen vom Vesuvausbruch verschütteten Städten*, Recklinghausen: 279-290.

Turnheim, Y. (2004). "Visual art as text: The Rape of Ganymede", in Fano Santi, M. (ed.), *Studi di archeologia in onore di Gustavo Traversari* II. Rome: pp. 895-905.

Ulisse (1996). *Ulisse: il mito e la memoria*, Roma, Palazzo delle Esposizioni, 22 febbraio – 2 settembre 1996, Rome.

Ungaro, L. (2002). "Il Foro di Augusto", in De Nuccio, M. and Ungaro, L. (eds), *I marmi colorati della Roma imperiale: Roma, Mercati di Traiano, 28 settembre 2002 – 19 gennaio 2003*, Venice: 109-121.

Vanden Berghe, L. and Schippmann, K. (1985). *Les reliefs rupestres d'Elymaïde (Iran) de l'époque parthe*, Gent.

Van der Spek, R. J. (1998). "Cuneiform documents on Parthian history: the Rahimesu archive. Materials for the study of the standard of living", in Wiesehöfer, J. (ed.), *Das Partherreich und seine Zeugnisse*, Historia Einzelsch-riften 122, Stuttgart: 205 – 258.

Veblen, T. (1899). *The Theory of the Leisure Class: An Economic Study of Institutions*, New York.

Vermaseren, M. J. (1982). *Mithraica III: The Mithraeum at Marino*, Etudes préliminaires aux religions orientales dans l'empire romain 16, Leiden.

Visser, E. (1998). "Ganymedes", in *Der Neue Pauly* IV. Stuttgart , Weimar: 781-782.

Vos, M.F. (1963). *Scythian Archers in Archaic Attic Vase Painting*, Groningen.

Vout, C. (2003). "Embracing Egypt", in Edwards, C. and Woolf, G. (eds.), *Rome the Cosmopolis*, Cambridge: 177-202.

Waldenfels, B. (2001). "Spiegel, Spur und Blick: Zur Genese des Bildes", in Boehm, G. (ed.), *Homo Pictor*, Colloquium Rauricum 7, Munich, Leipzig: 14-31.

Walker, S. (1997). "Athens under Augustus", in Hoff, M. C.and Rotroff, S. I. (eds.), *The Romanization of Athens: Proceedings of an International Conference held at Lincoln, Nebraska (April 1996)*, Oxbow Monograph 94, Oxford: 67-80.

Wallace-Hadrill, A. (2004). "The golden age and sin in Augustan ideology", in Osborne, R. (ed.), *Studies in Ancient Greek and Roman Society*, Cambridge: 159-176.

BIBLIOGRAPHY

161

Wallinga, H.T. (2005). *Xerxes' Greek Adventure: The Naval Perspective*, Mnemosyne Supplementum 264, Leiden, New York.

Walser, G. (1966). *Die Völkerschaften auf den Reliefs von Persepolis*, Berlin.

Walter, U. (2006). "Die Rache der Priamos-Enkel? Troia und Rom", in Zimmermann, M. (ed.), *Der Traum von Troia: Geschichte und Mythos einer ewigen Stadt*, Munich: 89-103, 233-234.

Wang, H. (2004). *Money on the Silk Road: The Evidence from Eastern Central Asia to c. AD 800*, London.

Watkins, C. (1995). *How to Kill a Dragon. Aspects of Indo-European Poetics*, New York, Oxford.

Weber, E. (1972). "Die trojanische Abstammung der Römer als politisches Argument", in *Wiener Studien: Zeitschrift für Klassische Philologie und Patristik*, Neue Folge 6: 213-225.

Welters, L. (1995). "Ethnicity in Greek dress", in Eicher, J. B. (ed.), *Dress and Ethnicity: Change Across Space and Time*, Berg Ethnic Identities Series, Oxford , Washington: 53-77.

Westergaard, N. L. (1852-54). *Zendavesta or the Religious Books of the Parsis* I, Copenhagen; repr. Wiesbaden, 1994.

Wheeler, E. L. (2002). "Roman treaties with Parthia: Völkerrecht or power politics?", in Freeman, Ph. *et al.* (eds.), *Limes: 18. Proceedings of the XVIIIth International Congress of Roman Frontier Studies held in Amman, Jordan, September 2000,* British Archaeological Reports, International Series 1084 (II), Oxford: 287-292.

Whitehead, R. B. (1914). Catalogue of Coins in the Panjab Museum, Lahore, I. Indo-Greek Coins, Oxford.

Wiesehöfer, J. (1994). *Die 'dunklen Jahrhunderte' der Persis* (Zetemata, 90), Munich.

— (1995). "Zum Nachleben von Achaimeniden und Alexander in Iran", in Sancisi-Weerdenburg, H., Kuhrt, A. and Root, M.C. (eds.), *Achaemenid History VIII: Continuity and Change*, Leiden, 389-397.

— (1996). "Discordia et Defectio - Dynamis kai Pithanourgia. Die frühen Seleukiden und Iran", in Funck, B. (ed.), *Hellenismus. Beiträge zur Erforschung von Akkulturation und politischer Ordnung in den Staaten des hellenistischen Zeitalters*, Tübingen: 29-56.

— 1998. "Zeugnisse zur Geschichte und Kultur der Persis unter den Parthern", in Wiesehöfer, J. (ed.), *Das Partherreich und seine Zeugnisse* Historia-Einzelschriften 122, Stuttgart: 425-434.

— 2001a. *Ancient Persia*, second ed., London / New York

— 2001b. "Frataraka", *EncIr* X, 195.

— (2002). "Die 'Sklaven des Kaisers' und der Kopf des Crassus. Römische Bilder des Ostens und parthische Bilder des Westens in augusteischer Zeit", in Freeman, Ph. *et al.* (eds.), *Limes: 18. Proceedings of the XVIIIth International Congress of Roman Frontier Studies held in Amman, Jordan, September 2000,* British Archaeological Reports, International Series 1084 (II), Oxford: 293-300.

— (2003). "Iraner und Hellenen: Bemerkungen zu einem umstrittenen kulturellen Verhältnis", in Conermann, S. and Kusber, J. (eds.). *Studia Eurasiatica: Kieler Festschrift für Hermann Kulke zum 65. Geburtstag*, Asien und Afrika, Beiträge des Zentrums für Asiatische und Afrikanische Studien (ZAAS) der Christian-Albrechts-Universität zu Kiel 10, Hamburg: 497-524.

Wilhelm, R. M. (1988). "Cybele: the great mother of Augustan order", *Vergilius, The Journal of the Vergilian Society of America, Inc.* 34: 77-101.

Winter, E. And Dignas, B. (2001). *Rom und das Perserreich: Zwei Weltmächte zwischen Konfrontation und Koexistenz*, Berlin.

Wiseman, T.P. (1984). "Cybele, Vergil and Augustus", in Woodman, T., and West, D. (eds.), *Poetry and Politics in the Age of Augustus.* Cambridge: 117-128.

Wissemann, M. (1981). *Die Parther in der augusteischen Dichtung*, Frankfurt am Main, Bern, New York.

Witzel, M. (2000). "The home of the Aryans", in Hintze, A. and Tichy, E. (eds.), *Anusantatyai. Festschrift fur Johanna Narten zum 70. Geburtstag*, Dettelbach: 283-338.

Wolff, F. (1910). *Avesta. Die heiligen Bücher der Parsen*, Strassburg (repr. Berlin, 1960).

Wood, M. (1997). *In the Footsteps of Alexander the Great*, London.

Woolf, G. (1994). "Becoming Roman, staying Greek: culture, identity and the civilizing process in the Roman east", in *Proceedings of the Cambridge Philological Society* 40: 116-143.

Wroth, W. (1903). *British Museum Catalogue of the Coins of Parthia*, London.

Ye'or, B. (2005). *Der Niedergang des orientalischen Christentums unter dem Islam: Vom Dschihad zum Schutzvertrag*, second edition. Gräfelfing (first published 1991: *Les chrétientés d'Orient entre "jihad" et dhimmitude : VIIe-XXe siècle.* Paris).

Yu, Taishan (1992). *Caizhongshi yanjiu*, Beijing.

— (1995). *Liang Han Wei Jin Nan Bei chao yu xiyu guanxi shi yanjiu*, Beijing.

— (2005). *Liang Han Wei Jin Nan Bei chao zhengshi xiyuzhuan yaozhu*, Beijing.

Zaehner, R. C. (1961). *The Dawn and Twilight of Zoroastrianism*, London.

Zanker, P. (1969). *Forum Augustum: Das Bildprogramm*, Monumenta Artis Antiquae II, Tübingen.

— (1988). *The Power of Images in the Age of Augustus*, Ann Arbor (= *Augustus und die Macht der Bilder*, Munich 1987).

— (2000). "Die Gegenwelt der Barbaren und die Überhöhung der häuslichen Lebenswelt, Überlegungen zum System der kaiserzeitlichen Bilderwelt", in Hölscher, T. (ed.), *Gegenwelten zu den Kulturen Griechenlands und Roms in der Antike*, Munich, Leipzig: 409-433.

Zizi tongjian (by Sima Guang, 1019-1086), Zhonghua shuju edition, repr. Hong Kong 1971.

CPSIA information can be obtained
at www.ICGtesting.com
Printed in the USA
LVHW081641311221
707636LV00017B/1176